THE FIRST
FIFTY YEARS

i

The Bible Study Textbook Series

NEW TESTAMENT

The Bible Study New Testament Ed. By Rhoderick Ice	**The Gospel of Matthew** In Four Volumes By Harold Fowler (Vol. IV not yet available)	**The Gospel of Mark** By B. W. Johnson and Don DeWelt
The Gospel of Luke By T. R. Applebury	**The Gospel of John** By Paul T. Butler	**Acts Made Actual** By Don DeWelt
Romans Realized By Don DeWelt	**Studies in Corinthians** By T. R. Applebury	**Guidance From Galatians** By Don Earl Boatman
The Glorious Church (Ephesians) By Wilbur Fields	**Philippians · Colossians Philemon** By Wilbur Fields	**Thinking Through Thessalonians** By Wilbur Fields
Paul's Letters To Timothy & Titus By Don DeWelt	**Helps From Hebrews** By Don Earl Boatman	**James & Jude** By Don Fream
Letters From Peter By Bruce Oberst	**Hereby We Know (I-II-III John)** By Clinton Gill	**The Seer, The Saviour, and The Saved (Revelation)** By James Strauss

OLD TESTAMENT

O.T. History By William Smith and Wilbur Fields	**Genesis** In Four Volumes By C. C. Crawford	**Exploring Exodus** By Wilbur Fields	**Leviticus** By Don DeWelt
Numbers By Brant Lee Doty	**Deuteronomy** By Bruce Oberst	**Joshua - Judges Ruth** By W. W. Winter	**I & II Samuel** By W. W. Winter
I & II Kings By James E. Smith	**I & II Chronicles** By Robert E. Black	**Ezra, Nehemiah & Esther** By Ruben Ratzlaff & Paul T. Butler	**The Shattering of Silence (Job)** By James Strauss
Psalms In Two Volumes By J. B. Rotherham		**Proverbs** By Donald Hunt	**Ecclesiastes and Song of Solomon** — By R. J. Kidwell and Don DeWelt
Isaiah In Three Volumes By Paul T. Butler		**Jeremiah and Lamentations** By James E. Smith	**Ezekiel** By James E. Smith
Daniel By Paul T. Butler		**Hosea - Joel - Amos Obadiah - Jonah** By Paul T. Butler	**Micah - Nahum - Habakkuk Zephaniah - Haggai - Zechariah Malachi** — By Clinton Gill

SPECIAL STUDIES

The Church In The Bible By Don DeWelt	**The Eternal Spirit** By C. C. Crawford	**World & Literature of the Old Testament** Ed. By John Willis	**Survey Course In Christian Doctrine** Two Bks. of Four Vols. By C. C. Crawford
New Testament History — Acts By Gareth Reese	**Learning From Jesus** By Seth Wilson		**You Can Understand The Bible** By Grayson H. Ensign

THE FIRST FIFTY YEARS

A Brief History

of the

Direct-Support Missionary Movement

by

David Filbeck

Lincoln Christian Seminary
Lincoln, IL 62656
USA

College Press Publishing Company, Joplin, Missouri

Library of Congress Catalog Card Number: 0-89900-060-6
International Standard Book Number: 80-65966

To Deloris
My Wife and Partner
in the
Great Commission

v

Table of Contents

Preface

Researching this book on the Direct-Support missionary movement has been a delight. History, especially in tracing one's heritage, can be fascinating. Since I was reared in the Restoration Movement, and specifically in the Direct-Support missionary movement, I found that reading again, this time from original documents, the events and reasons which led to the Direct-Support method were even more interesting. I think you will find this history equally interesting.

Two publications made my research a pleasant task. They are the *Index to the Christian Standard* and the *Index to the Christian Evangelist,* both published by the Historical Society of the Disciples of Christ. Those who made it possible for the publication of these two Indexes are to be commended. But while the Indexes to these two journals were indispensable, I was handicapped in researching every aspect of this history because no such index has been made for the *Gospel Advocate.* I was able to obtain microfilm on the early years of the *Gospel Advocate* from the Abilene Christian University Library, but having no index I had to spend many hours reading through them just to obtain a small amount of material. Being short on time I was forced to limit my research in this journal. It is hoped that someone will soon sponsor an indexing of the *Gospel Advocate* because I believe that no adequate history of the Restoration Movement can be written without having full access to the pages of this journal, an access which only an index can provide.

W. T. Moore, Disciples of Christ historian at the turn of the century, once wrote that the Restoration Movement has no Bishops, only editors. As you read this history of Direct-Support missions, you will see what he meant. Editors of the three main-journals in the Restoration Movement have played major roles in our history, and this is no less true in missions. Opinions expressed through editorials in the *Christian Standard, Christian Evangelist* and *Gospel Advocate* have down through the years set the course for missions and at times have even changed the course missions took in the Restoration Movement. In order to conserve both time and space, I have not for the most part included the names of editors in references whether in the text or footnotes. This is especially true for the *Christian Standard,* since many more references are made to editorials from this journal than from any other. However, we should not overlook the men who wrote these editorials. They are, and the years each served as editor of the *Chrisitan Standard:* Isaac Errett (1865-1888), Russell Errett (1888-1900), J. A. Lord (1900-1909), S. S. Lappin (1909-1916), George P. Rutledge (1917-1922), Willard Mohorter (1922-1929), Edwin R. Errett (1929-1944), Burris Butler (1944-1957), Edwin Hayden (1957-1978). For the *Christian Evangelist,* only James Harvey Garrison, the founding editor of the Journal figures prominently in our discussion. For the *Gospel Advocate,* only David Lipscomb similarly plays a role in our discussion.

There is one journal that, if we had access to a complete set of all its copies, would be a great help in researching the early years of independent missions among the Disciples of Christ. That journal is the *Tokyo Christian,* the monthly newsletter published by W. D. Cunningham beginning in 1901. Only a few individual copies are available for inspection. Hopefully a complete set of the *Tokyo Christian* is still in existence somewhere in the world and will be made available for research. W. D. Cunningham was one of the most dynamic missionaries of the Restoration Movement. Having his newsletters to study will greatly help us in understanding the beginnings of the Direct-Support missionary movement.

PREFACE

I am indebted to many friends and colleagues in writing this book. I am grateful to colleagues of Lincoln Christian Seminary for help and encouragement, especially to Dean Wayne Shaw for making more time available for research and writing, and to Enos Dowling for furnishing data on early missions in the Restoration Movement. Also, I am thankful to the following students who, through their own class research, furnished additional information which I have incorporated: Jan Messersmith, Charles Perry, James Poll and Steve Burris. I am especially grateful to Clifford Dull for suggesting many valuable editorial improvements in the book. Many people have read this book and have suggested corrections and improvements. I have incorporated many of their suggestions. None of these, however, should be held responsible for the mistakes that doubtlessly remain in the book. I alone stand responsible for these mistakes.

Introduction

Direct-Support Missions of the Christian Churches/ Churches of Christ have been operating in earnest for over fifty years. They did not just suddenly "crop up" on their own, however. On the contrary, Direct-Support Missions came into being—and still exist today—as a result of certain forces, tendencies, even dilemmas which themselves have existed in the Restoration Movement from the very beginning. Indeed, many of these tendencies and dilemmas go back to Alexander Campbell himself as he sought to initiate and then guide a religious movement dedicated to breaking out of the fetters of rigid ecclesiasticisms and denominationalism into the "freedom [for which] Christ has set us free" (Gal. 5:1 RSV).

Consequently, the missionary method which we have espoused as Direct-Support Missions is heir to a long-standing debate within the Restoration Movement, viz. how much organization beyond and above the local congregation is needed or allowed—if indeed such is allowed at all!—to carry out the Great Commission of discipling all nations, baptizing them and teaching them to observe all things which Jesus Christ has commanded (Matthew 28:19-20)? The debate began apparently as early as the establishment of the Mahoning Association in 1820. The Mahoning Association was not started by Alexander Campbell but soon after its formation he, along with the Church where he was a member, was invited to join. The Association, though, did not prosper until the hiring of Walter Scott in 1827 to be the Association's first evangelist. This cooperative venture among the various congregations of the Mahoning Association was very successful in that many people became Christians and several new churches came into existence. Yet, in spite of these successes, there were some who opposed this venture.

Even though the cause was apparently prospering under the work of the Mahoning Association, some brethren became anxious as to whether or not such an organization could be defended by the scriptures.[1]

The Campbellian Dilemma

This debate continued throughout and beyond Alexander Campbell's life, and has lasted until our day although in more muted tones. As with any debate, the question of how much para-congregational organization is needed or allowed presented problems to be solved, problems which more often than not resulted in a dilemma involving a choice between two equally cruel alternatives. This dilemma, which I have chosen to characterize as the Campbellian Dilemma, was first established when Thomas Campbell, the father of Alexander Campbell, wrote his *Declaration and Address.* The *Declaration and Address,* first published in 1809, was written in reaction to the ecclesiastical situation which Thomas Campbell found during his time. What he observed was essentially this: the local congregation was all but buried from sight in a maze of warring sectarian and denominational structures. The task, therefore, was to strip away all the accretions of structural overlay and restore the local congregation to its proper and primary position in God's scheme of human redemption. There was, moreover, Thomas Campbell argued, a Biblical justification for this restoration, for the Scriptures clearly speak of Christ building "His church" but nothing about the creation of supra-church structures. And since it was these supra-church structures

---

1. Earl I. West, *The Search For The Ancient Order* (Nashville, Tenn: Gospel Advocate Company, 1949), vol. I, p. 150.

which were at the root of the cause of division among Christians, Thomas Campbell urged that they be eliminated from the Church of Christ.[2]

Not long after this concept of restorationism was formulated, and the Restoration Movement inaugurated, a dilemma in the formulation became apparent. Simply stated, the subsequent dilemma that many of the Campbellian Restoration Movement have found themselves in is this: Given the goal of restoring the Christianity found in the New Testament, we find no explicit "thus saith the Lord" or precedent in scripture for any organizational structure beyond the local congregation for the purpose of evangelizing the lost; on the other hand, if we do not have such para or multi-congregational machinery the task of obeying the Scriptures in evangelizing our neighbors throughout the world is done inadequately, if at all. A. T. DeGroot, a leading figure within the Disciples of Christ wing of the Restoration Movement, also recognized the long-standing nature of this problem.

> . . . In Campbell's program there was a duty for Christians in separate congregations to become involved in the whole growth-by-study and effective witness-by-work which they could do only by voluntary cooperation in and beyond their local churches. Specifically at issue was the task of undertaking missions "unto the uttermost parts of the world."[3]

---

2. See Propositions number 11 and 12 of *Declaration and Address* (Lincoln, IL: Lincoln Christian College Press, 1971, reprint of 1809 ed.) (in *Historical Documents Advocating Christian Union*, Chicago, IL: The Christian Century Co., 1904). Compare also Dean E. Walker's summary of these two propositions:

"If human innovations are removed Christians will find themselves united — to remove these innovations and to discover what are innovations, means, practically, the restoration of the Church pictured in the New Testament" *Adventuring For Christian Unity* (Cincinnati, OH: Standard Publishing, 1935), p. 21.

3. A. T. DeGroot, *New Possibilities for Disciples and Independents* (St. Louis: Bethany Press, 1963), pp. 20-21.

The problem or dilemma thus presented is not one that a conscientious Christian can ignore. It must be solved.

A dilemma, of course, creates tensions, and tensions in turn create dynamics for their resolution. Direct-Support Missions of today represent one solution of the above dilemma which has been tried in the Restoration Movement. Therefore, to properly understand Direct-Support Missions, we must know what it is they are trying to solve. We must know where we came from and why we traveled the road we did in coming from there. To be sure there have been other solutions tried in the course of the Restoration Movement begun by Thomas and Alexander Campbell. Most of these solutions, which differ from the Direct-Support method in preferring one horn of the dilemma over the other, are likewise in operation. However, in studying the history of Direct-Support Missions, we are not interested in these other solutions except as they touch directly upon the formation of the Direct-Support Missionary Movement or may serve as points of reference by which Direct-Support Missions may be compared and contrasted with respect to methodology, structure and purpose.

Purpose and Plan of Book

In other words, my purpose in writing this book is not to compile a detailed history, whether of the causal antecedents or subsequent developments, of Direct-Support Missions. There are two reasons for this. First, such detailing of events has already been done by several historians or readily available through the various missions agencies of the Restoration Movement, and any reader interested in such may easily consult these sources. Second, it is more profitable and interesting to study the history of Direct-Support Missions in terms of precedents which have resulted in enduring and popular trends in the task of fulfilling the Great Commission. Since the number of Direct-Support missionaries have increased from just a handful to over 2,000, it would be impossible to detail their every move and progress. On the other hand, despite the large number of Direct-Support missionaries both here and abroad, a great deal of similarity in methodology and purpose in mission work exists among them. So it is my purpose, in a book of this nature, to detail only those significant developments which have shaped and continued to shape the Direct-Support Missionary Movement among Christian Churches.

To achieve this purpose, I have divided the book into four parts:

In Part I, the Historical Antecedents of Direct-Support Missions, we are interested in exploring one basic question: *What were the developments in the early days of the Restoration Movement that cast the mold for Direct-Support Missions and which will continue to help mold the shape of things to come in the years ahead?* In the period to be covered, encompassing just over 75 years (1849-1926), several significant developments transpired which gave rise to the Direct-Support Mission method espoused and supported today by Christian Churches and Churches of Christ.

In Part II, we take special note of a development in missions which took place in the Restoration Movement during the same time period covered in Part I, namely the rise of missionaries and mission enterprises conducted independently of the para-church structures specifically created for missionary outreach. From 1891 to 1926, there were several who served as independent missionaries, and, in effect, were the forerunners to Direct-Support missionaries of later years. The main question of this section, therefore, is: *What were the dynamics created and pioneered by the early independent missionaries that became the model for fulfilling the Great Commission in the Direct-Support Missionary Movement of later years?* The emphasis in this section is upon the words *created* and *pioneered*, because the missionary scene which these early independents found in the Restoration Movement was one totally dominated by para-church organizations. And before the Direct-Support Missionary Movement could succeed among Christian Churches a period where certain new mission dynamics could be initiated and tested was first needed. This period was comparatively brief, spanning only thirty-five years; nevertheless, it provided the time necessary for the transition from a total reliance on para-church missionary organizations to a more direct way of supporting the world-wide missionary outreach of the brotherhood.

Part III deals with the fifty years following 1926. In this book, the year 1926 is taken as the beginning for Direct-Support Missions among the Christian Churches, even though there were missionaries among Disciples of Christ working independently of any missionary society before this. From 1926 to 1976, several developments have occurred in the independent mission work of the Christian Churches. In this section, therefore, the main question is: *What have been the significant developments in Direct-Support Missions since 1926 which in turn established the precedents that Direct-Support missionaries in the years to come will likewise follow?* Besides its obvious interest from a historical perspective, the question is important from another perspective: What are the trends and patterns in Direct-Support Mission methodology that must be evaluated in the light of the realization that an increasingly large portion of the world's population is unevangelized and will likely remain so under present operations? It is this last question that is ultimately of more importance for the fulfillment of the Great Commission by Christian Churches and Churches of Christ in today's world. But, before any such re-evaluation can take place, the preceding question must be answered.

Part IV presents a brief evaluation of the first fifty years of the Direct-Support Missionary Movement. There has been phenomenal growth in Direct-Support Missions and missionaries since 1926. The basic question of this section is simply *What is the nature of this growth?* Growth usually brings problems, and there are problems associated with the growth that has taken place in Direct-Support Missions. While Part IV is not an extensive evaluation of the Direct-Support Missionary Movement, it does take a close look at some of the strengths and weaknesses of the movement, not only the strengths and weaknesses inherent in the very nature of the movement, but also those which the movement shares with missions in general.

As can be seen from the above, this book is intended to be more than a history of the Direct-Support Missionary Movement of the Christian Churches and Churches of Christ. It is also a brief history of missions in the Restoration Movement, more precisely a history of early Restoration Missions whose tensions and dynamics led to the emergence and development of Direct-Support Missions. There are now three main segments to this Movement, and each segment has its own program for missionary outreach into the world. For this reason, writing a complete history of missions in the Restoration Movement is beyond the scope of this book. Yet, without this history of Direct-Support Missions, it would be impossible to write a complete history of Restoration

Missions. In other words, this book is a history which recognizes that the Direct-Support Missionary Movement of today has its roots deep in Restoration history and is therefore kin to all else in the Restoration Movement. It is such a contribution which I hope this book will make to a more general study of missions in the Restoration Movement.

While I believe this is the correct way to write about the history of the first fifty years of the Direct-Support Missionary Movement, I must confess to a problem of maintaining objectivity. This becomes apparent in the choice of certain terms, which of themselves are neutral enough but, when used by one who served as a Direct-Support missionary for several years, may sound more pejorative than neutral. Moreover, in reliving through research the controversies which were the immediate antecedents to our Direct-Support Missionary Movement, it is clear that my sympathies are on the side of Direct-Support Missions. I make no apology for this, since, given my service to missions in the Restoration Movement, I could not do otherwise. All I request from readers, who perhaps do not share my sympathies, is an understanding of my perspective and, above all, of my commitment to the Direct-Support Missionary Movement as an instrument that God has and will continue to use to bring glory to His name among many tribes and nations of this world.

Part I

HISTORICAL ANTECEDENTS

(1849-1926)

Alexander Campbell

James T. Barclay

J. W. McGarvey

W. T. Moore

Chapter 1

ALEXANDER CAMPBELL AND
THE MISSIONARY SOCIETY

On October 23, 1849, Alexander Campbell was elected president over a church convention which, three days later, was named the American Christian Missionary Society (ACMS). That such a curious occurrence should have taken place has been an understatement which has plagued historians of the Restoration Movement ever since. For Alexander Campbell, the religious iconoclast of the American frontier, to be elected head of any religious organization — especially a missionary society — is truly remarkable for several reasons.

First, Alexander Campbell was widely known, and often feared, as a critic of the formal, religious organizations of his day. Missionary societies especially were subjected to his caustic commentary in sermon and print. For example, in the very first volume of the *Christian Baptist*, in answer to a letter which had mildly protested his criticism of missionary societies, Alexander Campbell wrote:

> Our objections to the missionary plan originated from the conviction that it is unauthorized in the New Testament; and that, in many instances, it is a system of iniquitous peculation and speculation. I feel perfectly able to maintain both the one and the other of these positions. What charity, what lawless charity would it require to believe that a Reverend Divine, for instance, coming to the city of Pittsburgh some time since, under the character of a missionary, and after "preaching four sermons" of scholastic divinity to a few women and children in the remote corners of the city, called on the treasurer of the missionary fund in that place, and actually drew *forty dollars* for the *four sermons*: I say, what lawless charity would it require to consider such a man a

3

servant of Jesus Christ, possessed of the spirit of Paul, or Peter, or any of the true missionaries!! My informant is a very respectable citizen of Pittsburgh. He assured me he had the intelligence from the treasurer's own lips. Ten dollars for a sermon one hour long! Preached to the heathen in the city of Pittsburgh by a regularly educated, pious missionary!! How many widows' mites, how many hard earned charities were swallowed in one hour by this gormandizer!! Tell it not in Gath, publish it not in the streets of Askelon! "But," say an apologist, "it required the good man a week to study it; besides, he gave them prayers into the bargain." A week to study a sermon! For a graduate at college too!! Why his sermon was not worth a cent! There is not a lawyer in Pittsburgh who could not prepare an orthodox sermon in a week, and deliver it handsomely too for *ten dollars*. From the prayers and sermons of such missionaries may the pagans be long preserved![1]

Naturally such criticism, did not endear Alexander Campbell to the religious world of his day. In fact, W. W. Sweet names Alexander Campbell along with two others of his day as the "unholy trinity of American anti-missionism."[2] But in spite of this reputation he was elected and served as president of a missionary society.

Second, because of his active past in opposing missionary organization, Alexander Campbell no doubt realized that there would be a number of his own colleagues who had formerly been won over to his cause because of such opposition but who would now turn against him, opposing the missionary society over which he had been elected president.

---

1. Alexander Campbell, ed., "To Mr. Robert Cautious," *The Christian Baptist*, vol. 1. (Bethany, VA: Alexander Campbell, 1827; reprint ed., St. Louis: Christian Publishing Co., 1889), pp. 53-54.

2. A. T. DeGroot, *Disciple Thought: A History* (Ft. Worth, TX.: Texas Christian University, 1965), p. 199.

This opposition would, in effect, destroy any pretense to unity among Christian brethren which Alexander Campbell was hoping to achieve through the Restoration Movement. In other words, this election would cause division within the ranks of the brotherhood. Yet, in spite of the division such a move would create, he advocated the formation of the American Christian Missionary Society (ACMS) or some similar organization as a necessary means of propogating the Gospel:

> I am of the opinion that a Convention, or general meeting of the churches of the Reformation is a very great desideratum . . .
>
> The purposes of such a primary convention are already indicated by the general demand for a more efficient and Scriptural organization—for a more general and efficient co-operation in the Bible cause, in the Missionary cause, in the Education cause.[3]

And when he was elected president, he expressed satisfaction over what had taken place.

> Our expectations from the Convention have more than been realized . . . Denied the pleasure of having been present on this interesting occasion by an usually severe indisposition, I am peculiarly gratified with the great issues of deliberation. . . . The Christian Missionary Society—will be a grand auxiliary to the churches in destitute regions, at home as well as abroad, in dispensing the blessings of the gospel amongst many that otherwise would never have heard it. . . . we cannot but hail [the ACMS] as greatly contributing to the advancement of the cause we have been so long pleading before God and the people.[4]

---

3. Alexander Campbell, "Convention," *Millennial Harbinger* (1849): 476.
4. Campbell, "The Convention of Christian Churches," *Millennial Harbinger* (1849): 694-695.

To Jerusalem — And Back!

In retrospect, it should not surprise us that the Disciples, meeting in Cincinnati, Ohio in 1849 would elect to form a missionary society instead of a general convention for the brotherhood. It was, after all, in the middle of what Kenneth S. Latourette has termed The Great Century.[5] It had been, for example, only fifteen years since William Carey, after spending forty years in India, had died. Robert Morrison, famed missionary to China, had also died the same year. Adoniram Judson, frail from his missionary work, had only three years previously spoken to crowds in Boston about how the church had grown to over 1000 converts in Burma. For the joy of seeing the church planted in Burmese soil, Judson had suffered the loss of two wives, languished in jail and was suffering from bad health. Moreover, on his return to Burma in 1848, he took sick, and on a long sea voyage in 1850 to regain his health, he died and was burned at sea. The faith and work of these, plus the scores of other missionaries who also served in the first half of the 19th Century, could not fail to attract the attention and admiration of the Disciples of Christ as they met to consider what to do next in the restoration of New Testament Christianity.

Neither was the mission method of these early missionaries lost on the Disciples, because these missionaries had not been sent out individually from local congregations but had gone out under the auspices of missionary societies. William Carey had gone to India under the Baptist Missionary Society, which was established in 1792 and supported by contributors and subscribers who believed in the purpose of the

---

5. Kenneth Latourette, *A History of the Expansion of Christianity*, vol. 4: *The Great Century: Europe & U.S.A.* (Grand Rapids: Zondervan Publishing Co., 1937), p. 45.

society. Adoniram Judson first went out under the American Board of Commissioners for Foreign Mission (established 1810) but changed to the American Baptist Missionary Union (established 1814) because of his conviction that immersion is the correct form of baptism. Robert Morrison went to China under the London Missionary Society (established 1804). Missionaries serving under the London Missionary Society led in the Christianization of the South Pacific islands. Tahiti had become Christian in 1812 after the Society had initiated special prayer for the conversion of Pomare, a powerful Tahitian Chief who had formerly successfully opposed the missionary John Williams. Mr. Williams, also of the LMS, had successfully evangelized in the islands of Hualune, Raiatea, and Rarotonga, and was finally martyred in the new Hebrides in 1839. In 1845, because of the London Missionary Society's work, a revival swept through the Fiji islands resulting in a formerly barbarous people turning to Christianity.

Because of such success in preaching the Gospel on foreign fields, new missionary societies were continually being formed. In addition, denominations began to form their own missionary societies.[6] In England, for example, the Welsh Calvinistic Methodist established a society in 1849, the Presbyterians in 1847, and the Primitive Methodists in 1842. In the United States, the Episcopalians began mission work in 1835, the Presbyterians in 1837, and the Lutherans in 1838.

In short, the Disciples who met in 1849 could not escape the spirit of the time. The excitement of missions, along with

---

6. *The Encyclopedia of Missions*, 2nd ed., s.v. "Modern Protestant Missions" (New York: Funk and Wagnalls Co., 1904), p. 479.

the news of victory and martyrdom on the mission field, were inspiring Christendom to greater effort in bringing the Faith to every nation on the earth. It is small wonder, then, that the Disciples of Christ were similarly caught up in the same spirit—Alexander Campbell and his (former) anti-missionary society bias notwithstanding! As James DeForest Murch has accurately pointed out:

> As the sessions of the 1849 convention progressed, it became evident that the real reason the delegates had come together was to discover ways and means of developing a missionary enterprise.[7]

The Restoration Movement had to be proclaimed beyond the American frontier into other lands. And if the successes of recent history proved anything, it demonstrated that establishing a missionary society was the best method of achieving the goal.

Interestingly enough, the idea of a para-church mission organization was not without precedent in the Restoration Movement. In 1845 D. S. Burnet had organized the American Christian Bible Society to promote the dissemination of the Scriptures without comment.[8] This society, however, remained marginal in the overall work of the Disciples, and so D. S. Burnet joined the call in 1849 to establish another society. The name originally suggested for this new organization was The Chrisian Home and Foreign Missionary Society. The name finally adopted, though, was the American Christian Missionary Society, a name similar to the older American Christian Bible Society. It was thought that the familiarity of the older organization would bode well for

---

7. James DeForest Murch, *Christians Only* (Cincinnati: Standard Publishing Company, 1962), p. 149.

8. Grant K. Lewis, *The American Christian Missionary Society*, (St. Louis: Christian Board of Publication, 1937), p. 6.

the new organization if a similar name were adopted. The name change did not alter the orientation of the society, for there was at the outset a Board of Managers for Home Missions and a Board of Managers for Foreign Missions. Yet, in spite of the existence of a Board for Home Missions, the first work of the ACMS — and for several years after it was established — was carried out on foreign soil.

Unfortunately, however, not much was accomplished in foreign missions during the early years of the American Christian Missionary Society. The year that the ACMS was incorporated (1850), J. T. Barclay, M.D. was sent out as the Society's first missionary. He wanted to go to Jerusalem for this missionary service, because "he believed that a Bible people should undertake their first mission work in the Holy City." [9] Consequently, on June 11, 1850, the ACMS appointed Dr. Barclay "to engage in teaching, preaching and the practice of medicine among the Jews of Jerusalem."[10] Dr. Barclay labored in Jerusalem and surrounding area for nearly four years, preaching and performing his duties as a physician. In 1852, he established a school and hospital in Bethlehem in response to a message that six hundred people in that city wanted to become Christians. He thought that by establishing a school he could lay a better foundation for baptizing this many people (he was opposed to baptizing them "en masse" without educating them first). However, his plan and school ran into persecution from both the Jews and Catholics of Bethlehem and before long the school closed. Still, by 1854, twenty-two persons had been baptized. Yet, the fact that only a few had been baptized

---

9. Murch, *Christians Only*, p. 149.
10. *Ibid.*

9

was disappointing to Dr. Barclay. On the home front, the ACMS had been unsuccessful in raising enough funds to adequately support Dr. Barclay, his family and his work in Palestine. The continuation of meager results on the mission field with inadequate support at home no doubt caused strains on Dr. Barclay's physical and mental health. Consequently, Dr. Barclay closed down the Jerusalem mission of the American Christian Missionary Society and returned to the United States in the summer of 1854.

Before Dr. Barclay returned home, the ACMS, sent out Alexander Cross in 1853 to Liberia. Alexander Cross was a black slave who had demonstrated an unusual amount of intelligence. His freedom was purchased and the church in Hopkinsville, Kentucky began training him to preach the gospel in Liberia.[11] Unfortunately, within a few weeks of arriving in Africa, Alexander Cross died of overexertion in the tropical heat.

In 1858, Dr. J. T. Barclay was reappointed by the American Christian Missionary Society to return and revive his former mission work in Jerusalem. This reappointment nearly created the first formal division in the Restoration Movement. Dr. Barclay was a slave owner, having inherited slaves upon his father's death. Even though there were strong anti-slavery sentiments among a number of influential men in the Restoration Movement, it was the stated policy of the ACMS to be neutral on the slavery issue. However, the neutrality of the ACMS was not sufficient to mollify the anit-slavery brethren, and when a slave owner was selected as its first — and second — foreign missionary, it was more

---

11. West, *The Search for the Ancient Order*, vol. I, p. 220.

than they could endure. Consequently, in 1859 several anti-slavery brethren convened in Indianapolis, Indiana to form the Christian Missionary Society.[12]

Two rationales laid behind the establishment of this second missionary society. First, it was argued, brethren who considered American slavery a crime were being prevented, as a matter of conscience, from cooperating in the mission work of the Restoration Movement because the neutrality of the ACMS toward slavery had resulted in the selection of a slave owner as its first missionary. Second, to quote from the business meeting of the first CMS convention:

> The true policy of the Christian Church is to encourage the formation within the pale of her communion of as many missionary societies as by reason of the convenience of locality, and facilities of social and religious intercourse, may be deemed necessary to call out the full liberality of the brethren, and interest and engage them all, as far as practicable, in the missionary work.[13]

The new society appealed for funds, and the following year, 1860, sent its first missionary, Pardee Butler, to Kansas. In addition to Kansas, missions to Minnesota, Texas, New England, as well as several other States, and Canada, were contemplated. The Christian Missionary Society, including its first missionary work in Kansas, was short-lived, however. The Civil War broke out soon after its formation, and the resulting economic strains placed on the churches prevented the society from raising enough funds to support

---

12. Eileen Gordon Vandegrift, *The Christian Missionary Society: A Study in the Influence of Slavery of the Disciples of Christ,* unpublished M.A. Thesis (Indianapolis: Butler University, 1945), p. 46.

13. *Ibid.*

adequately Pardee Butler, let alone open up other missions contemplated. The society ceased to function early in 1863 and, by the time the Civil War ended in 1865, there was no further rationale for its revival and continuation.

In addition to the appointment of Dr. J. T. Barclay, the American Christian Missionary Society, sent J. O. Beardslee as a missionary in 1854 to the island of Jamaica. While the outbreak of the Civil War caused Dr. Barclay to return to the United States in 1860, Beardslee was able to continue his mission work in Jamaica until 1864, at which time he returned to the United States. There is disagreement among historians in the Restoration Movement about how successful the mission in Jamaica really was. Grant T. Lewis, who wrote the history of the American Christian Missionary Society, stated, "Like the Jerusalem Mission, the Jamaica mission was not productive of many converts and was for a time discontinued.[14] William Thomas Moore concurred in this assessment.[15] On the other hand, James B. Carr, in a privately published history of mission work of the Christian Church, claims that Beardslee's labors in Jamaica were successful, at least more so than the other efforts promoted by the ACMS. Carr states that during the first three years of Beardslee's missionary work in the island, thirteen churches containing 640 converts were established.[16] In 1866, J. B. Beardslee attempted to return to Jamaica as a missionary for the ACMS, but lack of funds prevented his going.[17]

---

14. Grant T. Lewis, *The American Christian Missionary Society*, p. 16.
15. William Thomas Moore, *A Comprehensive History of the Disciples of Christ* (Chicago: Fleming H. Revell Co., 1909), p. 483.
16. James B. Carr, *The Foreign Missionary Work of the Christian Church* (privately published, 1946), p. 3.
17. *Ibid.*

While few notable results were accomplished on foreign fields during the first fifteen years (1850-1865) of the American Christian Missionary Society, there were some significant developments within the Restoration Movement on the home front due to its existence. One development, already noted, was the increased and heightened opposition to the missionary society which emerged during these same years. Even though Alexander Campbell supported the ACMS and served as the Society's president until 1866 (the year of his death), his active support did not check the flow of criticism and opposition directed against the ACMS. From the very beginning, when the ACMS was first organized, Jacob Creath, Jr. questioned the legitimacy of any organization which existed in addition to the local church through which the church may perform its missionary task. Again, through the pages of the Gospel Advocate, established in 1855, both Tolbert Fanning and William Lipscomb began stating their doubts about the scriptural legitimacy of para-congregational cooperation in general and the missionary society in particular.[18] Doubts soon turned into objections, and it was not long before objections to the concept of para-congregational cooperation became quite vocal and sustained.

It is interesting at this point to digress and take notice of a perennial question that has bothered historians of the Restoration Movement ever since the beginning of the American Christian Missionary Society. That question is this: Was Alexander Campbell inconsistent in his advocacy and support of the missionary society? Both "yes" and "no" answers have been given to his question. During Alexander Campbell's lifetime, those who opposed the missionary

---

18. West, *The Search for the Ancient Order*, p. 205.

13

society accused him of being inconsistent because of his former vocal criticisms of missionary societies and ecclesiastical organizations. Alexander Campbell answered his own critics by stating that it was only the abuses of such that he was against and that his former objections should not be construed as being in opposition to para-congregational organization per se. In general, this explanation of an apparent inconsistency has stood up well in the Restoration Movement. On the other hand, to some historians this explanation did not fully exonerate Alexander Campbell. David Lipscomb, an early opponent to the missionary society, asserted that by 1849 Alexander Campbell had become somewhat mentally incompetent. As Earl West describes the opinion of several of that time:

> Alexander Campbell was, in his older days less the mental giant of his former days and was therefore an easy victim of younger men who influenced him in favor of the Societies according to their point of view.[19]

The argument of course is that if Alexander Campbell had retained his mental powers, he surely would not have been led astray into the unscriptural position of supporting a missionary society. That he supported the missionary society is considered evidence of loss of mental powers, and so he indeed was led astray. Yet the argument is tenuous at best and does not seem to be popular today. Rather, as the facts clearly show, Alexander Campbell was fully in favor of the missionary society. However, this has not satisfied modern-day critics of para-congregational missionary organizations in the Restoration Movement. To these critics it is

------

19. *Ibid.*, p. 187.

inconsequential whether Alexander Campbell was inconsistent or mentally incompetent with respect to the scriptural
legitimacy of the American Christian Missionary Society.
As Earl West, a member of this school of critics, sums up
the matter of Alexander Campbell and the Missionary Society:
"Campbell believed in them [i.e., human organizations
including the missionary society], but Campbell was wrong.
This is our conviction."[20]

Dispite this, it would be a mistake to conclude that lack
of success on the foreign mission field and heightened opposition on the home front were the only characteristics of the
formation and early years of the American Christian Missionary Society. As stated above, significant developments
occurred in the Restoration Movement because of the establishment of the ACMS. The most notable of these was the
effect that the establishment and survival of the ACMS had
on other organizational efforts in the Restoration Movement. In a real sense, the opposition to the missionary society
in its early years had a positive effect upon these efforts,
because even though the opposition raised crucial questions
regarding the scriptural legitimacy of such para-congregational organizations, the questions were adequately answered
to the satisfaction of many in the brotherhood. Reinforced
in the belief that their organizing efforts were indeed legitimate,
leaders in the Restoration Movement forged ahead to organize the brotherhood for more inter-church cooperative
ventures in spreading the restoration of New Testament
Christianity. The object of this increased organizational
activity among churches of the Restoration Movement was
not foreign missions as much as the American frontier. In

---

20. *Ibid.*, p. 195.

a few short years after the establishment of the American Christian Missionary Society, the frontier was being evangelized and churches after the primitive order of the New Testament were being planted. The fact that the frontier was being evangelized is not the major concern here; rather, it is *how* the frontier was evangelized, or, more precisely, how congregations and individual Christians, especially east of the ever westward moving frontier, were organized as the frontier was evangelized.

The *modus operandi* used by the Restoration Movement in the period beginning with 1850 onward to evangelize the frontier was the formation and establishment of State (Missionary) Societies modeled after the parent organization, the American Christian Missionary Society. Lewis calls the ACMS the "Mother of Cooperating Organizations."

> The American Christian Missionary Society is often called "The Mother Society." It was not only the strong bulwork against religious anarchy and a narrow sectarian legalism that imperiled the very life of "the Movement," but it also became the instigator and defender of a well-organized cooperative life that spread throughout the brotherhood.
>
> In this more extended life the state missionary societies were of major importance.[21]

Indeed, one resolution proposed and adapted during that first convention of churches of 1849 was:

> *Whereas,* It is essential to a general union in the furtherance of the cause of our blessed Redeemer, that the brethren should confer with each other in the search after truth; and, whereas, the cultivation of the social and religious sympathies is necessary to bring into zealous and efficient actions the energies of the brethren, therefore,

---

21. Lewis, *The American Christian Missionary Society,* p. 17.

> *Resolved,* That we respectfully recommend to the churches the propriety of forming among themselves state and district meetings, to be held annually and quarterly, in such a way as may seem expedient, and that the churches in their primary assemblies be requested to send to their annual meetings by this messenger the number of members in their respective congregational with the name of the post office.[22]

The organization of the American Christian Missionary Society opened the way for the establishment of similar para-congregational societies on the state and district level. State societies were thereafter organized; in some cases certain state-wide or regional meetings which were already meeting on a regular basis were organized to become state societies. As an example of the latter, W. T. Moore states that:

> It is perhaps impossible to determine, with definite certainty, as to which state took the lead in this important matter of organizing statewide meetings into state societies. In several of the states yearly meetings were held, but these did not aim at any systematic, definite co-operation of churches. The meetings were mainly for preaching the Gospel and social enjoyment. Both Ohio and Missouri excelled in these yearly meetings. . . . In Missouri we have a record of these meetings, as far back as 1837, but the first state meeting in Missouri was held at Fayette, September 10, 1841. . . . These meetings continued to be held annually even before the organization of the General Missionary Society [i.e., the ACMS]. However, after 1849, these meetings began to take on a more distinctly business character.[23]

---

22. *Ibid.,* p. 9.
23. Moore, *A Comprehensive History of the Disciples of Christ,* p. 451.

17

FIGURE 1
FORMATION OF THE
VARIOUS STATE MISSIONARY SOCIETIES

State	Year Evangelistic or Informal State/Regional Convention Began	Year State Missionary Society was Formally Organized/Incorporated
Alabama	1874	1887
Arizona	1886	1907
Arkansas	1859	1883
California	1865	1876
Colorado	------	1873
Delaware	------	1884
Florida	------	1892
Georgia	1849	------
Idaho	1890	1901
Illinois	1832	1856
Indiana	1832	1856
Iowa	1846	1848
Kansas	1857	1858
Kentucky	1832	1850
Louisana	1851	1892
Maryland	------	1878
Michigan	1859	1869
Minnesota	1854	1877
Mississippi	1828	1883
Missouri	1841	1861
Montana	1881	1881
Nebraska	1861	1867
New York	1864	1878
New England Christian Missionary Society	------	1865
New Mexico	------	1907
North Carolina	------	1883
North and South Dakota	------	1884
Ohio	------	1852
Oklahoma	------	1907
Oregon	1846	1891
Pennsylvania	1834	1929
South Carolina	1879	1881
Tennessee	1840	1878
Texas	1836	1886
Utah	1891	------
Virginia	1850	1875
Washington	------	1888
West Virginia	------	1870
Wisconsin	1865	------
Wyoming	1868	1916

18

Figure 1 (p. 18) presents a list of states where state missionary societies were organized or incorporated and the year of their incorporation. As can be seen from the middle column, evangelistic and/or informal organizational efforts in each state usually preceded the formal organization of the State Missionary Society, in a number of instances by several years.

In other words, the lack of success in evangelism on foreign soil coupled with the rapid growth of the church on the American frontier caused the evangelistic efforts of the Restoration Movement to turn inward, and leave its original vision of proclaiming New Testament Christianity in other nations for the task of evangelizing its "own backyard."

This development inevitably led to the decline of the American Christian Missionary Society as a foreign missionary society among the churches of the Restoration Movement. Funds given to the Society by churches and individuals fell off drastically in the 1860's. In 1869 the ACMS adopted the "Louisville Plan" to raise funds needed for foreign evangelism. The plan was a brotherhood-wide fund raising scheme, which was rejected by the brotherhood almost as soon as it was promulgated, and perhaps rightly so. In order to be a brotherhood-wide plan,[24] the creation of a great deal of machinery to administer the collection, supervision, and disbursement of the monies as well as to enforce the plan and penalize in some way if necessary those churches that fail to participate would have been necessary. Those mentioned above who opposed any para-congregational organization naturally had a "field day"

---

24. *Ibid.*, p. 564. It was estimated by that time that the Restoration Movement in America had grown to 500,000 or more people many of whom were scattered all over the American frontier.

denouncing the Louisville Plan as unscriptural, but even those who did not oppose such organization or any scriptural principles saw in the plan a bureaucratic nightmare and decided not to support it. So the ACMS was right back where it started, declining even more in its ability to carry out foreign missionary work.

This turn of events from outward to inward evangelism should not be too harshly criticized, however, for the job of establishing New Testament Churches on the American frontier had to be done. The ACMS, as a brotherhood organization of its time, deserves credit for stepping in the breach and mobilizing as well as organizing the Restoration Movement for planting new churches as the American population moved westward. In retrospect, we may question the wisdom, perhaps even the legitimacy, of the top-heavy bureaucratic structures which ultimately resulted from the formation of so many state missionary societies, but we cannot deny the phenomenal advances and growth made by the Restoration Movement on the American frontier because these state societies were organized. Indeed these were glorious years of growth for the Restoration Movement in America.

Foreign Missions Revived

These years of national growth, however, did not mean that foreign mission concerns were forgotten in the Restoration Movement. To the contrary, foreign missions were still close to the heart of several brotherhood leaders and concern for the need of Christian Churches to preach the Gospel to those in other lands was often expressed by these leaders. Consequently, in the 1870's there was movement on two fronts to correct the imbalance that had emerged from a near total emphasis on evangelism in America.

For example, in 1872, the Annual Report, issued by the General Missionary Convention,[25] called for the brotherhood to review the work of foreign missions as soon as possible.[26] Nothing came of this call until the 1874 General Missionary Convention, which was held in Cincinnati, Ohio. At this convention W. T. Moore invited several brotherhood leaders to a special meeting to discuss the need for further organizational efforts among the churches so that the message of the Restoration Movement could be carried to other lands, since

> up to 1874 very little effort had been made through any organization to do any missionary work in foreign lands . . . so there was a growing feeling that the time had come when the Disciples should begin a foreign missionary work in earnest, as such a work would react upon the home churches, and would probably do more to stimulate missions activity at home, as well as abroad, than anything else that could be done.[27]

A committee was formed and met the following year to prepare a Constitution for a new missionary society. At the 1875 General Missionary Convention (held in Louisville, Kentucky), the Constitution was adopted and the Foreign Christian Missionary Society (FCMS) was born.

---

25. It was during the creation of the Louisville Plan, and written into its Constitution, that the ACMS was renamed the General Christian Missionary Convention. While the financial and bureaucratic scheme of the plan was never fully realized, the new name survived. In the literature we find that after 1869 the original ACMS was referred to as the General Convention, the General Missionary Convention, the General Christian Missionary Convention, or the General Society.

26. Archibald McLean, *The Foreign Christian Missionary Society* (New York: Fleming H. Revell Co., 1919), p. 31.

27. Moore, *A Comprehensive History of the Disciples of Christ*, p. 617.

While W. T. Moore was contemplating the organization of a new foreign missionary society, Mrs. Caroline Neville Pearre of Iowa City, Iowa, conceived the notion that the women of the Restoration Movement should band together to foster a missionary spirit in the brotherhood and to raise funds for both home and foreign missionary enterprises.[28] Mrs. Pearre's idea was advertised, and some seventy-five women met during the 1874 General Missionary Convention to organize the Christian Woman's Board of Missions (CWBM). Even though organized at the same Convention, the CWBM differed from the FCMS in that the former was dedicated to both home and foreign missions while the latter was designed only for foreign missions. There was one other aspect in which the CWBM differed from the FCMS: its business was managed entirely by women. Throughout its history, all officers of the CWBM (Presidents, Vice Presidents, Secretaries, Treasurers) were women, an especially remarkable accomplishment since it was achieved when women in the U.S.A. had yet to win the right to vote.[29]

The formation of two new missionary societies met with general acceptance among the Disciples of Christ. This approval was due in large measure to the work and influence of one man, Isaac Errett, who was Editor of the *Christian Standard* during this time.[30] In 1867 Errett wrote that the

---

28. Ida Withers Harrison, *Forty Years of Service, History of the Christian Woman's Board of Missions from 1874 to 1914* (St. Louis, MO: Christian Board of Pub., 1915), pp. 22-23.

29. Mrs. O. A. Burgess, President of the CWBM in 1880 and again from 1890 to 1902, exclaimed that "the Christian Woman's Board of Missions was unique . . . in that the business of the Society was managed entirely by women. For years we were not aware that other women's Societies did not proceed in the same way." (*Ibid.*, p. 25.)

30. Before he became editor of the *Christian Standard*, Isaac Errett served as Corresponding Secretary of the ACMS from 1857 to 1860. He also was a strong supporter of the Ohio Christian Missionary Society, one of the many state societies that sprang up after the ACMS was organized.

Christian Standard was the only weekly advocating missionary societies.[31] When he learned of Mrs. Pearre's plans for the CWBM, he wrote an editorial urging churches and individuals to help in its formation.[32] When the Foreign Christian Missionary Society was formally organized in 1875, Isaac Errett was its first president, and continued to serve as the society's president until his death in 1888. In fact, upon his death Isaac Errett was recognized as "our wisest master-builder in the reconstruction" of the Restoration Movement.[33] Which meant that, after the days of destruction in doing battle with the sects, it was Isaac Errett who, as a second-generation leader, did the most to consolidate the gains of the Restoration Movement via the various missionary societies. This pivotal role which Isaac Errett played during this period was long afterwards recognized by the Disciples of Christ. Writing in 1909, E. V. Zollars said that,

> Perhaps Isaac Errett's most valuable contribution to our work as a people was the impetus that he gave us in the way of organization. Circumstances, as well as his personal fitness for the task, enable him to assist largely in rescuing our movement from chaos and in organizing our forces so as to best develop our latent possibilities . . . In short, he is responsible, perhaps more than any other man, for saving us from the folly of ultra-conservatism or anti-ism.[34]

The foreign missionary societies — initiated, we may say, along sexist lines in the Restoration Movement! — began immediately to renew the spirit for foreign missionary work

---

31. Isaac Errett, "Tell It As It Is," *Christian Standard*, March 2, 1867, p. 68.
32. Errett, "Help Those Women," *Christian Standard*, July 11, 1874, p. 220.
33. Hugh McDiarmid, "Isaac Errett," *Christian Standard*, December 29, 1888, p. 838.
34. E. V. Zollars, "Isaac Errett," *Christian Standard*, September 11, 1909, p. 1594.

by Churches of the Restoration Movement. Their first efforts, however, did not auger well for such a renewal. The first mission fields which the FCMS entered were England, Denmark, France and Turkey. Only in England did the Restoration Movement take root as a result of these efforts; mission work in the other three countries was eventually closed. The CWBM first chose Jamaica, a mission field first entered by the American Christian Missionary Society but later abandoned because of lack of funds. The CWBM sought to revive this work but little progress for the first ten years and consequently, during these years there were frequent turnovers in personnel. The tide turned in 1881 when the FCMS and CWBM agreed to send missionaries to India, an agreement which was carried out the following year when the FCMS sent its first missionaries to India followed by the first CWBM missionaries three years later in 1885.[35] From this time onward, both societies grew, sending an ever growing missionary force throughout the world: Figures 2 and 3 present foreign mission fields entered and the year of entry of these two societies between the years of 1875 and 1918. During these 44 years, the FCMS sent out a total of 436 different personnel while the CWBM sent out over 200 different foreign missionaries plus a host of others for home missions.

The Christian Woman's Board of Missions established and carried on an extensive home mission work during these years. Schools for the underprivileged in the mountains of Kentucky, West Virginia and Tennessee were started. Mission work among Orientals in California and Oregon was also begun. Negro educational institutes and social work were established in Mississippi, Kentucky, Alabama,

---

35. Harrison, *The First Forty Years*, pp. 42-44.

Virginia, Tennessee, Texas, and Indiana. In addition to these states, Negro evangelistic work was also carried on in Arkansas, Georgia, Missouri, Oklahoma and South Carolina. The CWBM was the first agency of the Restoration Movement to recognize that the secular university was a legitimate home mission field. Consequently, Bible Chairs were established at the University of Michigan (1892), University of Virginia (1897), University of Kansas (1901), University of Texas (1904), and Tri-State College of Angola, Indiana (1908).

FIGURE 2		FIGURE 3	
CHRISITAN WOMAN'S BOARD OF MISSION		FOREIGN CHRISTIAN MISSIONARY SOCIETY	
Mission Field	Year Entered	Mission Field	Year Entered
Argentina	1905	Belgian Congo (Zaire)	1897
Canada	1909	China	1886
India	1882	Cuba	1901
Jamaica	1876	Denmark	1876
Liberia	1905	England	1876
Mexico	1895	France	1877
Paraguay	1918	Hawaii	1899
Puerto Rico	1900	India	1882
		Italy	1875
		Japan	1883
		Panama	1893
		Philippines	1901
		Tibet	1902
		Turkey	1879

Of the two societies, the Christian Woman's Board of Missions surged ahead of the Foreign Christian Missionary Society in mobilizing and organizing the Disciples of Christ for mission work; only the American Christian Missionary Society outperformed the CWBM in this respect. Early in its history, for example, the CWBM began to mobilize the youth of the Christian Churches in the support of missions.

> A study of the old records of the CWBM shows that very early in its history our missionary mothers felt that the training of the children in the knowledge and work of missions would be fundamental to the permanent success of the work.[36]

A magazine, titled *Missionary Tidings,* was soon started for the youth and a Young People's Department, with a National Superintendent at its head, was established. This Department established Mission Bands and later Junior and Intermediate Societies as auxiliaries to the Christian Woman's Board of Mission in church after church in America. The object of each auxiliary,

> shall be to develop the spiritual life of its members; to lead them into active personal service "For Christ's Sake"; to instruct them in the purposes, methods and results of missions, and to train them in habits of systematic giving in support of missionary enterprises.[37]

Through these youth auxiliaries the CWBM was able to raise funds for the building of hospitals, school buildings and homes for missionaries throughout the world.

During the reorganization of the CWBM in 1914, a constitution was adopted which allowed the creation of several types of auxiliaries on the state, district and local levels. Since many of these auxiliary organizations were already in existence, the new constitution merely recognized them and gave them a formal basis for existing. One of the more significant types of auxiliary which sprang up during this time was the Women's Auxiliary Missionary Society of the

---

36. Harrison, *The First Forty Years,* p. 90.
37. *Ibid.,* p. 159.

local congregation. Women of a local church could band together to form the Christian Women's Missionary Society of
that church. These local auxiliaries proved to be so popular
that they were carried over in later years into Direct-Support
Missions as an essential feature of missionary mobilization.
In addition to Women's Societies, there were also Young
Women's Mission Circles organized in local congregations.

Another significant contribution which the Christian Woman's Board of Missions made to the missionary outreach of
the Disciples of Christ was the establishment of the College
of Missions, which formally opened its doors to students in
1910 in Indianapolis, Indiana.[38] The College was a training
institution for missionaries and its curriculum was drawn up
according to recommendations on missionary education emanating from the World Missionary Conference which was
held at Edinburgh in 1910.

> A curriculum of more than sixty courses was provided,
> including some offered by a neighboring institution, Butler
> College, and made available, when necessary, for College of
> Mission students. The courses are arranged in eight main
> groups, as follows: (1) Missionary Science and History; (2)
> Biblical Literature, History and Interpretation; (3) The World's
> Religions; (4) Philosophy and Education; (5) Social Science
> and Home Missions; (6) Economics and Political Science.
> Besides these a number of subsidiary courses by "special
> lectures" are given each year.[39]

The College of Missions continued its operation until 1944
when it was moved to Yale University.

---

38. *Ibid.*, p. 85.
39. *Ibid.*, p. 87.

The FCMS and CWBM were not the only organizations created in the Restoration Movement after 1874. In 1833, at the General Missionary Convention, it was suggested that efforts be organized to provide funds for mission churches on the frontier to build church buildings. The Convention provided $5,000 for this fund, and the venture was so successful that by 1888 the Board of Church Extension was formally organized with headquarters in Kansas City, Missouri.[40] At about the same time, the National Benevolent Association was formed (incorporated in 1887) and headquartered in St. Louis, Missouri. Other brotherhood-wide organizations formed during this period were:

The Board of Ministerial Relief (organized in 1843, discontinued in 1886 but finally resurrected and incorporated in 1897)

Commission on Christian Unity (which began in 1871)

The Temperance Board (established in 1907)

The Social Service Commission (began in 1911)

The Committee on Rural Churches (established in 1894)

These organizations, as can be seen from their names, grew out of home mission concern within the Restoration Movement.

A Divided Movement

Meanwhile, however, the existence of so many national and state organizations, all made possible in the Restoration Movement because the American Christian Missionary Society had previously been organized and more importantly had survived in one form or another, created a swirl of tensions

---

40. Lewis, *The American Christian Missionary Society*, p. 21.

in the Restoration Movement which in turn unleased certain dynamics which are still today very much a part of the Restoration Movement. For with the formation of an increasing number of societies on the international, national and state levels, the opposition correspondingly increased, thereby creating a repulsion effect within the Disciples of Christ, where, as in physics, like bodies repel one another. As one part of the Movement rushed headlong into planning and creating para-church structures to advance the cause of the Movement, another part rushed off in the other direction in opposition.

The tension, resulting from the establishment of the ACMS in 1849, immediately broke out into an open debate which was carried by brotherhood journals. Before the Civil War,[41] for example, brotherhood periodicals, such as the Gospel Advocate opposed the para-congregational structures while the *American Christian Review* edited by Benjamin Franklin supported them.[42] Franklin, however, soon changed his mind and began to use his paper to speak out against the ACMS and state societies that had sprang up around it.[43] Franklin's conversion was a setback for the pro-society side of the debate, but with the establishment of the Christian Standard after the Civil War, under the editorship of Isaac Errett, the cause of para-congregational structures was once

---

41. James R. Wilburn, *The Hazard of the Die* (Austin, Texas: Sweet Publishing Co., 1969), pp. 176-181.

42. "One of the Societies' staunchest supporters at their beginning was Benjamin Franklin. . . . He served as a corresponding secretary of the ACMS and used his paper to speak on behalf of its efforts. His paper might almost be considered the mouthpiece of the society during its first years." (*Ibid.*, p. 249.)

43. For an account of why Franklin changed his mind on the society debate, see *The Hazard of the Die*, pp. 249-250.

more advocated through a brotherhood journal.[44]

The opponents of para-church organizations advanced four main arguments against the various missionary societies which had emerged in the Restoration Movement.[45]

First, there was opposition to the *methods used in financing the societies.* The three major missionary societies, the ACMS, CWBM and FCMS, sold memberships as a way of raising funds for their operations. This, it was claimed, was an unscriptural method in that the Apostle Paul advocated something quite differently (I Cor. 16:1-4) and that it would allow (in theory at least) denominationalists and even infidels to buy into the societies and thus gain control over the task of spreading the plea of the Restoration Movement around the world. Later, when special congregational collections for the societies were instituted, opponents still objected stating that a congregational offering coerced them, as

---

44. James R. Wilburn, writing from a Church of Christ (non-instrumental) perspective, presents an interesting interpretation of the establishment of the Christian Standard at this time.

". . . The *Christian Standard* was a new weekly designed to rekindle the waning interest in the Missionary Society." (*Ibid.,* p. 229.)

"When Franklin began to speak out against the Missionary Society, the effect was staggering. For a while the organization floundered for lack of financial support. Had it not been for the artificial respiration by the new *Christian Standard* (which struggled, even then, depending upon heavy gifts from supports of the society), the church might remember the national society as a part of the story of the Civil War epoch which, by itself might not have inflicted as deep divisional wounds. But, as it happened, the society remained as a reminder of the feelings nourished during those senseless years of hysteria and hate, and hostilities remained with some even after they had forgotten their origin." (*Ibid.,* p. 250.)

45. For two contemporary summaries of these arguments cf. "Touching Grounds of Withdrawal," *Christian Standard,* January 22, 1887, p. 28, where A. C. Bartlett raised questions about the legitimacy of the society and H. McDiarmid gave answers in defense.

members of the congregations, into supporting something which they did not approve.

Second, opponents claimed that all para-church structures were human innovations and therefore, unauthorized by the New Testament. To create such organizations was to fall back into the dark ages of clericalism and ecclesiasticalism out of which the Restoration Movement had come. That is, para-church organizations were a threat to the autonomy and supremacy of the local congregation. Moreover, since Jesus Christ had established only the church, a para-church organization could not possess the Spirit of Christ; hence, the para-church structure was, at the most, a useless and lifeless appendage to the Church of Jesus Christ.

Third, opponents argued that the *local church was God's missionary society.* The church was ordained and sufficiently organized to be God's agency for evangelistic outreach into a sinful world. In this case, not only was the para-church missionary society an unnecessary addition to God's plan, it was also a demonstration of man's unfaithfulness to that plan.

Fourth, since the church embodied the divine method for evangelizing the world, *to establish, advocate and support the para-church missionary societies was heretical and schematic.* It was heretical because it proposed a method of evangelism other than what God had instituted, and schismatic because it effectively divided brethren, who otherwise would be united, into pro- and anti-society parties. Furthermore, it was argued, the proponents would be the cause of the division since it was they who advocated a para-church plan in place of God's plan for mobilizing Christians to evangelize the world.

Proponents of the para-church structures among the Disciples of Christ, of course, rose up to answer these objections. The journal which they most often used for their

31

defense of the missionary societies was the *Christian Standard*. The *Christian Evangelist,* another major journal of the same period, also supported the cause of missionary societies, but not as extensively as the *Christian Standard*. For example, in its second full year of publication (1867), the *Christian Standard* published twenty-three articles and editorials just on the debate alone, nearly all of them in defense of the missionary societies;[46] this count does not include a great number of other articles which simply reported the news of the societies. By comparison, the *Christian Evangelist* did not reach the same number of articles published on the debate until 1883.[47]

The defense which proponents of the missionary societies gave was not a one-on-one answer to the objections put forward by the opponents. There were, to be sure, answers to a few specific objections, but more generally the defense took on the characteristics of an offense. That is, proponents defended their para-church organizational efforts by pointing out weaknesses inherent in an anti-society position, weaknesses moreover which the missionary society, as a para-church structure, avoided in an admirable way.

Proponents of the missionary societies advanced two main arguments in behalf of their cause.

First, as an argument designed to meet the objections put forward by opponents and to go beyond them in significant ways, proponents claimed that *the church has the freedom to organize and use "expediencies" as missionary societies to fulfill God's plan*. Robert Milligan, writing in the *Christian Standard* in 1866, advanced thirteen theses

---

46. Claudia E. Spencer, ed., *Christian Standard Index* (Nashville: Disciples of Christ Historical Society, 1972), p. 2237.

47. Spencer, ed., *The Christian Evangelist Index* (Nashville: The Disciples of Christ Historical Society, 1962), pp. 962-963.

in defense of the missionary society. Essentially Milligan, in these theses, conceded that the church was indeed God's missionary society and that every member of the church is a missionary. But, he went on to argue, if each congregation is a missionary society, then the whole brotherhood is likewise a missionary society. How, then, shall the brotherhood realize its potential as a missionary society? This potential could be realized only by local churches exercising the expediency of appointing representatives to come together to plan and organize for the task. Since a para-church organization existed only for a specialized task, it could not dictate policy or doctrine to the churches. Since the Scriptures did not specifically prohibit such expediencies, churches in different locations had the freedom to associate together in any form that seemed reasonable to accomplish the task which God has given the church, viz. the evangelization of the world.[48, 49]

Second, proponents argued that *the missionary societies were allowing the churches to fulfill the Great Commission while the anti-society position of the opponent actually prevented them from fulfilling the last command of Jesus Christ.*

Those who favor missionary societies have no objection to individual congregations sustaining evangelists by weekly contributions: *but let us see them do it.* We cannot save the

---

48. Robert Milligan, "Missionary Societies," *Christian Standard*, November 10, 1866, p. 250.

49. Robert Richardson, on the other hand, took a different view than Robert Milligan's. Writing in 1867, Richardson asked, ". . . Is it true, then, that the Church is already organized with a view to missionary work? . . . I remark, that it is entirely a mistake to suppose that *the* Church is already organized for missionary work . . . *the* Church is not organized *at all* for any such purpose whatever." ("Missionary Work No. 2," *Christian Standard,* June 29, 1867, p. 201.)

world by theories. Give us *deeds*. . . . Let brethren who prefer other methods to organized societies follow their own convictions; but let their arguments against the societies be the superior results of their mode of operating. At the present stage of our history, an ounce of demonstration is worth a ton of theory in this matter.[50]

In short, the do-nothingness of the anti's demonstrated the very weakness of their arguments while the positive accomplishments of the missionary societies, in evangelizing the American frontier and sending missionaries to foreign nations, more than justified the utilization of para-church organizations.[51]

Other arguments in favor of the missionary societies were also advanced through the pages of the *Christian Standard* and *Christian Evangelist*. Both journals, for example, carried articles on Alexander Campbell and the missionary society pointing out that Campbell had spoken and written in favor of congregations banding together to accomplish certain tasks, whether those tasks be building a church building or sending out an evangelist. However, proponents of the missionary societies did not appeal too often to Campbell in support of their cause, for opponents could also appeal to an "earlier Campbell" in support of their position, at which point the debate would have devolved into a counterproductive argument of whether Alexander Campbell was inconsistent, had changed his mind, or had simply grown senile and didn't know any better than to advocate para-church organizations!

---

50. *Christian Standard,* April 21, 1866, p. 20.

51. In all fairness it should be noted that during these years of controversy there were churches which were opposed to the missionary society but which also supported evangelists and home missionaries (cf. Wilburn, *The Hazard of the Die*, p. 186).

Unfortunately the debate over the legitimacy of the missionary societies in the Restoration Movement was not confined to the pages of brotherhood journals. It was carried over into local churches where it was acted out often in bitter and hostile terms. Both sides — those in favor of the societies and those opposed to them — were guilty of agitating for their respective position on the debate to the point that congregational unity and harmony in church after church was greatly disrupted. The aggressive tactics of both sides, moreover, succeeded in only making a bad situation worse. Anti-society brethren in churches began to complain that representatives of the societies were too "pushy" and insensitive in trying to force the anti's to contribute via congregational offerings to the support of the societies; when they did not give, they were made to feel like second-class citizens in the Kingdom. Those in favor of the societies, on the other hand, complained of traveling "anti" evangelists who would split churches over matters of Sunday Schools, prayer meetings and, above all, the missionary society, even going so far as physically locking out those who were in favor of such things.[52] Obviously a brotherhood-wide division was in the making.

The first formal call for division over the issue of the missionary society (including other items of debatable legitimacy) was not long in coming. On August 18, 1889, there was issued in Shelby County, Illinois, the Sand Creek Address and Declaration, which said in part:

> There are among us those who do teach and practice things not taught or found in the New Testament . . . viz. that of

---

52. J. H. Garrison and B. W. Johnson, eds., "The Churches vs. Missionary Societies," *Christian Evangelist*, May 5, 1887, p. 283. The letter, from where the above information is taken, closed with the words, "They have made the missionary question here a test of fellowship."

the church holding festivals of various kinds . . . the use of the musical instrument in the worship; the select choir (to the) abandonment of congregational singing. Likewise the man-made society for missionary work and the one-man imported preacher. . .

. . . We state that we are impelled from a sense of duty to say that all such as are guilty of teaching or allowing and practicing the many innovations and corruptions to which we have referred . . . if they will not turn away from such abominations [we] cannot and will not regard them as brethren.[53]

The publication of this Declaration had a powerful impact throughout the Restoration Movement. Many were now truly alarmed that the debate over the missionary society, instead of solving the question over the legitimacy of para-church organizations, was leading only to a divided Movement. Churches throughout the land were beginning to line up on either one side or the other, or worse still, were splitting into competing congregations, one pro-society and the other anti-society.

In order to avert what seemed the inevitable, J. W. McGarvey, a leading preacher and scholar in the Restoration Movement of the late 1800's, offered through the pages of the *Christian Standard* a compromise titled, "Mission Work: A Word For Peace."[54] In his compromise, McGarvey called for a halt to the aggressive promotion for funds in congregations by agents of the missionary societies until a more sober judgment of the societies' scriptural justification

---

53. For the full text, see West, *The Search For The Ancient Order*, pp. 430-432.

54. J. W. McGarvey, "Mission Work: A Word For Peace," *Christian Standard*, February 7, 1891, p. 114.

could be made by the brotherhood. Being pro-society but anti-musical-instrument in worship, McGarvey perceived himself in an unique position to avert division and bring peace: both sides would surely listen to him. McGarvey's compromise called on everyone to allow the freedom to band together in para-church organizations but that such organizations had no inherent right to other people's money. The missionary societies had the freedom to solicit money from those in favor of the societies, but "agents of societies should conscientiously abstain from so pressing their claim upon these anti-society brethren as to give them complaint."[55] If the pro-society brethren would only yield on this last point, McGarvey pleaded, the coming division could be avoided.

Reaction to McGarvey's suggested compromise was instant and forceful. Both proponents and opponents of the missionary society claimed that the compromise did not go far enough either way! There was even agitation for both sides to divide immediately and each go its own way.[56] But despite such reactions, a few brotherhood leaders still hoped that the compromise would be accepted. M. C. Kurfees, for example, whose sympathies laid more with the opponents of the missionary societies, wrote in the *Christian Standard* urging the brotherhood to consider McGarvey's compromise as the way to peace.[57] Kurfees called on the brotherhood to "yield" to those who oppose the missionary societies, i.e. to collect for the societies on an individual basis and not force a whole church to contribute. "This will satisfy the anti's," Kurfees promised.

---

55. *Ibid.*

56. Cf. the letter written by F. M. Green in the *Christian Standard,* March 14, 1891, p. 228 ("Correspondence: in Mission Work: A Word for Peace").

57. M. C. Kurfees, "Mission Work: Yielding Can Stop Here," *Christian Standard,* February 28, 1891, p. 181.

Kurfees' plea, even though published through the pages of the *Christian Standard* was not to be realized, for the strongest reaction to McGarvey's peace compromise came from the *Christian Standard* itself. In a sharply worded editorial, the *Christian Standard* pointed out three weaknesses to the compromise: 1) yielding cannot consistently stop with giving up church collections (the brotherhood would also have to yield on Sunday Schools, musical instruments, paid preachers, church buildings, etc., to eventually satisfy the anti's); 2) the Bible does not command a church in congregational action, to yield to the convention of a few in all things that cannot be enforced by the authority of the Scriptures; 3) yielding on this issue would prevent congregational instruction on the church's duty, as a corporate body, to support missions (i.e. mission work is much more at the nexus of the Gospel than eating or drinking over which brethren are urged to yield for the sake of weaker brethren).[58] Because of this last point, the editorial argued that giving up church collections for the missionary societies would not only endanger the missionary outreach of the Restoration Movement, but it would also be unscriptural. It was the duty of the brotherhood to promote the missionary societies because it was through these para-church structures that the Restoration Movement was fulfilling the Great Commission.

The "time for sober judgment" which J. W. McGarvey pleaded for did not come. Neither side yielded on any of the issues raised in the debate: both sides felt that too much had been invested in their respective positions. From the

---

58. Hugh McDiarmid, "That Word For Peace," *Christian Standard*, April 4, 1891, pp. 290-291.

perspective of the anti-society brethren, too much had been invested ideologically to allow the thesis that other brethren had the freedom to organize para-church structures in order to carry out specific tasks. From the perspective of the society brethren, too much para-church machinery had been created to exempt part of the brotherhood from the responsibility of paying for it; the burden should be borne by all and not just by those who happen to be in favor of such machinery. So with the publication of the Sand Creek Declaration (calling for division), McGarvey's Word of Peace (calling for sober judgment), and the Christian Standard's rejection of this Word (calling for corporate responsibility in fulfilling the Great Commission), the two positions — anti-society vs. pro-society — became polarized, and it wasn't long before the tension between the opposing position became strained even to the breaking point.

The tensions thus produced by the plethora of para-congregational organizations set an unfortunate precedent in the Restoration Movement, namely that, if such tensions cannot be resolved, then there must be separation of the Movement into opposing religious parties. At times, though, it can rightfully be argued that following such a precedent, unhappy as it may be, is a necessary correction to going overboard along organizational lines and becoming overly bureaucraticized. Whatever one's evaluation of this precedent may be, we must nevertheless recognize that it has happened, as according to a modern proverb, that division has become the order of the day whenever tensions cannot be resolved in the Restoration Movement.

Consequently, in the final decade of the 19th century, the tensions created in the Restoration Movement grew tauter until, at the opening of the 20th century, the strain could be borne no longer and the first major division occurred.

In 1906, a number of churches and brethren declared that that part of the Restoration Movement which advocated and used para-congregational religious societies to perform the work of God's Kingdom was hopelessly apostate, and so formally withdrew to form the Churches of Christ (non-instrumental). To be sure, there was more at stake in the division than just the missionary society. The musical instrument in worship was also involved, for by 1906 a number of churches in the Restoration Movement had purchased and were using organs to aid singing in the worship service. This too was considered unscriptural by many. But while the anti-organ issue has over the years grown to overshadow the society issue as a *cause celebre* between the Church of Christ and the rest of the Campbellian Restoration Movement, it was nevertheless only a co-factor, if not a secondary factor, in relation to the missionary society underlying the division of 1906.

The division resulting in the Churches of Christ needs no longer to occupy our attention with respect to our subject, the Historical Antecedents to Direct-Support Missions in the Restoration Movement. Undoubtedly, several historical and ideological parallels between why the Churches of Christ separated from the rest of the Restoration Movement and the later emergence of Direct-Support Missions can be drawn. But these are outside the scope of this volume. That being the case, we leave this part of the history of the Restoration Movement to proceed more directly into the developments which led to the creation of Direct-Support Missions.

Isaac Errett

W. E. Garrison

Chapter Two

THEOLOGY AND THE MISSIONARY SOCIETY

With the coming of formal separation over the issue of whether or not para-congregational missionary societies were legitimate means by which the Great Commission could be carried out, the Restoration Movement was divided into two camps, the Disciples of Christ and the Churches of Christ. For the Churches of Christ, the missionary society and the principle of the local, autonomous church were antithetical, since in the Scriptures there was precedent for the latter but none for the former. To these brethren and churches, therefore, it was more important to maintain the principle of the local congregation even if it meant, for the time being at least, a neglect of formulating a method whereby the Churches of Christ could evangelize the nations. Maintenance of this principle, however, placed these brethren in the unenviable dilemma of having a command to obey (the Great Commission) but having no plan to carry it out because the plan would be a human invention and therefore unscriptural.

For the Disciples of Christ, on the other hand, the missionary society was not antithetical to the principle of the local, autonomous congregation, but rather the society was a strategy whereby the churches could obey and carry out the Great Commission of evangelizing the nations; moreover, the strategy, or method, for obedience was as necessary as the command was important, for without the strategy the command could not be implemented and carried out. To state the argument from a theological perspective, to fail to carry out this last command of Jesus Christ because of a fear that the strategy would be an unscriptural human invention would be as bad as the servant who hid his one

41

talent (Mt. 25:14-30). The servant was condemned not because he had used a method of his own invention to earn more talents, but because he had failed, yea even refused, to employ a plan of his own creation to gain more talents for his master. At the least he could have employed the method of investing the money and returning it plus the interest to his master.

Two Theological Perspectives

While missionary societies were an acceptable strategy or method among the Disciples of Christ before and after the beginning of this century, the basis of this acceptance was not as simple as the above words indicate. If it were, there perhaps would be no Direct-Support Missions today. But it was more complex, and it wasn't long before a significant number of brethren within the Disciples of Christ came to view the missionary society, and all the other para-congregational organizations evolving therefrom, with disfavor and even alarm, while others came to view these organizational structures as something more than a strategy to fulfill a command. The first group of brethren viewed these organizations as utilitarian, expedient and, therefore, expendable: such organizations were servants of the churches enabling the churches to carry out the task of evangelism in the modern world. The other group, however, viewed these organizational developments from a teleological perspective; that is to say, the maturing and fulfillment of the Restoration Movement were not to be found in the restoration of autonomous New Testament Churches, but in the emergence of brotherhood wide agencies and organizations.

The utilitarian or pragmatic viewpoint of the missionary society was the earlier of the two viewpoints mentioned above. In an oft-quoted passage, Isaac Errett, then editor of the *Christian Standard*, wrote in 1867 illustrating this view:

> The *Standard* is the only weekly paper among us now that advocates Missionary Societies; and we want the brethren to know this fact. Where there is a great end to be accomplished—a scriptural end—and the Word of God does not shut us up to any special routine of operations, we go from the best expedients that the united wisdom of the brethren in a given District, State or Nation, may suggest . . . But we have no idolatrous attachment to the General Missionary Society. If it can do the work proposed, we will encourage it. If it fails to command sufficient confidence and sympathy to enable it to do its work wisely and well, we shall go in for whatever form of associated effort the general wisdom of the brotherhood may approve.[1]

The theological view of para-church organizations often emerged in the pages of the *Christian Evangelist*. Of this journal, Disciples of Christ historians, W. E. Garrison and A. T. DeGroot, state:

> The *Christian Evangelist* became strong and efficient through the conviction that the accomplishment of the purposes of the movement demanded cooperation, and that Christian unity is more likely to be found along the road of union in work than through the air lanes of theological inquiry and uniformity.[2]

The first editor of the *Christian Evangelist*, James H. Garrison, who was editor from 1869 to 1912, was an able promoter of this view of missionary societies. According to William E. Tucker, James H. Garrison began his ministry in the Restoration Movement as a "Flaming Conservative" but

---

1. Isaac Errett, "Tell It As It Is," *Christian Standard*, March 2, 1867, p. 68.
2. Winfred Ernest Garrison and A. T. DeGroot, *The Disciples of Christ, A History* (St. Louis: Christian Board of Publication, 1948), p. 361.

soon underwent a "radical change of mind" emerging as an "Ecumenical Saint."[3] His change of mind was soon reflected in how he came to view the cooperation of churches through the missionary society, a view which he himself often expressed through the pages of the *Christian Evangelist*. For example, in an 1894 editorial, J. H. Garrison proclaimed that

. . . . if we are to be loyal to Christ's great commission to evangelize the world and not triflers with this solemn duty, we will have missionary societies and boards with which to carry on our work in an orderly and systematic way, and will hold them to the purpose for which they have been created.[4]

There were others among the Disciples of Christ, moreover, who advocated the same view of the para-church missionary societies that had emerged in the Restoration Movement. A striking example of this is from the pen of E. C. Browning who wrote a four-part article on the subject for the *Christian Evangelist* early in 1894. Browning began his series by declaring that the emergence of missionary societies in the Restoration Movement was inevitable:

The present status of our mission work is a growth from the concept (of cooperation) . . . Out of it inevitably grew Missionary Conventions, or Conferences, general or national, and State and National Boards, etc.[5]

3. William E. Tucker, *J. H. Garrison and the Disciples of Christ* (St. Louis: The Bethany Press, 1964), pp. 162-165.

4. J. H. Garrison, "Prerogatives of Mission Boards," *Christian Evangelist*, May 24, 1894, p. 322. Compare also these words from another editorial of the same year: ". . . But it is evident that other and more general organizations of (our) churches are *necessary* (italics supplied) in order for wider cooperative effort and to the successful fulfillment of the mission of the church." (*Christian Evangelist*, Oct. 11, 1894, p. 642).

5. E. C. Browning, "What Kind of Missionary Organization Shall We Have," *Christian Evangelist*, May 24, 1894, p. 550.

A more eloquent statement of the teleological perspective, however, is an excerpt from a message which was delivered at the 1899 Kansas City General Convention. In this address the speaker compared the pre-society days of the Restoration Movement to the forty years of desert wandering of the Israelites after their exodus from Egypt.

> It was forty years from the Declaration and Address (given by Thomas Campbell) to the organization of the American Christian Missionary Society, the exact period of the time the Israelties wandered in the wilderness before entering upon the conquest of Canaan.[6]

These two viewpoints — the utilitarian and the teleological — soon posed a dilemma for the Disciples of Christ. Even though the dilemma of whether or not para-congregational organizations were legitimate means of fulfilling the Great Commission had been settled in favor of such organizations, the question arose as to whether these organizations should be treated as dispensible addenda to the churches, or should they be treated seriously as part of the whole church? If the former, then the evangelistic outreach could also be dispensed with; but if the latter, then the church was in danger of being supplanted in importance and power by the organization. While the dilemma was real enough, it did not lead immediately into a full-scale debate and division among the Disciples of Christ. Rather, the two viewpoints, including their respective advocators, existed amicably side-by-side for many years. Isaac Errett, in a letter often quoted by modern day Disciples of Christ historians, wrote to James Garrison:

---

6. "Some Lessons From Our Past," *Christian Evangelist*, Jan. 4, 1900, p. 8.

We have been together from the beginning of this missionary work. We have stood shoulder to shoulder . . . and the two most effectual instrumentalities in educating our people and bringing them into active cooperation in spreading the gospel in all lands have been the *Christian Evangelist* and the *Christian Standard*; and indeed, upon all points of doctrine and practice and expediency you and I have worked on the same lines in perfect harmony.[7]

Even as late as 1908, J. A. Lord, editor of the *Christian Standard*, was still reiterating Standard's pragmatic viewpoint toward the missionary methods by advocating not only liberty on the part of the individual church as to method — whether to support missionaries through one of the societies or independently[8] — but also to switch methods from the cooperative to the congregational, or vice versa, if the church so desires. Hence, J. A. Lord went on to emphasize,

The *Christian Standard* will rejoice to hear of churches selecting their missionaries on the field, and sustaining them without reference to the missionary society, and we will rejoice if churches and individuals multiply the receipts of the missionary societies, to enable them to do still greater things in bringing men out of darkness into the Kingdom of God's dear Son.[9]

The existence side-by-side of these viewpoints on the para-church missionary organization — the pragmatic and

---

7. Garrison and DeGroot, *The Disciples of Christ, A History*, p. 364.

8. By 1908 there were a few Disciples of Christ missionaries serving independently of the societies. See below, Chapter V, *From the Incidental to Model*, for a brief survey of independent Disciples missions between 1900 and 1926.

9. J. A. Lord, "The Standard and Missionary Methods," *Christian Standard*, Oct. 3, 1909, p. 1666.

the teleological—was not directly responsible for the emergence of Direct-Support Missions among the Disciples of Christ soon after the opening of the 20th Century. To find the most immediate antecedent for Direct-Support Missions we must look further afield, but in looking elsewhere we shall have to return to this issue once more and investigate the role it played in producing the Direct-Support Missionary Movement.

A New Theological Dimension

What was the immediate and most direct antecedent for the emergence of Direct-Support Missions within the Disciples of Christ? It is to be found in relation to the rise, among the Disciples of Christ, of a new dimension in the theological understanding of the Bible. This dimension was theological liberalism.

In retrospect it seems strange that liberalism should be the most immediate cause of Direct-Support Missions among the Disciples of Christ. Liberal theology and the missionary evangelism of the non-Christian in other cultures and lands are unrelated if not antithetical to each other. Liberal theology takes and applies a rather extreme form of cultural relativism while missionary evangelism seeks boldly to convert non-Christians. Cultural relativism is judging a person (of another culture) in terms of the culture available to him and not in terms of our own culture which is not available to him. The application of this principle in liberal theology is that if Christianity is not available to a person as part of his culture, then it is morally wrong to persuade that person to accept Christianity which, of course, is not part of his culture. Missionary evangelism, on the other hand, states that Christianity is not cultural in origin but has been given by revelation from

God. The task of the missionary, therefore, is to introduce Christianity into the culture so that it indeed may be available to the people of that culture for acceptance and salvation. Yet, despite their seeming antithetical nature, the use of liberal theology among the Disciples of Christ during the height of far reaching missionary activity, leads in a direct line to the emergence of Direct-Support Missions, not only becoming the major cause for their emergence but also providing the subsequent rationale for their structure and as a method of strategy whereby Christian Churches and Churches of Christ can be assured of having the Great Commission faithfully carried out.

What is theological liberalism? The terms liberal and liberalism are used in several different contexts — e.g. liberal politics, social liberalism, philosophical liberalism — in addition to theology. However, liberalism does not necessarily mean the same in every context, nor is there any necessary carry-over of an essential meaning of the term from one context to another. This can be illustrated by the fact that a person may believe and expouse liberalism in politics while at the same time not being a theological liberal. The converse may also be true: a theological liberal may hold to and advocate conservative politics. Moreover, theologies can be constructed to support either combination. On the other hand, we must admit that, while there is not an intrinsic relationship between theological liberalism and other types of liberalism, on the practical level theological liberalism has commonly been associated with political and social liberalism. But, it should be remembered, the relationship between the various contexts of liberalism is one of association and not of necessity.

In the 19th Century the term liberalism emerged in theological circles as a descriptive term referring to newly introduced ways of interpreting the Biblical record. Previously there were only two ways: believe the Bible and interpret the Biblical record at face value, or reject the Biblical record altogether. Correspondingly, if the Bible were believed and understood accordingly, then it was assumed that God exists and that His power could perform any type of miracle including all those recorded in the Bible; but if the Bible were rejected, it was assumed that there are naturalistic explanations for the supranaturalism of the Bible and the question of whether a deity existed or not was superfluous. In the 19th Century there developed, between these two extremes, other alternatives as to how to understand the Bible; alternatives which drew upon scholarly research in other disciplines such as Comparative Religion, Anthropology, Literature, etc. One early alternative used in interpreting the Biblical record was the concept of *myth*.

Myth in religious studies is a technical term and should not be understood as it is used in ordinary usage, i.e. a fanciful and untrue statement, or an event that never occurred. As a technical term, myth refers to an explanation of why the world or some part of the world is the way it is or came to be the way it is. Every tribe and people have myths which explain, for example, how the world came into existence, how the different races came to be, why the monkey has a long tail, etc. As such, myth is not primarily studied for its truthfulness (whether it actually occurred that way or not), but for its ideological and functional value in society (e.g. social control, entertainment, socialization, etc.). Even though the truth-value of a myth is secondary from this perspective, it is still an underlying assumption that the event or events that a myth describes is in all probability legendary.

49

This concept of myth enabled the liberal theologian of the 19th Century — a century that was fast eschewing metaphysics from its basic assumptions about the world and the processes of life — to take a nontraditional look at the Bible and reconcile the Biblical record with an increasingly secular and naturalistic outlook on life and the world.[10] For example the miracles and other supranatural events (e.g. the Virgin Birth) of the Biblical record could now be classified as myths whose function was not to preserve actual, historical events; rather their function was sociological and cultural in nature. That is to say, myths, for example, provided for the ancient Hebrews explanations of how the world came to be formed, why they were a different ethnic group from everyone else in the world, why they were to refrain from work on the seventh day, etc. Furthermore, these mythical portions of the Biblical record were not applicable to our modern age not because their truthfulness was highly questionable according to naturalistic assumptions, but because they simply were not relevant to an age of secularism. Yet, by classifying such portions as mythical in character, the Bible needed not to be rejected in its entirety as in the past but could be retained, taught, and applied in a modern age. From this perspective theological liberalism also came to be known as Modernism.

It is at this point where we can understand how theological liberalism came to be easily associated with social liberalism.

---

10. "The genius of liberal theology was its openness to all truth and its insistence on genuine dialogue between church and world. Fearing nothing more than an outmoded faith, liberals reconstructed Christian theology in order to harmonize it with prevailing currents in philosophy and science." Lester G. McAllister and William E. Tucker, *Journey in Faith* (St. Louis: Bethany Press, 1975), p. 362.

If the supernatural portions of the Biblical record are classified as myths, then there is little left to proclaim — i.e. the kerygma of the New Testament — about the supernaturalness and power of God to a fallen world. That being the case, only social relationships, which are also taught in the Bible, are left to be proclaimed. Since social liberalism is likewise concerned with social relationships (i.e. social justice, etc.), theological liberalism early found common cause with this type of social philosophy, an association that has lasted to this day.

Not only was the term liberalism used to describe new ways of interpreting the Biblical record, but it also came to denote a basic approach to the Bible and religious truth in general. That approach was rationalism. Rationalism, as both a philosophy and methodology, claimed that truth can be known by means of the mental processes of the mind. During the 18th and 19th Centuries, rationalism had scored several notable victories in answering a number of questions that had plagued mankind from the beginning, and in presenting, perhaps for the first time in history, a satisfactory nonmetaphysical model of the world. That being the case, rationalism, so it was proposed, held promise of answering some questions about the Biblical record that had likewise plagued Biblical scholars. For example, what was the significance of the two names of God, YAHWEH and ELOHIM, in the Old Testament? Why are there differences between Leviticus (the first book on the Mosaic Law) and Deuteronomy (the second book)? Why did the four Gospels divide themselves into two groupings, The Synoptics and John? These and a host of other questions about the Bible were subjected to the methodology of rationalism, and of course answers were formulated accordingly. The answers, however,

51

suffered from a serious defect that infects rationalism as a philosophy, viz., they tended to be critical of the Biblical record even to the point of being destructive in many instances.

In other words, liberalism in theological circles was a term amalgamating under its cover a number of nontraditional approaches to the Bible and its message for the world. Any theologian or minister, therefore, subscribing to any or all of these approaches was termed a liberal, modernist or even rationalist. As an approach to the Bible, theological liberalism became popular with religious leaders in many denominations and churches before and after the turn of the 20th Century. Religious leaders within the Restoration Movement were also not left unaffected by liberalism and its various methodologies for interpreting and applying the Bible in a secular age. Earl I. West reports that late in 1889, R. C. Cave delivered a sermon filled with rationalism to the Central Christian Church in St. Louis.

> Cave asserted that Abraham and Moses were grossly ignorant of the true character of God, and denied both the virgin birth of Jesus and the bodily resurrection of Christ. He described the Bible as an evolution, not a revelation, and declared that there was no such thing as a divinely-given "plan of salvation."[11]

This sermon created a great deal of controversy in the Restoration Movement, yet the very fact that it was preached — and could be preached! — in a Christian Church of that time reveals how far theological liberalism had infiltrated the Movement.

---

11. Earl I. West, *The Search for the Ancient Order* (Nashville, Tenn: Gospel Advocate Company, 1944), vol. I, p. 259.

Over the next two decades, after R. C. Cave had preached his sermon, liberals within the Christian Churches mobilized to disseminate their theology among the Disciples of Christ. For example,

-in 1892, Disciples of Christ students attending the Yale Divinity School organized the Campbell Club with the purpose of investigating traditional religious problems in the light of liberal theology;[12]

-in 1894, the Divinity House, a liberal theological school of the Disciples of Christ, was established in connection with the University of Chicago;[13]

-in 1896, the Campbell Institute was organized by Disciples influenced by the liberalism of Yale and the Chicago Divinity House;[14]

-in 1899, the first "Congress" was convened in St. Louis to discuss religious, theological, scientific and social problems according to liberal philosophy;[15]

-in 1901, the Christian Century was first published, covertly espousing the liberal cause;

12. James DeForest Murch, *Christians Only* (Cincinnati: Standard Publishing, 1962), pp. 238-239.

13. McAllister and Tucker, *Journey in Faith*, p. 374. Herbert L. Willett was elected as the first Dean of the Disciples Divinity House. He was followed by Winfred E. Garrison and Edward Scribner Ames respectively. "Joined by Charles Clayton Morrison, long-term editor of the *Christian Century* in Chicago, these men literally constituted the intellectual center of the Disciples for many years. Brilliant and determined, they led the Stone-Campbell movement into and through the heyday of American liberal theology."

14. *Ibid.* "As a liberalizing force in the life of Disciples . . . the Campbell Institute's influence was out of proportion to its size."

15. *Ibid.*, p. 375. The precursor of the first Congress was an editorial by J. H. Garrison in the *Christian Evangelist* (May 1, 1890, p. 274) in which he asked "What are the modifications, if any, which Time and Experience have made Necessary, in the Doctrinal Aspects of our Movement?"

-in 1908, the Christian Century instituted a policy of frank
and open commitment to liberalism within the Restoration
Movement.[16]

But theological liberalism was not without its opponents
in the Restoration Movement. Conservatives immediately
took up the battle against theological liberalism. Notable
among these was J. W. McGarvey, who began in 1893 a
series of popularly written articles in the *Christian Standard*
under the title of "Biblical Criticism." In these articles McGarvey
exposed the naturalistic assumptions underlying liberal
theology and the rational approach to the Bible. Thus a
debate between liberals and conservatives within the Disciples
of Christ began; it was a debate that ultimately ranged over
the full scope of brotherhood activities, from the local congregation to the state and national societies and on to the
foreign mission fields, and was to last hot and heavy over
the next fifty years.

That the Liberal-Conservative controversy over the Bible
should have afflicted the Restoration Movement is, from
one viewpoint, odd indeed. The oddity stems from the high
view that the Restoration Movement has had concerning the
Scriptures, i.e. if the Bible is truly the only rule of faith and
practice, then this should leave no room for rationalistic
interpretation of the Biblical record. From another viewpoint, however, this controversy is not strange but should
have been expected, especially if certain safeguards were
not instituted. From this latter perspective we may consider

---

16. Murch, *Christians Only*, p. 239. By 1918, the *Christian Century* had
become so liberal theologically that many people within the Disciples of Christ
had ceased subscribing to it. Consequently, the journal left the Restoration
Movement and became an interdenominational journal "where it became the
outstanding advocate of liberal thought."

the incisive logic Alexander Campbell and others used in criticizing creeds and lifting up the Scriptures above human opinion and dogma, for the same critical method could be turned against the Biblical record itself — as it had been turned against creeds in a previous generation — with the same result; destroying any reason to believe in the credibility of the record itself.

Earlier it was pointed out that theological liberalism and missionary evangelism are antithetical to each other. Yet, both became closely associated with each other in the Disciples of Christ in the beginning years of this century, an association which soon resulted in a drastic change in the very character of Disciples of Christ missions. This raises an interesting and important question: Within the Restoration Movement, how could two antithetical ideologies become so closely associated? The answer is to be found in relation to how the national and state missionary societies — as para-congregational organizations — were viewed in the Disciples of Christ. As noted in the previous section, these para-congregational organizational developments in the Restoration Movement, more specifically in the Disciples of Christ wing of the Movement, were viewed in either of two ways: from a utilitarian and pragmatic viewpoint, or from a teleological viewpoint. It was through the latter viewpoint that theological liberalism became closely associated with the missionary societies organized in the Restoration Movement, for there was in reality a natural affinity between theological liberalism of that time and the teleological interpretation of organizational development.

Of the many characteristics of theological liberalism at the turn of the 20th Century, there was one distinguishing mark: a firm commitment to evolution as the explanatory principle underlying all social and human processes.[17] Evolution under the impetus of Darwin had captured the day in the biological sciences, and because of that was fast becoming just as widely accepted in the social sciences. Moreover, a characteristic feature of evolution as a theory about change and process was similarly a commitment to teleology; all change was conceived as functional and leading to useful goals and ends. For example, in the biological sciences, the evolution of the wing on the bird or the long neck on the giraffe was conceived by evolutionists as achieving some useful end necessary for survival; in the social sciences, Hegel propounded that the modern nation-state with its bureaucracy is the epitome of cultural evolution while Marx protested claiming that the goal of cultural evolution, socialism, was yet to be reached.[18] In liberal theology, teleological evolution was a basic assumption and methodology in constructing new ideas about the Bible, e.g. YAHWEH of the Old Testament was merely a tribal and rather a cruel god but by the time of the New Testament the idea of deity in human development had evolved into a much higher concept, viz. a loving God. Similarly religion was viewed teleologically with Christianity, as one of the three "higher religions" (Buddhism and Islam being the other two), being the goal of the religious strivings of man

17. "With increasing acceptance of the theory of evolution and the doctrine of progress, the root of the restoration ideal was cut. . . . Drawing on Campbell's distinction between the covenants and his sermon on the Progress of Revealed Light, some Disciples now found it helpful to speak of 'progressive revelation.' " (Ronald E. Osborn, "Dogmatically Absolute, Historically Relative," in *The Renewal of the Church*, Vol. I, W. B. Blakemore, editor. St. Louis: Bethany Press, 1963, p. 283).

18. Henri Lefebvre, *The Sociology of Marx* (N.Y., N.Y.: Vintage Books, p. 123.

down through the ages, i.e., Christianity with its mono-theism and high moral code was a type of religion mankind was evolving toward all along.

In fact, in the theological liberalism of the early 20th Century, every development in Christianity was interpreted according to the frame of reference that teleological evolution afforded. Religious organizations were not exempted, especially those organizations that had only recently emerged on the scene. Since, therefore, the missionary societies within the Resto-ration Movement were in reality not only para-congregational but also supra-congregational in character, those espousing theological liberalism in the Disciples of Christ came to look upon this organizational development as that to which the Restoration Movement was evolving and progressing. The establishment of local congregations was merely a stepping stone to a greater and higher stage of religious develop-ment and maturity. In other words, liberals perceived eccle-siastical and institutional development as the real goal of the Restoration Movement.[19]

Since liberal Disciples of Christ leaders saw in the mis-sionary societies that to which the Restoration Movement was maturing, it was natural for these leaders to gravitate toward these para-congregational organizations. In fact, there was real motivation for this attraction, for if these organizations truly represented the direction the Disciples of Christ were moving and progressing, then it was imper-ative for the liberal to help guide this progress toward that ultimate end as defined by theological liberalism. Others in

---

19. David Edwin Harrell, Jr., *The Social Sources of Division in the Disciples of Christ 1865-1900, A Social History of the Disciples of Christ*, Vol. II (Atlanta: Publishing Systems, Inc., 1973), p. 100. "Probably the most important innova-tion to come of the new social liberalism among Disciples was the building of institutional churches."

the Disciples of Christ who viewed the missionary societies from a utilitarian viewpoint unfortunately felt no such compulsion to help direct the para-congregational development of the Movement by formulating a comparable conservative theology of organizational development; consequently, they tended to pay little attention to these developments and left largely by default the leadership of these organizations to those who were vitally concerned.

And there was no one more concerned in the institutional development, structure and role of these para-congregational organizations than the Disciple Liberal!

With the attraction of Disciple Liberals to the missionary organizations that had developed in the Restoration Movement, it was not long before they had a decisive voice in directing the progress of the Disciples of Christ in their missionary outreach. The direction, of course, was in service of theological liberalism as it was perceived in the early part of this century. This merging of theological liberalism with the organized missionary enterprises of the Disciples of Christ now led in a direct line to the emergence of Direct-Support Missions in the Disciples of Christ.

Theology, Unity and the Missionary Societies

During the time that Liberal Disciples were being attracted to the para-congregational organizations of the Disciples of Christ, another development within these organizations was taking place, a development which, when ultimately finished, and likewise closely associated with the liberal wing of the Disciples of Christ, was to set the final stage for the emergence of Direct-Support Missions. This development was a growing realization in many quarters that there were too many missionary organizations among the Disciples of Christ and thus there was a need for streamlining these operations. The method whereby this streamlining was to be accomplished was unification of the three missionary societies: The American Christian Missionary Society,[20] the Christian Woman's Board of Missions and the Foreign Christian Missionary Society.

The call for the unification of missionary societies was not unique to the Disciples of Christ. William Carey, perhaps foreseeing such a day, proposed in 1806 the holding of a pan-mission conference every ten years.[21] Now, toward the end of the 19th Century, scores of missionary societies were established and operating throughout the world. Concern for greater unity among the many societies was growing. Many people thought that, if the whole world was to indeed hear the Gospel, there must be better coordination and less competition among the missionary societies. Accordingly, John R. Mott, a leading missionary statesman of the day, led in the establishment in 1893 of the Foreign Missions Conference of North America, which later in 1908 became the Federal Council of Churches,[22] Mott continued his work of promoting unity in mission outreach, and in 1910 led in holding the first pan-mission conference at Edinburgh, England, in which 1,355 delegates representing 153 missionary societies met to plan the 20th Century's strategy for evangelizing the world.

---

20. In 1895 the General Missionary Convention changed its name back to the American Christian Missionary Society (see chapter 1, footnote 26).

21. J. Herbert Kane, *Understanding Christian Missions* (Grand Rapids: Baker Book House, 1974), p. 179. Carey proposed that the first conference be held in 1810 in South Africa. The idea, however, was dismissed by other mission leaders, only to be fulfilled 100 years later in the Edinburgh Conference of 1910.

22. *Ibid.*, p. 178.

Picking up on this same theme, J. H. Garrison, through the pages of the *Christian Evangelist,* first began promoting the unification of the Disciples' missionary societies in 1892.[23] Seven years later Garrison again wrote an editorial urging the consolidation of the various missionary societies and benevolent agencies of the Disciples of Christ.[24] In this latter editorial he listed four reasons for consolidation: 1) mission work, whether at home or abroad, is one, so there is no Biblical justification for the division of labor between the home boards (e.g. the ACMS) and foreign boards (the FCMS and CWBM); 2) economy of administration, i.e. greater efficiency in performing missionary work would ensue and several practical problems which had risen because of several and overlapping organizations would be solved; 3) consolidation would simplify convention reporting, and instead of several reports from the various societies and boards there would be only one unified report given at the General Convention; 4) consolidation would reduce a number of financial appeals to the churches, for all appeals from the various agencies could be systemized into an orderly procedure.[25] Before long committees were formed to discuss the possibility of unifying both home and foreign missions of the Disciples of Christ.[26] Reports issuing from these discussions were favorable to unification.

23. J. H. Garrison, "Promoting Unification in 1892," *Christian Evangelist,* Sept. 8, 1892, p. 576.

24. Garrison, "Consolidation of Missionary Society," *Christian Evangelist,* July 6, 1899, p. 837.

25. "For some time the numerous agencies, state and national, which had come into being to administer the various programs of missions, education, and benevolence, had found themselves competing for support. Each organization depended heavily on one or more special days in the church calendar for an offering to its cause. Ministers and congregations were weary from repeated appeals." (McAllilster and Tucker, *Journey in Faith,* p. 344.)

26. McAllister and Tucker, *Journey in Faith,* p. 344.

Even though there was competiton among the various missionary organizations for funds, the annual meeting of the American Christian Missionary Society nevertheless had become the general meeting where all the missionary organizations and other agencies reported their activities. In fact, this meeting was often called the General Convention, and it was the hope of many Disciples of that time that "this would provide the means for a church-based convention and a connectional relationship from the local congregation through the district and state to the national level."[27] This hope was not realized immediately, but the fact that churches and individuals continued to treat the meeting as the General Convention of the Disciples of Christ paved the way for its realization.

The General Convention provided a sufficient if semi-official platform from which to discuss, issue reports, and propose plans to tighten up the organizational life of the Disciples of Christ. Since the Convention was both a missionary and brotherhood convention, it was natural to proceed in modifying all organizational structures, missionary or brotherhood, simultaneously. As the Convention was becoming the National Convention of the Churches (and the forerunner of the International Convention of Disciples of Christ), the Convention also tackled the problem of various missionary organizations competing for money.

A calendar committee was appointed at The Buffalo Convention in 1906. Its mandate was to reduce the number of special days. The committee went beyond its assignment and proposed that the various boards and societies should be united into one organization with one board of administration.[28]

---

27. Loren E. Lair, *The Christian Church and Their Work* (St. Louis, MO: Bethany Press, 1963), p. 132.
28. McAllister and Tucker, *Journey in Faith*, p. 345.

The problem of competing special days for funds for the various missionary organizations and what to do about it, was discussed for a few years. However, nothing concrete came out of the discussion. One reason for this lack of action was the Centennial Convention of 1909: every organization was too busy preparing for the biggest celebration the Disciples of Christ ever had or have had since to worry about the problem and what to do about it.

Despite the delay caused by the Centennial Convention, sentiments for the unification of the various societies and boards of the Disciples of Christ continued to grow. Indeed, to a number of Disciples, the fragmentation and division of the church's missionary task among several societies and boards was antithetical to the Disciples of Christ plea for church unity. In other words, the Disciples of Christ, in spite of their own plea, were not themselves united, and because of this their witness calling for the unity of Christendom at large was inconsistent. Therefore, before the Disciples could without hypocrisy influence Christendom toward that unity for which Jesus Christ prayed, they must first "clean up their own house" and become united themselves. It was argued that only by first consolidating the many para-church societies and boards into one unified operation would the Disciples of Christ have the proper theological credentials for promoting their long stated goal of Christian unity among the denominations and sects. This perspective for the unification of the missionary societies and benevolent boards was early expressed by J. H. Garrison in a *Christian Evangelist* editorial.

> . . . The congregational organization is an essential manifesta-
> tion of the Christ-life. . . . But it is evident that other and
> more general organization of these churches are necessary

in order for wider cooperative effort and to the successful fulfillment of the mission of the church.

. . . Our plea for unity requires cooperation or united effort among our own churches in all missionary work. . . . Opposition to such missionary cooperation would be an entire contradiction of our plea for union.[29]

Not only was unification viewed as necessary "house cleaning," it was also proclaimed as being the will of the Restoration Fathers, as this late *Christian Evangelist* editorial stated:

It was according to the ideal of our pioneers, both in the sense of fundamental doctrines to be impressed upon the world and in solving the problems of organization incidental to a new religious movement, that the missionary societies which they organized were ultimately to be merged and operated as one single organization under the direction of the churches. After many years we have come back to their wisdom on this point. . . .

This is not only in line with the best thought and experience of the age on efficient and economic organizations, but it is in accordance with the feelings of the brotherhood in general, and in agreement with purpose of unity written down in the New Testament.[30]

---

29. J. H. Garrison, "What Kind of Missionary Organizations Shall We Have?," *Christian Evangelist*, Oct. 11, 1894, p. 642. Compare also these comments written in 1918 by George W. Brown, Disciples of Christ missionary to India. "Missionaries are in favor of unification for another reason. We stand for Christian Union — with big letters. Then why not practice it to the utmost among ourselves? What a splendid example of unity will the unfication of our boards be! And what a commentary on our plea is disunity! We do not feel that the establishment of separate boards was a mistake in the beginning. These boards have done good work; they are still doing it. Perhaps their work could have been accomplished in no other way. But now we are in the day of better things, of greater things. On with unification!" ("A Missionary View of Unification," *Christian Evangelist*, Nov. 21, 1918, p. 207).

30. "The United Missionary Society," *Christian Evangelist*, Sept. 11, 1919, p. 931.

Such sentiments and arguments for unification, however, were not universally accepted among the Disciples of Christ. There were a number of Disciples who, while not opposing the legitimacy of missionary societies and benevolent boards, did oppose their unification, an opposition which the *Christian Standard* likewise expressed and increasingly spearheaded. In a 1906 editorial titled "The Nature and Limits of our Missionary Societies," readers were reminded that missionary societies were but agencies of the churches and were established for the specific purpose of service to the churches in the area of evangelism. Moreover, according to the thinking of the *Christian Standard*, the theological reasons advanced in behalf of unification amounted to nothing more than a veiled disguise for an unscriptural assumption of authority and power of these agencies over the churches. The article closed with a note of sadness over the planning for unification that was beginning to be promoted in the brotherhood.

It is, therefore with no little sorrow that we see signs multiplying that there is a determined effort on foot, through the manipulations of the officials of these societies, with the connivance of certain editors, to commit our societies to a policy directly the reverse of that to which they are sacredly pledged, and to induce them to interfere in matters, not only never committed to their keeping, but positively prohibited by the very terms of their existence. The proposition of the editors of the *Pacific Christian* and the *Christian Evangelist* to make the missionary societies the medium of official surveillance of our churches and members, is not the only item in this unholy scheme. It is far more comprehensive, and embraces a plan to control our colleges and the very literature of the brethren. If it were possible for them to carry out their scheme, it would place in their hands the education of our preachers, the editorship of our weekly journals, and the preparation and distribution of our Sunday-school supplies.

. . . They will know that this scheme will begin the most bitter and determined controversy ever waged among us, and that it will provoke division and schism wherever its effects are felt.

. . . Meanwhile let them prepare to act quietly and orderly and determinedly, and frown down any attempt, no matter what it may be, that is made to divert our Missionary Societies from their great and sole object.[31]

The main fear of unification held by many Disciples, including J. A. Lord, then editor of the *Christian Standard,* was twofold. On the one hand it was feared that the societies would be diverted from their original purpose of evangelism,[32] which on the other hand would in turn lead into ecclesiasticism over the churches.

In spite of the dire warning emanating from the *Christian Standard* of a bitter battle and division, plans for developing greater organizational unity of both the brotherhood and its

---

31. "The Nature and Limits of our Missionary Societies," *The Christian Standard,* August 22, 1906, pp. 1202-1203.

32. In a much later editorial (1924), the *Christian Standard* lamented this very development in the United Christian Missionary Society. Under the title, "Missionary Aims" (Feb. 9, 1924, p. 433), the UCMS was compared with the Presbyterian and Southern Baptist mission boards with respect to purpose. While the two denominational boards stated their aims to be evangelism, the UCMS "posed as the benevolent work of the Disciples of Christ." The editorial ended: "It is a sad day for the Restoration Movement when the missionary agency which is ambitious to appear before the world as representative of the missionary spirit is far behind the agencies of the sects in the emphasis it places on evangelism.

missionary enterprises continued hand in hand. The conventions of 1907 and 1908 each dealt with the problems involved in unification. The 1909 convention appointed a special committee which reviewed the issues involved and proposed the following resolution:

> That this committee address itself to the task for one general delegate convention of our people, the Societies becoming boards thereof, and that we aim at the unification of our missionary, educational, and benevolent organizations, a reduction in the number of offerings, and a general reduction of the expense of administration.[33]

The resolution was adopted by the 1910 convention but because of opposition was unable to implement it; i.e. the convention was prevented from beginning a delegate convention with authority to bring about the unification of the missionary societies. Within the Disciples of Christ there was still a sizeable number of people who wanted their national convention to be a mass meeting of interested Christians and not an ecclesiastical body where only delegates attend not to share in a common fellowship but to transact business of and for the brotherhood.

Seeing that unification, along with its attendant proposal to create a delegate convention for the Disciples of Christ, was progressing in spite of its opposition, the *Christian Standard* at this point announced in an editorial of the same name "A New Missionary Policy."[34] Actually the editorial enunciated not so much a new missionary policy as it did a new policy toward existing missionary work as it was being carried on by the various agencies and boards. Although

---

33. Lair, *The Christian Churches and Their Work,* p. 133.
34. "A New Missionary Policy," *Christian Standard,* July 31, 1915, pp. 1376-1377.

stated in twenty-three points, in essence the editorial laid down three principles on which its new policy would henceforth be based. First, the editorial signalled a change in *Standard's* role in the missionary program of the Disciples of Christ, namely from that of advocacy of the missionary societies to that of watchdog over their power and impact over the churches. Second, the editorial outlined the proper role which the missionary societies must exercise vis-a-vis the church, i.e. the societies are business facilities and not religious institutions, and that the organization of each society is individually based and not ecclesiastical in nature. Third, the new policy reaffirmed the *Standard's* long pragmatic and eclectic orientation to method in mission work, reiterating that a plurality and variety of societies, agencies and boards each confined to accomplishing specific tasks of and for the church, were best for the Disciples of Christ. In the weeks which followed the publication of this editorial, the *Christian Standard* received several responses and comments, many of them expressing agreement and sympathy for the principles set forth in the new policy. It was hoped that this would begin discussion which would result in preventing not only unification but also the convention of the American Christian Missionary Society from becoming a delegate convention.

Sentiments for a delegated convention (as a means of developing a greater unity among the churches) continued, however. Many Disciples, in advocating unification, felt that, if unification were to be accomplished, there had to first be a para-church governing body—i.e. a delegate convention—which would have the power to authorize unification. Finally, in the 1917 General Convention, a compromise was worked out which integrated the two opposing viewpoints. The General Convention would still be a general assembly of all who wished to attend, but in addition there would be a Committee For Recommendations which was in effect a delegate body whose members were elected by the state societies. All organizations and agencies were to report to this committee, and it was through this committee that all business items had to be cleared. From this date the convention was known as the International Convention of Disciples of Christ.

The *Christian Standard* was critical of the formation of the International Convention[35] even though Frederick D. Kershner, a respected conservative among the Disciples, was the one responsible for the compromise which allowed this particular reorganization of the convention.[36] The criticism, however, did not stem from any question over the scriptural legitimacy of the convention — conservative Disciples and *Christian Standard* were still pragmatists on the question — but from certain "tendencies" observable in the administration of the convention. The main tendency which alarmed the *Christian Standard* was the appointment or election of men who belonged to the Campbell Institute to important positions of leadership in the convention. In a 1918 editorial entitled, "Further Evidences of the 'Tendencies,' "[37] the *Christian Standard* pointed out that of sixteen delegates to a special committee on peace (in reaction to World War I which was in progress), ten were members of the Campbell Institute. Of the remaining six delegates, only

---

35. *Christian Standard*, September 7, 1918, p. 481. An editorial in this issue titled "A Small Convention Period" criticized the plans for a small convention where "the most revolutionary measures known to the present generation of Disciples of Christ are to be decided upon. . . . These plans are not in line with true Restoration progress. Hence they should be thwarted."

36. Tucker, *J. H. Garrison and the Disciples of Christ*, p. 205.

37. George Perry Rutledge, "Further Evidences of the 'Tendencies,' " *Christian Standard*, April 20, 1918, p. 925.

three were considered conservatives. The *Christian Standard* wondered why a (liberal) club having only 200 members got ten delegates while 6,000 Disciple preachers and thousands of businessmen only got three — unless, of course, the over-representation from the Campbell Institute wasn't just another piece of evidence that the leadership of the convention was tending ever more to a theological liberal stance.

With the establishment of a delegate body within the International Convention, having the authority to transact business even if on a limited basis for the brotherhood, the stage was set for finalizing the plans calling for the unification of the missionary societies. Now, the various missionary societies and benevolent boards could themselves petition the Committee on Recommendations of the International Covention to merge their various enterprises thus achieving greater efficiency in operations. The Committee could then pass on the petition and recommend to those assembled at the International Convention to vote on and approve the unification scheme. This was done and accomplished during the 1919 convention which was held at Cincinnati, Ohio, and which resulted in the formation and organization of the United Christian Missionary Society (UCMS).

The UCMS brought together into one organizational structure the following six societies and boards: The American Christian Missionary Society, The Christian Woman's Board of Missions, The Foreign Christian Missionary Society, The Board of Church Extension, The National Benevolent Association, and the Board of Ministerial Relief. Upon unification the work of these six societies and boards was reorganized and distributed among four divisions: and Administrative Division with Departments of Foreign Missions,

Home Missions, Church Erection and the Ministry; and Educational Division with Departments of Religious Education and Missionary Education; a Promotional Division; and a Service Division which included the treasury and office management.[38] Of foreign missions, the UCMS, in 1919-1920, inherited and assumed the administration of ten mission fields, 275 missionaries, and 23,711 church members on foreign soil.[39] From the Christian Woman's Board of Mission, the UCMS inherited missions fields in Jamaica, India, Mexico, the Belgian Congo (now Zaire), Argentina, and Paraguay. From the Foreign Christian Missionary Society, the UCMS assumed control over mission work in India, China, Japan, the Philippines, and Puerto Rico.[40]

The merger of all Disciples of Christ mission work, both foreign and home, under the auspices of a single organization did not proceed without opposition. Just as the *Christian Standard* had opposed the formation of the International Convention, so did it lead in opposing the formation of the UCMS. Moreover, since the creation of these two organizations had proceeded simultaneously, the opposition of the *Christian Standard* often took on the character of a double-barrel attack in opposing the International Convention and UCMS at the same time. When, for example, it was announced that the 1919 International Convention would consider the formation of the UCMS, the *Christian Standard* called for a preconvention rally to protest the proposed merger of the missionary societies which doubtless

---

38. McAllister and Tucker, *Journey in Faith*, p. 349.
39. Lair, *The Christian Churches and Their Work*, pp. 196-197.
40. Carr, *The Foreign Missionary Work of the Christian Church*, p. 11.

would be approved by the convention. A large number of Disciples attended and registered a strong opposition to the upcoming International Convention.[41] In the end, however, the *Christian Standard* reserved its most vocal attacks for the UCMS.

There were several reasons why the *Christian Standard*, and many within the Disciples of Christ, opposed the UCMS. In less than a year after the UCMS had been organized, the *Christian Standard* initiated a discussion of these reasons with respect to the UCMS which lasted in reality not the three months which the *Christian Standard* promised but for several years. However that may be, the opening discussion contained an editorial entitled "The Issues Stated," with the subtitle, "Will the Societies Defend Them."

The Christian Standard proposes to present the arguments affirming the following propositions in a series of signed articles. We offer the societies criticized equal opportunity to defend their positions:

That the constituent boards of the United Christian Missionary Society were guilty of ecclesiastical character to commit the independent churches of Christ to membership, as a body, in an association of denominations (sects) only.

That the constituent boards of the United Christian Missionary Society compromised the Restoration plea when they attempted to enroll churches of Christ in the Interchurch combination as a "denomination" (i.e., sect).

That the constituent boards of the United Christian Missionary Society betrayed the cause of primitive Christianity when they lent their sources and expended trust funds to further a movement intended to raise $324,000,000 for the promotion of sectarian creeds, and only $12,000,000 for "the creed that needs no revision."

---

41. Murch, *Christians Only,* pp. 246-247.

That the constituent boards of the United Christian Missionary Society were false to their trust when they hazarded $600,000 of trust funds, and untold expenses, on the slender chance of obtaining the subscription of less than $1,500,000 in five installments from the non-Christian public.

That the constituent boards of the United Christian Missionary Society violated the plain dictates of business morality when they joined in soliciting ministers of the gospel to make secret reports on the financial standing of the church membership.

That the contributions of the membership to the funds of the constituent boards of the United Society can not be used to liquidate the deficits of the Inter-church Movement without misappropriation of funds.

That, by their endorsement of Association for the Promotion of Christian Unity, through its inclusion in the United Budget, the constituent boards of the United Christian Missionary Society have made themselves participants in the policy and misrepresentations of that association.

That, through the endorsement of the Board of Education, by the inclusion of said Board in the United Budget, the constituent boards of the United Christian Missionary Society have lent encouragement to unscriptural and antiscriptural teaching in our colleges.[42]

At the heart of these issues was the UCMS' participation in various interdenominational movements. Participation as a missionary organization was perhaps not too objectionable. But now, by being the only brother-wide organization, the UCMS was more than a missionary organization; it was

---

42. George Perry Rutledge, "The Issues Stated," subtitle "Will the Societies Defend Them," *Christian Standard,* July 3, 1920, p. 988.

the representative of the Disciples of Christ in these movements. In fact, to the outside denominational world the UCMS was the Disciples of Christ. Consequently, the *Christian Standard* charged, participating in these movements made the Disciples just another denomination. Furthermore, there was a cost to participation. For example, in joining the Interchurch Movement, which was started under the influence of John R. Mott as a result of his Edinburgh Missionary Conference of 1910, the UCMS was soon tagged with its share of a $12,000,000 debt. The Interchurch Movement had borrowed this sum to promote church federations, hold seminars on evangelism, pay salaries, and a host of other expenses. But the program was overly ambitious and its leaders too optimistic about its acceptance by the denominational world. It wasn't long before the Movement ran into trouble and several denominations began to pull out.[43] This left those that remained, including the UCMS, with the loan to pay back. Since the money had been spent to promote federation and not unity on a Scriptural basis, many in the Disciples of Christ thought that any payment the UCMS would make on the debt would amount to misappropriation of the churches' money.[44]

After this opening salvo, however, two other issues concerning the UCMS emerged which quickly overshadowed the above issues in emotion and importance. These two isues were theological liberalism, with its accompanying teleological interpretation of organizational development,

---

43. See "Interchurch Snags," *Christian Standard,* March 20, 1920, p. 632.

44. However after the collapse of the movement, the *Standard* proposed that the whole brotherhood cooperate in paying the UCMS' share of the debt. See "Let's Clear Away the United Society's Inter-Church Debt," *Christian Standard,* Nov. 20, 1920, p. 1525.

and open membership, i.e. accepting into church membership people of denominational or sectarian background
who had not been immersed. Of the two issues, the latter
soon became the *cause celebre,* of conservative Disciples,
symbolizing all that was evil about the former.

Theological liberalism in the missionary enterprises of the
Disciples of Christ was unfortunately one of the things that
the UCMS had inherited from the older Disciple societies.
In 1908 Guy W. Sarvis, who espoused the new liberal theology, was apointed by the Foreign Christian Missionary
Society to serve as a missionary in China. He arrived in
China in 1911 but because of opposition to his appointment
resigned from the FCMS the following year. However, the
gain resulting in Sarvis' resignation was short-lived, for
blazened across the top of the page of an August 7, 1920,
Christian Standard article, in large letters, were the words
DOES CHINA MISSION ENDORSE OPEN MEMBERSHIP? The
headline hit like a bombshell, not because it appeared in
the *Christian Standard* but because it was the title of an
article written by R. E. Elmore, who at that time was serving
as Recorder (i.e. Recording Secretary) of the Foreign Christian Missionary Society which, of course, was scheduled
later that year to become a part of the United Christian Missionary Society. The *Christian Standard* had been taking
pot-shots at the missionary work, especially the China mission, of the societies for some years but without much success
at arousing the brotherhood concerning mission practices
which were considered questionable. Now, however, an
FCMS insider, the Recorder of the minutes of Executive
Committee itself, raised the same question that the *Standard*
had been asking all along. Elmore, in his article quoted at
length a 1919 communique from Frank Garrett, director of

74

the FCMS China mission, to the Executive Committee which in effect request permission from the committee to institute and practice, in accordance with a union plan in association with paedo-baptist mission groups, open membership. Garrett assured the committee that the proposed practice had the unanimous consent of the field executive committee. Elmore, as Recording Secretary for the FCMS Executive Committee, responded negatively to Garrett's request, but the issue refused to die, for the FCMS received more request to practice open membership in China. Therefore, Elmore counterproposed in a resolution that the Executive Committee recall Frank Garrett and all other FCMS missionaries "who favor this unscriptural practice." The resolution was not seconded, however; rather, a substitute resolution was adopted which expressed gratification over the prospects of union among the various groups in China. Elmore responded to this letter resolution by publishing the whole series of events in a 12,000 word article in the *Christian Standard!*[44]

Not three weeks after Elmore's article had appeared in the *Christian Standard,* moreover, there appeared in the *Christian Century,* a statement claiming that most, if not all, of the mission churches of the Disciples in China had been for some time receiving unimmersed Christians into their membership.[45] Alarmed, P. H. Welshimier, the young but influential minister of the First Christian Church of Canton, Ohio addressed an "Open Letter to the Executive

---

44. R. E. Elmore, "Does China Mission Enclose Open Membership?," *Christian Standard,* Aug. 7, 1920, pp. 1107-1109. The article appeared even more impressive due to the size of paper (10½ inches by 12½ inches) which was used in publishing the *Standard* during this time. Elmore's article was three pages long, over half of it in small 8 point print.

45. *Christian Century,* Aug. 26, 1920.

Committee of the Foreign Christian Missionary Society," which was published in the *Christian Evangelist,* asking if the *Christian Century* statement was true.[46] If so, Welshimier warned, the Canton congregation would withdraw its yearly support of $4,000 to the FCMS, plus the $1,000 which the church also gave each year to the Christian Woman's Board of Mission. Two weeks after Welshimier's Open Letter, the *Christian Standard* reprinted a 1919 article from the *Christian Century* which claimed that every Disciple mission station in China, with the exception of one, was at that time practicing open membership.[47]

Because of these revelations, the battle was on. Conservatives cited reports of open membership on the mission field and called for cessation of the practice while society officials denied it was being practiced, or, as it became customary in later years, defended the practice as a legitimate means of performing mission work in an environment where circumstances more readily threw together Christians of various backgrounds.

> The situation on the mission field, as a rule, is quite different from that here at home, as the different communions usually have their own distinct territory which they have chosen. Because the field is so large and much of it entirely unoccupied, there is hardly any overlapping. As a consequence, there are very few churches of different communions in the same community, except in the larger cities like Nanking, Shanghai, and Peking.[48]

---

46. P. H. Welshimier, "An Open Letter To The Executive Committee of the FCMS," *Christian Evangelist,* Sept. 16, 1920, p. 929.

47. "Is China Practicing Open Membership?" *Christian Standard,* Oct. 9, 1920, p. 1345.

48. Stephen J. Corey, *Fifty Years of Attack and Controversy* (St. Louis: Committee on Publication of the Corey Manuscript, 1953), p. 71.

The idea of open membership was not new to the Restoration Movement. Indeed, the idea can be traced back to Alexander Campbell himself and his infamous Lunenberg Letter. Ever since that time the question of how we should consider the "pious unimmersed" has been debated in the Restoration Movement. To many Disciples, of course, the question had been settled and the issue was no longer a debatable one: even the pious unimmersed had to be immersed in order to be fully in accord with the Biblical teaching on baptism. But the introduction of theological liberalism with its teleological interpretation of social and religious processes into the Disciples of Christ resurrected the question and made it once more legitimate in a way previously not thought possible. The argument in favor of open membership now ran as follows: If the goal toward which the Restoration Movement was evolving was the supra-congregational organization as the UCMS, then it must be that the goal toward which all Protestant bodies were moving was the all-church union, i.e., a super-church federation encompassing all denominations. Since nonimmersionist bodies were likewise evolving in the same direction and moving toward the same teleological goal of organizational union, it was obvious, theologically speaking, that the mode of baptism was playing no part in the evolution toward the organizational unity of all Protestantism. Therefore, it was necessary for the Disciples of Christ as an immersionist body to accept the nonimmersed on an equal basis in order not to thwart the ultimate achievement of this goal. Rather, in order to be in harmony with the direction in which Protestantism was moving, it was essential for the Disciples of Christ, again theologically speaking, to accept the nonimmersed believer.

Federation of denominations was a favorite theme of discussion in American Protestantism in the early part of this century. As among the Disciples of Christ, theological liberalism with its emphasis on teleology gave impetus to such discussions. In 1901 there came into existence the Federation of Churches and Church Workers. Accordingly, at the 1902 General Convention of the Disciples of Christ it was proposed that the Disciples look with favor on the federated plan as a means of achieving that unity to which the Restoration Movement had always aspired.[49] In 1905 several Disciples attended the Inter-Church Conferences on Federation in New York, a conference which eventually led into the establishment of the Federal Council of the Churches of Christ in America.[50] However, such attendance was opposed and, moreover, since there was no one agency legally empowered to represent the brotherhood, nothing of significance was accomplished. The federation concept was similarly unsuccessful on the interdenominational level — except on the foreign mission field where different conditions made federation of the various religious bodies much more possible than in America. Consequently the missionary societies of the Disciples, and later the UCMS, looked with favor upon the plans for federation on the mission field.[51] But this required, as a matter of personal and organizational policy, a shift from a strict stance on immersion to an open-membership position for the Disciples of Christ.

Because of the growing influence of liberalism, the above shift was easier to accomplish for the missionary agencies of the Disciples of Christ than was expected.

---

49. Garrison and DeGroot, *The Disciples of Christ,* p. 487.

50. *Ibid.,* pp. 408-409.

51. Cf. "Foreign Missions and Christian Unity," by Robert E. Speer, *Christian Evangelist,* May 12, 1910, p. 661. See also "A Day Vision," a *Christian Evangelist* editorial on this article, May 19, 1910, p. 711.

Chapter Three

LESLIE WOLFE AND THE MISSIONARY SOCIETY

With reports coming from the Far East that Disciple missions and missionaries were indeed practicing open membership, the focus of brotherhood tension, which had originated in the differing theological perspectives on the nature of the para-church organization vis-à-vis the local congregation, now shifted from the organizations themselves to the mission field. Heightened emotions followed this shift; it was one thing to debate the proper function and goals of the para-church organization relative to the church in the Disciples of Christ but it was something else again to debate the perceived shortcomings of such an organization in proclaiming the principles of the Restoration Movement to others.

The perceived shortcoming, of course, was the practice of open membership on the mission field. The restoration of the Biblical form and purpose of baptism was one of the salient features of the Disciples of Christ: immersion for the remission of sins therefore was not a negotiable item in proclaiming the reformation. Since the day of Walter Scott this view of baptism had been preached in the pulpit, proclaimed on the frontier, expounded in the journals, and argued in debates with the sects. Immersion for the forgiveness of sins was distinctively Christian Church and Church of Christ doctrine, for it set apart the Restoration Movement from both the Roman Catholics and the many Protestant bodies: from the Roman Catholics in that immersion and not also sprinkling or pouring was for the forgiveness of sin, and from Protestant bodies in that immersion was for the remission of sins and not a rite which one undergoes after sins are forgiven. From this perspective on baptism, the

Restoration Movement, and more specifically the Disciples of Christ, had something to say to all concerned, whether Roman Catholic, Protestant or nonbeliever. To retreat from this emphasis on baptism via the practice of open membership—accepting the nonimmersed as full members of Christ's Church—was in effect to have nothing to say to the world or contribute to the understanding of God's Will. Small wonder then that when it was alleged that open membership was being practiced on the mission field, emotions ran high in the brotherhood, for many Disciples saw in the practice the loss of all they had achieved in escaping from the encrustments of denominationalism.

The Christian Standard and the UCMS

Between the years of 1920 and 1925, each time the International Convention met, the reports of open membership on the mission fields of the Orient were hotly discussed. After the 1921 convention emotions over the issue were so enflamed that John T. Brown, a member of the UCMS Board of Managers, proposed to travel himself to the Disciple missions fields of the Orient to investigate the truth or falsity of the reports. He left early in 1922 and returned the same year, having visited the Disciple mission fields of India, China and the Philippines. On his return he issued a report on his findings which indicted the UCMS for practicing open membership in the China and Philippines mission fields.

Brown first gave his report to the UCMS Board of Managers, but nothing appeared in print concerning the situation he found. When he saw that the Board of Managers was not going to recognize, much less act upon, his report, he

80

submitted the report for publication in the *Christian Standard*.[1] The report amounted to some 35,000 words and created no little concern in the brotherhood. The UCMS Board of Managers sought to discredit Brown's report by saying that his report was unauthorized, since in reality he had traveled to the Far East on his own. This and other attempts to discredit Brown's report, however, did not stem the flow of reports and articles highly critical of the UCMS written by Brown and published in the *Christian Standard*. For example, in a sensational series of eleven articles entitled, "Why I Resigned From the UCMS," published in the *Christian Standard* in 1923 and 1924, Brown outlined the reasons why he could no longer support the organized mission work of the Disciples of Christ. After this series was completed, Brown published another article in the Standard under the title, "The UCMS Self-Impeached."[2]

John T. Brown was not the only person during this period writing in the *Christian Standard* about the United Christian Missionary Society. In fact, between the years of 1919 and 1925 the *Christian Standard* carried on a vigorous opposition to the UCMS. Over this seven year period, according to a count made in the *Christian Standard Index*,[3] the *Standard* printed a remarkable 299 editorial and articles on the UCMS (an average of nearly one a week!).[4] Some of the more

---

1. John T. Brown, "John T. Brown Full Report," *Christian Standard*, Oct. 28, 1922, pp. 109-126.

2. Brown, "The UCMS Self-Impeached," *Christian Standard*, May 31, 1924, p. 873.

3. Spencer, *Christian Standard Index*, pp. 3275-3277.

4. This number does not take into its total count articles critical of the International Convention or articles about China and the Philippines where open membership was being practiced. These would add appreciably to the total amount of space devoted to the UCMS and open membership during the years 1919-1925.

eye-catching titled published during this period were: "Canton, Ohio Church Withdraws Financial Support From the UCMS" (1921), "A Protestant Against Centralization" (1921, 1922), "Puncturing a Bubble" (1922), "The Latest Hoax" (1922), "The Missionary Crisis" (1923), "Icabod" (1923), "The Mischief of It" (1924), "The Wages of Modernism" (1924), "A New Order of Bishops" (1925), "Scraps of Paper" (1925), "Loyalty to Organizations vs. Loyalty to Christ" (1925). An interesting "nontitle" occurred in the December 16, 1922 (p. 310), issue of the *Christian Standard*. A large blank page appeared with only a small boxed-in caption at the bottom stating "This page is reserved for use of UCMS for frank defense of its positions, whenever it desires directly or through writers of its naming, to reach the 'Standard' readers." Well-known personalities of the brotherhood who wrote articles on the UCMS included P. H. Welshimier, S. S. Lappin, Z. T. Sweeny, R. E. Elmore, and R. C. Foster.

The early attacks on the UCMS by the *Christian Standard* were not answered in any direct way. For the most part, journals like the *Christian Evangelist*, which were sympathetic to the UCMS and the practice of open membership, largely ignored *Standard's* attacks and invitations to debate.[5] But in later years, Stephen J. Corey, who lived through this period and suffered through personal attack because of his association with the UCMS, entitled a book, *Fifty Years of Attack and Controversy*,[6] to characterize the feeling he and others had toward the *Christian Standard*. In this book Corey traced the opposition that the *Christian Standard* had

---

5. Cf. "Talking Behind Our Backs," *Christian Standard*, March 1, 1924, p. 552.

6. Stephen J. Corey, *Fifty Years of Attack and Controversy* (The Committee on Publication of the Corey Manuscript, 1953).

toward the International Convention and UCMS since the beginning of these organizations. More significantly, though, he laid the blame for dividing the Disciples of Christ at the doorstep of the *Christian Standard.*

It is indeed ironical that the ecumenical outlook, which was so evident in the minds of Thomas Campbell and Barton W. Stone, two of the most irenic of the movement's early leaders, has been so changed by certain groups in our history. . . . The first movement of this kind, largely led by Benjamin Franklin, resulted in the early non-cooperative separation that was centered in opposition to instrumental music. . . . The second, which we are now experiencing, is led by the *Christian Standard* in its attacks on biblical scholarship and its revival of opposition to missionary organizations and has developed a new division among Disciples of Christ.[7]

Stephen J. Corey, notwithstanding the personal anguish he went through, was wrong in his understanding and subsequent interpretation of the events which led up to the division whereof he wrote, viz. the beginning of Direct-Support Missions among the Disciples of Christ. To be sure, the *Christian Standard* agitated and clamored loud and long in opposition to the points Corey raised in the above quote, but it must also be admitted that no division in any organizational or structural sense resulted in the brotherhood. In the early 1920's the brotherhood remained intact despite the repeated attacks of the *Christian Standard.* Even the Restoration Congresses, called by the *Christian Standard* in opposition to the International Covention, failed to produce any division. Moreover, as was done in 1922, brethren continued to attend the International Convention regardless of whether the *Christian Standard* participated

---

7. *Ibid.*, p. 8.

or ignored it.[8] In this regard the *Christian Standard* was a failure.

In retrospect, therefore, we must absolve the *Christian Standard* of any success of causing division within the ranks of Disciples, in spite of the fact that a great deal of energy and printer's ink were expended in reforming the Disciples of Christ or advocating division if the reform did not take place. The real catalyst for the division—i.e. for the emergence of Direct-Support Missions—was not a religious journal but a person, Lesie Wolfe, missionary first under the Foreign Christian Missionary Society (1907-1920), then under the United Christian Missionary Society (1920-1926) to the Philippines.

The Philippine Mission

Christian Churches and Churches of Christ are indebted to Mark Maxey for a detailed account of the Philippine mission and of the crucial role it played in the emergence of Direct-Support Missions in his book, *History of the Philippine Mission.*[9] This book is essential for a grasp of the many undercurrents that flowed back and forth over the issues of open membership and (interdenominational) church federation with respect to the Disciples of Christ mission work in the Philippines, undercurrents which led to the Direct-Support Missionary Movement among the Disciples of Christ. Unless otherwise noted, the material in the rest of this chapter is taken from Maxey's book.

The first Disciples of Christ mission in the Philippines was established in 1901 under the direction of the Foreign

---

8. Murch, *Christians Only*, p. 256.

9. Mark Maxey, *History of the Philippine Mission* (San Clemente, CA: Go Ye Books, 1973).

Christian Missionary Society. The first two years were spent in getting the mission operational, but in 1903 the Disciples began to experience growth. In two more years, in 1905, the mission reported 750 members in fifteen churches; there were 319 baptisms that year alone. By 1910 the Disciples in the Philippines had grown to 4783 and 47 churches, with 1010 baptisms reported for that year. The FCMS missionary force also grew to meet the ever increasing opportunities of the Philippine mission field. By 1910 there were 14 Disciple missionaries serving in four locations and supervising nearly a hundred national workers. The FCMS had also, by 1910, established two Bible Colleges training 48 Philippine students for the ministry. In addition, three hospitals were in operation and a substantial church building program for Filipino congregations was underway. The work continued to grow, although at a slower rate, over the next decade. The peak of the Disciple mission work in the Philippine was reached in 1925 when the UCMS reported a membership of 9289, 81 churches, 651 baptisms, 37 people studying for the ministry (down from 97 the previous year), and 21 missionaries (down from a peak of 25 in 1923).

The Philippine mission, like other Oriental missions of the Disciples of Christ, was soon caught up in the utilitarian — teleological controversy, with its attendant problems of interdenominational federation and open membership regarding the missionary society. The controversy began for the mission when the Foreign Christian Missionary Society sent its Commission to the Far East in 1914. The Commission's first stop was the Philippines, after which it traveled on to visit FCMS mission fields in China and Japan. Knowing of the union work in theological education which was in progress with various denominational missions in China,[10] the Commission upon arrival in the Philippines recommended that the FCMS insitute a similar program with the Union Theological Seminary. In the report on UCMS missions in the Orient, which John T. Brown submitted in 1922 to the UCMS Board of Managers, the Philippine mission was singled out for special consideration. Brown reported that the Taft Avenue Disciples of Christ Church in Manila had two membership lists: one for immersed members and another for nonimmersed members. The report also recommended that this arrangement at the Taft Avenue Church be corrected. However, a letter of clarification on the situation from the church to the UCMS Board of Managers explained that, while two membership lists were indeed kept, nonimmersed people who were members were not elected to any important office.

> Those not baptized by immersion were chosen as members of the music and social committees. All were allowed to vote. . . . We receive Protestants of other churches as "guest member" . . . which gives them a real part in the congregational life of the church.[11]

This letter, which both admitted the practice of open membership and clarified its function, was acceptable to the UCMS Board of Managers. Consequently, the practice continued and those who had instituted it in the Philippines were not reprimanded by the UCMS. In 1923, the UCMS made a comity agreement with the Methodist mission in which some Methodist churches would come under the oversight of the

---

10. C. S. Settlemeyer, "Union in Educational Work in China," *Christian Evangelist*, May 26, 1910, p. 740.

11. Maxey, *History of the Philippine Mission*, p. 59.

Disciples, and in exchange certain Disciple churches would be under the control of the Methodists. This agreement, in turn, led to a number of unimmersed people being incorporated into the membership of the Philippine Disciples of Christ churches.

Not every UCMS missionary in the Philippines was in favor of these developments. W. N. Lemmon, a medical doctor who had first come to the Philippines in 1909, wrote a letter in 1924 to the UCMS protesting that these developments would result in a "betrayal of the brotherhood," but it was to no effect as Dr. Lemmon left the Philippine mission the following year to return permanently to the States. Another missionary, George Saunders from Australia, also protested, but again to no avail as he was immediately voted out of the UCMS mission by a majority of his American colleagues! A third UCMS missionary who protested was Leslie Wolfe.

Leslie Wolfe was born in 1876 in Ohio but grew to manhood in Illinois. He studied for the ministry at Eureka College and Drake University, both Disciples of Christ schools. After finishing his education, Wolfe ministered in several churches, but his heart was in serving on some mission field. In 1903, he married Carrie Francis Austin, and together they applied for missionary service with the Foreign Christian Missionary Society. Four years later they arrived in the Philippines where they were immediately assigned to work in the Manila area.

Mr. and Mrs. Wolfe were of determined and steadfast character, both in their commitment to the Restoration Movement and their service in the Philippines. During his service with the FCMS and UCMS, Leslie Wolfe helped establish churches in Manila, conducted evangelistic trips out into the Provinces, translated Bible material into the Tagalog language, and taught Filipino students in the Bible College which had been established in Manila. He early gained a reputation, with his fellow missionaries, of being a difficult person to work with, a reputation which grew as the utilitarian-teleological controversy intensified on the mission field. Indeed, it was in the context of this controversy that many of his colleagues were critical of him, for Wolfe had turned out to be an unreconstructed utilitarian regarding the proper role of the para-church missionary organization as well as a staunch conservative on the issues which were facing the Disciples of Christ mission in the Philippines. More significantly, though, he was in a position of power and seniority by virtue of having been stationed in Manila for all of his years of missionary service. From this position Wolfe vigorously agitated for strict adherence to the historic principles of the Restoration Movement in the evangelistic outreach of the Philippine mission, as well as being uncompromisingly opposed to the steps the UCMS was taking to involve, and eventually merge, the Disciples of Christ in an interdenominational federation in the country. Specifically of the latter, Wolfe was:

-opposed to closing down the Bible College in Manila where the majority of Filipino national preachers were trained (The college was closed in 1923 under the proposal that Disciples of Christ church leaders be henceforth trained in an union seminary.);

-opposed to selling the mission printing press which turned out Bible-related publications for the Filipino churches (The UCMS proposed that the press be closed out and Disciple publications be merged with denominational literature.);

-opposed to open membership (which many of his fellow UCMS missionaries, in conference, had voted in favor of);

88

-opposed to the proposal for establishing union churches instead of Churches of Christ in Kalinga Province (the UCMS had proposed to join with the Methodists and United Brethren in union churches instead of carrying out an evangelistic program of its own).

The UCMS viewed Wolfe's opposition to these joint efforts to established union churches as "unevangelistic." For example, in the 1924 *Year Book* of the Disciples of Christ (pp. 61-63), there was expressed the sentiment that "A strong man for the Manila evangelistic work is much needed." In the 1925 *Year Book* (pp. 71-73), it was stated that Wolfe was not that man: "Although we have asked constantly for an evangelistic missionary for the Manila district, Mr. Wolfe, fully occupied with other duties, has continued in charge of this work during the year." Wolfe remained undaunted in the face of such attempts to remove him out of his position of influence in the Manila district. Instead, he grew more vocal in his opposition to UCMS mission policy.

Wolfe's opposition now must have been even more vigorous and insistent than usual, for on April 4, 1925, nine of his colleagues signed a petition urging the Executive Committee of the United Christian Missionary Society to recall Mr. and Mrs. Leslie Wolfe. In a detailed letter to the committee, five charges were leveled against the Wolfe's:

1. Their incompatibility, i.e. they were unable to work with other UCMS missionaries;
2. Mr. Wolfe's frequent display of temper (e.g. Leslie Wolfe was arrested once on a charge of abusing a Filipino student in a fit of anger);[12]

---

12. Barton McElroy (in personal communication), former missionary to the Philippines, states that this incident was incorrectly reported. Wolfe did not slap a student but a man who was apparently intoxicated and using the front yard of Wolfe's house in Manila as a bathroom. After an investigation Wolfe was fully exonerated for his action.

3. His maintaining an uncompromising attitude of opposition to the plans and programs of the majority of the missionaries;
4. Their drumming up support from Filipino brethren for their opposition to UCMS plans;
5. The constant gossiping and nagging of Mrs. Wolfe.

A few days later, Wolfe likewise addressed a letter to the UCMS Executive Committee to answer the above charges. According to him the crux of the matter was not in his or his wife's attitude toward the progress of the mission but in the "new turn" the UCMS was taking with regard to baptism, church membership and toward "fundamentalists," of which he considered himself and which his UCMS colleagues did not like. In addition to his letter, a number of Filipino brethren also wrote to the UCMS Executive Committee in support of Mr. and Mrs. Wolfe.

The International Convention of the Disciples of Christ

More explosive than the letter written to the UCMS, however, were the letters Filipino brethren wrote to the *Christian Standard* expressing what was taking place with respect to Leslie Wolfe. The first letter was by L. M. Bana, a former Filipino advisor to the UCMS, who called the policy of open membership and comity agreements with the Methodist "deplorable," and ended his letter with a plea to the *Christian Standard:*

Anything you can render through the churches, progress and individuals in the United States in behalf of the "Christian brotherhood in the Philippines" who are clinging to the primitive teachings and principles of the New Testament Church, will be greatly appreciated by me.[13]

13. Maxey, *History of the Philippine Mission*, p. 81.

90

Bana's letter was duly printed in the *Christian Standard*. But before there was time for the UCMS to reply, a second letter from a Filipino brother arrived. This letter, from Vidal B. Barromeo, expressed confusion over why the UCMS had "non-open membership" missionaries as well as "open membership" missionaries. The confusion was compounded, Barromeo lamented, because he did not know which way to believe. He ended his letter asking the *Standard* to advise which way the Filipino Disciples of Christ should believe.

Printing these letters in the *Christian Standard*, of course, added more fuel to the fires of controversy which were raging in the States over the UCMS and open membership. An UCMS official, W. H. Hanna, who was on the Executive Committee, wrote an answer to Bana's letter which was published in the *Christian Standard*. Hanna in essence confirmed that comity agreements had been made with the Methodists in the Philippines, but he blamed this development more on the fact that the UCMS had insufficient funds to shepherd the Disciples in those areas given over to Methodist supervision; in fact, Disciples of Christ converts in these areas, Hanna stated, "Were free to choose their course, to seek to maintain their own church life, to go into Methodist Churches, to go back to Catholicism, or to go to the devil." The *Christian Standard* was not impressed with Hanna's reason, branding it as "the same old brand of open membership in vogue in Oriental missions of the UCMS." Because of the deteriorating situation in the Philippines, plus what was occurring in other UCMS missions in the Far East, the *Christian Standard* began a new publication called the "Spotlight," dedicated to discussing the UCMS. The first issue,[14] which was published in September, 1925,

---

14. After the first issue, the "Spotlight" was renamed the "Touchstone."

was devoted mainly to the Philippine situation. More letters from and about the Philippine situation were printed. To top it off, though, the "Spotlight" published a resolution passed by the Tagalog Convention which: 1) disapproved open membership and, 2) insisted that the UCMS send only missionaries who have been "reared in our own churches, thoroughly knowing and firmly believing in Restoration, and never send missionaries who are 'modernists' and 'liberalists.' "

With the deteriorating situation between conservative and liberal missionaries in the Philippine mission becoming widely known throughout the brotherhood, the tension between the utilitarian and the teleological viewpoint of the para-church organization broke out into open debate, threatening to polarize the two viewpoints into opposing — and irreconcilable — positions. On the one hand, those Disciples who held to the teleological view considered the developments toward interdenominational federation and open membership as "progression," while on the other hand those Disciples who held to the utilitarian view considered these same developments as "digression." Disciples on either side of the debate were now truly alarmed over what was transpiring on the mission field and more importantly the effect it was having on the brotherhood in the States. In other words, many were beginning to wonder how the brotherhood could remain intact much longer.

In order to avert what seemed the inevitable, the 1924 International Convention of the Disciples of Christ, which was held at Cleveland, Ohio, appointed a Peace Committee to arrive at a formula whereby both sides could avoid division and remain together as a single brotherhood. The Peace Committee was made up of members of the Executive Committee of the International Convention. Their duty was to hear from representatives from both sides in order to save the Restoration Movement — this time the Disciples of Christ — from another division over the issue of the missionary society. Their task, moreover, proved to be a crucial one, for by the time the 1925 Convention, which was held at Oklahoma City, rolled around, tempers were at the boiling point. Many Disciples showed up at the Convention[15] clamoring for something to be done, once and for all, about the problem of open membership being practiced by UCMS missionaries on the mission field.

Before the Convention convened, a group of conservative Disciples, led by Z. T. Sweeney, had presented to the Peace Committee a resolution, or formula, which would assure the continual unity of the brotherhood. Since no other formula had been presented, Sweeney's Peace Resolution, as it became known, was read before the Convention assembly. There were six articles to the Resolution.[16] The first article was the most important one of all for it proposed in two clauses:

1. That no person be employed by the United Christian Missionary Society as its representative who has committed himself to belief in, or practice of, the reception of unimmersed persons into the membership of Churches of Christ.

---

15. 4,030 were registered for the 1925 International Convention. The *Christian Evangelist* (Oct. 15, 1925, p. 1318) allowed this to be a fair cross-section of the brotherhood, "a truly representative gathering."

16. *Christian Standard*, October 24, 1925, p. 2235.

Before Sweeney's Resolution was read, the Committee on Recommendations, which had to approve what reports and resolutions should be read before the Convention, recommended that the first three articles be rejected and a weaker resolution be substituted. This was later made into a motion on the Convention floor but it died for lack of a second thus opening the way for the Convention to consider the original resolution on an article-by-article basis.

2. That if any person is now in the employment of the United Christian Missionary Society as a representative who has committed himself or herself to belief in, or practice of, the reception of unimmersed person into the membership of Churches of Christ, the relationship of that person to the United Christian Missionary Society be severed as employee. And this be done as soon as possible, with full consideration given to the interest of the person involved without jeopardy to the work of the society.

The remaining articles of the Resolution were elaborations of these two clauses so that there would be no possibility of misunderstanding or misapplication of the Resolution's intent:

-Article Two called upon all missionary and benevolent agencies of the Disciples of Christ to obey and follow the Resolution;

-Article Three stated that all previous Convention resolutions and interpretations thereof, concerning the issue of open membership upon adoption of this Resolution, were hereby annulled;[17]

-Article Four called upon all missionary and benevolent agencies to allow their financial records to be inspected by accountants;

---

17. There had already been two similar attempts at past International Conventions to avert division over open membership. In the 1920 Convention there was formulated what became known as the Medbury Resolution which urged UCMS missionaries to openly pledge allegiance to the historic position of the Disciples of Christ on the importance of immersion. This resolution was too weak to stop the practice of open membership, so at the 1922 Convention another attempt was made to assure that no open membership was being practiced. Unfortunately this attempt proved so inept that, in the end, it was made out to assert that all cases of open membership had ceased and no UCMS missionary was now practicing it!

-Article Five proposed that the constitution of the International Convention be amended to permit the Convention itself to amend matters from the floor;

-Article Six urged all agencies to, above all else, strive to maintain the unity of the brotherhood.

A heated debate on the convention floor followed the reading of the Resolution.[18] Both sides—those in favor of the Peace Resolution and those opposed to it—jockeyed for advantage in order to influence the Convention for the final vote on the Resolution. After five hours of debate, and an overnight adjournment, the question was called, and the chairman called for a voice vote. Both sides shouted from the floor their respective votes. So loud was the shouting of either side that the chairman was unable to decide which side was in the majority. A show of hands vote was immediately called for, and when the votes were counted, those in favor of the Peace Resolution were in the majority by at least a 10-to-1 margin. The Unity of the Disciples was saved—for the time being at least.[19]

Even though the Peace Resolution passed, one problem quickly emerged in implementing it: several executives and missionaries of the UCMS would have to resign. This ramification of the Sweeney Resolution was not lost on Stephen J. Corey, then foreign secretary of the UCMS, for he was ready to hand in his resignation when members of the UCMS

---

18. "Brethren Arise in Majesty," *Christian Standard*, Oct. 24, 1925, pp. 2237-2239.

19. The *Christian Evangelist* (Oct. 15, 1925, p. 1318), in an editorial on the vote commented: "The fact that its adoption was nearly unanimous is very strong prima facie evidence that it was wise (sic)." The *Christian Standard* (Oct. 24, 1925, p. 2239) commented: "There can be no question of the victory of conservative forces. They routed the forces of the Campbell Institute and did it in decisive manner."

Board of Managers urged him to wait until the resolution had been "interpreted!"[20]

The (UCMS) interpretation came two months later and stated that the resolution applied only to open agitation for open membership and not to privately held opinions on the issue. The conclusion of the matter was obvious: since no UCMS personnel was currently "openly agitating" for open membership, there was no one to sever from the organization. Moreover, it was further "interpreted," since the issue of open membership had been settled at the 1922 convention,[21] there was no such practice anywhere in the UCMS thus making the resolution superflous.[22] Since Stephen J. Corey was not being divisive, i.e. agitating for open membership, he was not forced to resign.

The Recall of Leslie Wolfe

While the Sweeney's Peace Resolution was being passed, and an interpretation being formulated, there was still the matter of the petition for Leslie Wolfe's recall to act upon. Accordingly the United Christian Missionary Society authorized in October of 1925 the Commission to the Orient to travel to the Philippines to investigate the charges against Leslie Wolfe. The Commission arrived in the Philippines in February of 1926. Unfortunately the Commission was composed of:

A friendly group of people, who are loyal supporters of the work and strong friends of the Society and the missionaries. . . . One of the chief plans will be to get a first-hand knowledge of the situation on the field and bring back to our people

---

20. Corey, *Fifty Years of Attack and Controversy,* pp. 104-105.
21. See footnote 17.
22. Murch, *Christians Only,* p. 249.

at home such a report as will educate them and bring them to a confidence in the missionaries and in the task on the field.[23]

It was no surprise then when, a few weeks later on March 12, 1925, the Commission cabled to the UCMS Board of Managers recommending that Leslie Wolfe be recalled immediately. On April 30, 1926, Wolfe was separated from UCMS employment, but stayed on for a few months in the Philippines to continue work as an "independent" missionary under the behest, and with the financial support, of conservative Disciples in the States.

Because of the interpretation of the Peace Resolution — an interpretation which violated the intent of the resolution — and the dismissal of Leslie Wolfe from UCMS employment, the final scene for an explosion which would rend asunder at the seams the thin fabric of unity holding together the Disciples of Christ was about to be played.

For a starter, the *Christian Standard* printed, upon his dismissal from the UCMS, an article titled "Keep Wolfe in the Philippines,"[24] in which the *Standard* called upon its readers to help raise a budget of $6,000 for Wolfe and his mission work. In addition to the article the *Standard* sent out special telegrams and letters to many of its readers asking for special contributions and for twenty men to pay Wolfe's salary ($1,200) for one year. Money for Wolfe began to pour in, and the *Standard* printed a running account of how much was being received, who the donors were, and calling for greater effort in order to meet fully Wolfe's budget.

---

23. Letter of Stephen J. Corey to Frank W. Stepp, written Oct. 31, 1925 and quoted in *The History of the Philippine Mission*, p. 100.

24. James DeForest Murch, "Keep Wolfe in The Philippines," *Christian Standard*, April 3, 1926, p. 319.

Following these appeals to underwrite the mission work of Leslie Wolfe, the *Christian Standard* carried in its August 14, 1925, issue a nine page supplement reviewing the action of the Commission to the Orient in dismissing Leslie Wolfe from the UCMS. The supplement began with "A Call To Action," an article which urged conservative Disciples to descend upon Memphis, Tennessee, where the 1926 International Convention was to be held, to protest and reverse the infamous "interpretation" which the UCMS had given to the Peace Resolution. The article was signed by W. R. Walker, P. H. Welsheimer, Mark Collis, W. E. Sweeney and S. S. Lappin. The remainder of the supplement was devoted to discussing the full report of the Commission to the Orient and its explanation of why Leslie Wolfe was dismissed. In essence, the *Standard* continued to call for a large gathering of conservative Disciples to attend the Memphis Convention. When it was learned that Leslie Wolfe himself, plus J. L. Baronia and Dr. F. S. Orlina, two Filipino co-workers, had set sail from the Philippines in order to attend and present his side of the controversy to the Convention, interest in the Convention reached fever pitch. In anticipation of a large crowd, and fearing that Wolfe and his companions would not be allowed to present their full case during the convention, *Standard Publishing* rented a Methodist Church in Memphis, paying the rent in advance by check,[25] to hold a preconvention Restoration Congress. However, Walter White, minister of the Linwood Avenue Christian Church, and chairman of local arrangement for the International Convention, brought local pressure upon the Methodist

---

25. "The Memphis Convention," *Christian Standard*, Oct. 30, 1926, p. 540.

church to cancel the rent agreement.[26] The Pantoges Theatre in Memphis was next rented, and for two days

> . . . the ambassadors from the Philippines told their story and leading ministers and educators restated the care of opposition to liberalism and open membership and the perfidy of the UCMS.[27]

The following week time was given to Leslie Wolfe and his companions from the Philippines to present their case to the International Convention. If tempers were at the boiling point during the 1925 Convention, the situation at the 1926 Convention was more like a boiling caldron. Emotions, unfortunately, were now running too high to rationally present either Wolfe's or the UCMS side and calmly consider sensible solutions. Brethren who were stirred up from having attended the sessions at the Pantoges Theatre were anxious to see Wolfe vindicated before the Convention, but those in favor of the UCMS were just as determined to see that no such vindication took place. So, when Wolfe received his opportunity to present the doctrinal issue which laid behind the Philippine controversy, he was given only a few minutes. Accordingly, to conserve time, he quoted only part of a resolution which had recently been adopted by UCMS missionaries in the Philippines as an example of open membership in that mission field. After returning to his seat, Wolfe was recalled to the platform to read the resolution in its entirety.

> Whereas, Members of the churches of other communions are often located in communities where we have the only church; and

---

26. Henry E. Webb, *A History of the Independent Mission Movement of the Disciples of Christ* (unpublished D.Th. Thesis, Southern Baptist Theological Seminary, 1954), p. 144.

27. Murch, *Christians Only*, p. 252.

Whereas, We wish to give them the fullest possible recognition in our churches; be it

Resolved, That it is the sense of the Christian Mission that evangelical Christians who have not conformed to our requirements for regularly entering the church should be listed as affiliated members while still retaining their membership in their churches it being made clear that they are not regular members of the local church.[28]

After Wolfe had finished reading the resolution, it was pointed out that the resolution in no way referred, as Wolfe alleged, to open membership. However, the wording of the resolution is ambiguous at best, and what Wolfe wanted to get across was that its very ambiguity was being used by the UCMS in the Philippines as justification for instituting and practicing open membership. But Wolfe had no more time in which to clarify this point, and seeing at this moment a chance to embarrass Wolfe the discussion was closed. In commenting on this scene which took place on the floor of an International Convention, James DeForest Murch wrote in the later years:

As "lambs for the slaughter," the Philippine delegation was easily disposed of in the main convention — evangelicals who dared to take the platform to state their grievances were insulted and made to appear as fools.[29]

---

28. Corey, *Fifty Years of Attack and Controversy*, pp. 120-122. Corey states that two hours were set aside for this presentation. Maxey, on the other hand, states that Wolfe personally was given only five minutes to state his case before the convention. (Maxey, *History of the Philippine Mission*, p. 167.) Henry Webb states that the Disciple conservatives were simply "outwitted from the start" by a determined liberal element still smarting from the Peace Resolution of the 1925 International Convention (Webb, *A History of the Independent Movement*, p. 144).

29. Murch, *Christians Only*, p. 253.

After this, the Report of the Commission to the Orient—the report which described in detail the reasons for dismissing Leslie Wolfe from the UCMS—was accepted without change by the business session of the 1926 International Convention, thus ending formally Leslie Wolfe's ordeal with the missionary society.

All emotions were now spent. The climax of the struggle, which had been building in intensity for two decades, had been reached but more crucially left unresolved. Conservative Disciples, many in disgust, left Memphis vowing never to participate again in the International Convention.[30] Edwin Errett, writing in the *Christian Standard,* branded the 1926 Convention "A Convention of Bad Faith"; and in the same issue an editorial sarcastically noted that those who believe the International Convention can still be reformed "are few in number compared to those who now regard the convention as a nuisance."[31]

More significant, though, than the disgust that conservative Disciples now felt toward the International Convention, was Leslie Wolfe's departure on December 25, 1926, to return to the Philippines to serve for the next twenty years as a missionary for the Christian Churches and Churches of Christ but independent of the United Christian Missionary Society.

---

30. *Ibid.,* p. 256. On October 12-16, 1927, the first North American Christian Convention was held, which conservatives in the Disciples of Christ attended.

31. Edwin Errett, "A Convention of Bad Faith," *Christian Standard*, Nov. 27, 1926, p. 631ff.

Part II

A NEW MISSIONARY DYNAMIC

(1890-1926)

Chapter Four

W. K. AZBILL AND THE FIRST BREAKTHROUGH

Before Leslie Wolfe accepted the invitation from certain Disciples in América to remain in the Philippines as a missionary independent of the United Christian Missionary Society, there were already other Disciples of Christ missionaries serving outside the auspices of the UCMS and its predecessors the Foreign Missionary Society and the Christian Woman's Board of Missions. Indeed, from the very early days of the Restoration Movement there had always been self or congregationally initiated evangelism and church planting in the United States, which were counted as mission work; but there was nothing similar that could properly be considered a comparable breakthrough for foreign missions until the final decade of the 19th Century. From the 1890's, and over the next thirty years, several such foreign missionary enterprises were inaugurated and sustained outside the normal channels of the established missionary societies.

Not much is known about these early independent missions and missionaries. The main reason for this ignorance is that, since they occurred in that transitional period from 1890 to 1926 when there was neither full sympathy for the missionary societies nor strong support for non-society mission work, they have largely been neglected by historians in the Restoration Movement. Obviously early historians of the missionary societies were not disposed to chronicle the progress of these independent missionaries. Likewise for equally obvious reasons, early and modern day Disciples of Christ historians say little, if anything, at all about these independent Disciples. Church of Christ (non-instrumental) historians, while sometimes referring to these independent missionaries, normally do not claim them. No doubt because, since they arose in the above named transitional period, most of them were not sufficiently "anti-society" to subsequently be legitimately considered Church of Christ missionaries.[1] This neglect is understandable. However, it is not understandable when historians of the Direct-Support missionary movement likewise fail to detail either this progress or recognize their significance for the subsequent emergence of the Direct-Support movement as a full-fledged system of missions among the Christian Churches.

Because these early independent missionaries are relatively unknown and unrecognized among us today, we shall at this point dip back into history to the 1890's and trace through the subsequent years the various dynamics of independent mission work which proved to be significant for the formation of the Direct-Support missionary movement. It will, in other words, bring us "up to date" regarding events and precedents which, because of their nature, were outside the mainstream of brotherhood activity but which were nevertheless destined to play a formative role in the missionary outreach of the Restoration Movement in later years. This dipping back into history is important to us for another reason. When a significant portion of the Disciples of Christ rejected in 1926 the para-church missionary organization as a proper and legitimate strategy for fulfilling the Great Commission, a void was created. This void had to be filled, otherwise this portion of the brotherhood would be remiss in not having a strategy by which to carry out the commands of the Great Commission. Fortunately, what was developing on the horizons of the Restoration Movement in the form of these early independent missionaries filled the void and became

---

1. Cf. Earl I. West, *The Search for the Ancient Order* (Gospel Advocate Company, 1944), Vol. II, pp. 457-459.

the strategy of evangelizing the world for a great number of churches in the Restoration Movement.

Consequently, contrary to our stated objective in the Introduction, we shall consider these early independent missionaries in some detail before continuing our history of the Direct-Support missionary movement from 1926 onward. This detailing is necessary in order to properly assess the impact these early missionaries had on the Direct-Support missionary movement. Yet, in spite of the amount written here, much more historical research and writing on these missionaries and their work remains to be done, especially if we are to understand their full impact, not only on Direct-Support missions, but also on missions in the Restoration Movement in general. Therefore, to the extent that is possible in this chapter and the next, their work is here surveyed, and their contribution to missions in the Restoration Movement recognized.

The First Volunteers

In the August 13, 1891, issue of the *Christian Evangelist* there appeared an announcement from Wilson Kendrick Azbill, already a veteran missionary in the Restoration Movement, of a plan to form a band of volunteer missionaries to travel to and evangelize in Japan. The plan called for each volunteer to:

> be selected with reference to his special fitness for the work, and those will be preferred who are deservedly beloved by all who know them, as being the more likely to succeed abroad and to be supported by the churches at home. Each as soon as he or she has decided to go, will proceed to solicit what will be needed for the journey and for the start on the

field. When all are thus prepared, and when I have gathered something for the houses that will be needed we will go.[2]

Azbill also announced that he would remain with his band of volunteers until they became settled in the work after which he would return to the States to form still other bands to evangelize other areas.

The plan was a bold one, not because of its originality (it was essentially what the "anti's" had been agitating for all along),[3] but because it was proposed in an environment entirely dominated by para-church missionary organizations. Yet, despite its boldness, such a plan was not unexpected when Azbill's life and ministry in the Restoration Movement are taken into account. He was born in 1848 in Madison County, Kentucky. Growing up in a Christian home, he entered Transylvania College and studied under J. W. McGarvey. After graduation he preached and led in establishing Columbia Christian College. From 1882 to 1886 he served as a missionary in Jamaica under the auspices of the Christian Woman's Board of Mission. After returning to the United States he was employed by the Foreign Christian Missionary Society to raise funds from churches in Indiana and surrounding states.[4] For several months in 1891 he worked

---

2. W. K. Azbill, "Faith and Foreign Mission," *Christian Evangelist*, Aug. 13, 1891, pp. 518-519. See also "Brother Azbill's Mission," *Christian Evangelist*, Aug. 20, 1891, p. 540: "I want suitable men and women to go with me. I want a band of young men and women, namely a doctor and wife, a carpenter and wife, a preacher and wife and three young ladies for teachers."

3. Cf. "(Azbill) now adopts this plan as the practical, direct, common-sense method, in which he sees the work can effactually be done. But in doing this, he adopts precisely the plan presented by the inspired apostles and long maintained by the Gospel Advocate." "Grounds on Which We Can Unite," *Gospel Advocate*, Nov. 28, 1891, p. 748.

4. *Christian Standard*, April 11, 1891, p. 317.

diligently traveling from congregation to congregation seeking to raise funds for the foreign mission work of the FCMS.

Azbill's experience first as a missionary and later as a fund raiser for foreign missions revealed to him, in spite of the growth and progress of the missionary societies, how much was not being done by churches of the Restoration Movement in foreign missions.[5] For example, Azbill claimed that only 663 congregations out of a total 5,288, or roughly 10% of the churches at that time, were contributing to the foreign outreach of the Restoration Movement. Anti-society sentiments among the churches partly accounted for this low percentage, Azbill asserted, but it was also "accounted for, in part, by failure of the missionary societies."

. . . Let us acknowledge that (the anti's) have been more successful in their opposition than we have been in our efforts to enlist our brethren in our missionary enterprises.[6]

It was true that the missionary societies had fund raisers and campaigns to raise funds from the churches, but these often turned out to be ineffectual, since many of the society personnel in fund raising appeared more interested in the techniques of fund raising than in the purpose of their techniques, namely foreign mission work. Azbill alleged that this superficial interest on the part of some official repelled many sincere individuals and churches, who would otherwise support missions, from giving money to the societies.

In view of these things, Azbill argued, many of the 4,625 churches which were not at that time supporting any foreign mission work would do so if a fresh approach to missions was made available to them. In other words, Azbill's plan was designed essentially to mobilize and incorporate the

---

5. W. K. Azbill, "Faith and Foreign Mission," *Christian Evangelist*, Aug. 13, 1891, pp. 518-519.
6. *Ibid.*, p. 519.

vast majority of churches (90% of the total) into the missionary outreach of the Restoration Movement which was being carried by only a small number of churches. Since his plan called for volunteers, going without stipulated pay,[7] hence without the encumbering machinery of a missionary society, many individuals and churches would now find missions in the Restoration Movement unobjectionable and would join the rest of the brotherhood in proclaiming the Restoration plea around the world.[8] The outcome to his plan, therefore, could only be a happy one for the Restoration Movement.

Azbill was no doubt acutely aware of the impending division in the Restoration Movement over the legitimacy of para-church missionary organizations.[9] The Sandcreek Declaration and Address, which was published a dozen years before this time and had called for a withdrawal of fellowship over the issue, was gaining more popularity as each year went by. Moreover, in another dozen years the division would become a sad reality. Yet, in all the promotion that Azbill put into his plan through the pages of the *Christian Evangelist* and *Christian Standard*, he did not propose that his

---

7. W. K. Azbill, "Going to Japan," *Christian Standard*, Nov. 21, 1891, p. 976.

8. In an editorial comment to Azbill's article "Faith and Foreign Missions" (*Christian Evangelist*, Aug. 14, 1891, p. 519), J. H. Garrison remarked: "Brother Azbill's method will at least give an opportunity for those who are yearning to do foreign mission work but who are opposed to missionary societies." In similar vein the Gospel Advocate called upon the churches which were not supporting the societies to now show to the brotherhood they were pro-missions by supporting Azbill. ("The Japan Mission—What it Signified." *Gospel Advocate*, Dec. 31, 1891, p. 827).

9. For example, in "Some Facts and Comments on Them" (*Christian Standard*, Dec. 17, 1892, p. 1058), Azbill asserted that the churches in the southern part of the United States were not anti-missionary, only anti-society.

plan would avert the coming division over mission methods, thereby preserving the unity of the Restoration Movement.[10] In spite of the obvious attraction his plan would have in this respect, Azbill promoted only the practical aspects of his plan, namely it would enlist more churches supporting the missionary outreach of the Restoration Movement. Perhaps he did have in the back of his mind hopes that his plan would in fact eventually prove to be the very key that would avert division in the brotherhood, but, if he did, the division that was pronounced in 1906 laid to rest permanently any hopes he may have had along this line.

The initial response to Azbill's plan for a band of volunteers to work in Japan was good. Immediately after he made his announcement in the *Christian Evangelist* eighteen volunteered to join his band.[11] Azbill wisely did not publish their names at first, because before very long many of them changed their minds and dropped out. Besides the response which came from individuals who wanted to join his volunteer band, many churches and church leaders also showed enthusiasm in the project.[12] J. H. Garrison expressed favor through the pages of the *Christian Evangelist*. As was expected, the *Gospel Advocate*, long an opponent to missionary

---

10. Even in promoting his plan through the Gospel Advocate, Azbill made no pitch that his plan could avert division over mission methods. Rather, his objective was entirely pragmatic: "After consultation with Brother David Lipscomb, I have decided to visit as many of the churches of Christ in your State as I can . . . to impart to you a more perfect knowledge of the proposed mission to Japan." ("The Volunteer Mission to Japan," *Gospel Advocate*, Dec. 3, 1891, p. 767).

11. "Azbill's Mission." *Christian Evangelist*, Oct. 1, 1891, p. 633.

12. "Going to Japan," *Christian Standard*, Nov. 21, 1891, p. 976.

societies, was also in favor.[13] Even a few officials of the missionary societies expressed favor in Azbill's plan.

By February of 1892, Azbill had selected the volunteers who would accompany him to Japan. The number of volunteers had dwindled from an initial high of eighteen to six.[14] They were Mr. and Mrs. J. M. McCaleb, Mr. and Mrs. L. L. Lindsey, Miss Lucia Scott and Miss Carmie Hostetter. Azbill recruited them through the Student's Volunteer Corps, a student mission group of Hiram College.[15] The volunteers gathered in Indianapolis, Indiana to begin their journey by train to San Francisco. On the eve of their departure, a fantastic reception was held by the Indianapolis churches for Azbill and his band. The Governor of Indiana was invited to speak and to give a toast to the departing band, but due to a mix up in scheduling on Azbill's part he was unable to attend. Azbill had raised enough funds to pay travel expenses to Japan. Since his wife was not accompanying him to Japan, but staying in Indianapolis, he instructed that funds for the band's support in Japan be sent to her. Letters to Japan should be sent to him in care of George T. Smith (FCMS missionary) in Tokyo. If individuals wanted to send money directly to him, they were to send the money in the form of bank drafts.

Upon arriving in Japan, Azbill and his band of mission

---

13. "We recommend most heartily Brother Azbill's proposed mission, because he is starting on scriptural lines, and we have faith he will not lead brethren into his support to betray them into the societies" ("Grounds on Which We Can Unite," *Gospel Advocate*, Nov. 28, 1891, p. 748).

14. "The Japan Volunteers," *Christian Evangelist*, Feb. 4, 1892, p. 76.

15. "The Japan Volunteer Band on Their Way," *Christian Evangelist*, Mar. 17, 1892, p. 166.

volunteers were met by Eugene Snodgrass, FCMS missionary.[16] They soon became settled in Tokyo and began their mission work of opening a Bible School for children and preaching points. In addition to evangelistic outreach on the field, Azbill, along with J. M. McCaleb, wrote and issued a constant stream of reports on their activities. These were printed in both the *Christian Evangelist* and *Christian Standard*. During 1892, their first year in Japan, Azbill wrote six letters from Japan while McCaleb wrote seven. Both men also reported their activities through the pages of the *Gospel Advocate*.

Bucking the System

In August, 1892, Azbill returned from Japan and issued the first annual report of his mission enterprise.[17] He counted Aug. 15, 1891, when he first conceived of his plan, as the beginning. For the year that followed, Azbill reported a total of $3,070.62 in contributions received from 14 states. Expenses were: travel, $1,656.52; salaries, $1,168.89; and provision on hand, $245.20. The Volunteer Band had, by Aug. 1892, established two Sunday schools and one preaching point in Japan. This report, which was sixteen pages long, brought forth editorial comment from the *Christian Standard*.[18] The *Standard*, long a staunch advocate and defender of the missionary societies in the face of strong attacks by the "anti's," considered Azbill's report as representing the anti's and then smugly welcomed them "to the

---

16. "The Volunteer Band on the Field," *Christian Evangelist*, May 26, 1892, p. 326.

17. "First Year of the Volunteer Mission Band," *Christian Standard*, Sept. 17, 1892, p. 797. Also in *Christian Evangelist*, Oct. 6, 1892, p. 633.

18. "A Volunteer Report," *Christian Standard*, Sept. 17, 1892, p. 792.

noble army of *doers* and trust that they have eternally deserted the ranks of cavillers." The *Standard* went on to "twit" the anti's because of the cost of Azbill's mission: any mission work, whether that conducted by a society or on a volunteer basis, the *Standard* said, costs money. Hopefully the anti's would now realize this and would henceforth cease opposing the missionary societies on the basis of their costliness. Azbill immediately answered the *Standard* by saying that his volunteer missionary band was not anti-society, neither should it be considered the long-awaited plan of the anti's in fulfilling the Great Commission.[19] In other words, Azbill still considered himself a member in good standing of that part of the Restoration Movement which was pro-society, and any attempt to assign him solely to the anti's on account of his mission methodology was an injustice both to him and his method.

Azbill's credibility in this regard was greatly weakened due to an unfortunate situation he found himself, by virtue of his independent status, drawn into soon after his arrival in Japan in 1892.[20] Eugene Snodgrass, FCMS missionary who had met Azbill at the boat upon the latter's arrival, had become embroiled in a bitter controversy with the FCMS field supervisor over what should be the proper policy in the face of a government order to close an FCMS mission school. Japanese law at that time prohibited foreign mission work from being done unless it was conducted in connection with an educational institution. Consequently the FCMS had established a school at Akita, not far away from Tokyo, and sent Snodgrass to live and work there as an evangelist.

---

19. "R. B. Tyler's Blunder," *Christian Standard*, Oct. 23, 1892, p. 894.
20. W. K. Azbill, "How not to Manage Missions," *Christian Standard*, April 14, 1914, p. 581.

With the subsequent closing of the school, Snodgrass considered it illegal to stay on in Akita and so informed his field supervisor that he was moving back to Tokyo. The supervisor ordered Snodgrass to stay on with his work on evangelism in Akita since the Japanese government rarely enforced this law. But Snodgrass refused to obey this order on grounds of conscience, upon which the supervisor stopped Snodgrass' salary. In the end both Snodgrass and the field supervisor were fired from the FCMS, but, under the influence of Azbill,[21] Snodgrass decided to stay on in Japan as an independent missionary. Azbill announced this decision through the *Christian Standard,* and furthermore stated his next task would be "to secure for this brother and his mission an adequate support from churches where he is well known."[22] A month later, Azbill announced the task accomplished.[23]

It was at this point that Azbill began to experience more than just passing opposition to his ideas and plans on missions in the Restoration Movement. From the beginning, of course, there were those who opposed his plan—even the *Christian Standard* refused to print the first announcement of his plan for volunteers for Japan.[24] Others had predicted failure because it did not have the financial undergirding that a missionary society enjoyed. It also turned out that, in his initial enthusiasm, Azbill misinterpreted the encouragement that officials of the missionary societies gave to him in forming a "para-society" band of mission volunteers to work in Japan. For example, C. L. Loos, President of the

---

21. Eugene Snodgrass, "Brother W. K. Azbill," *Gospel Advocate,* April 27, 1893, p. 270.

22. "Letter from Japan," *Christian Standard,* Jan. 7, 1893, p. 13.

23. "Eugene Snodgrass," *Christian Standard,* Feb. 4, 1893, p. 95.

24. W. K. Azbill, "Open Letter to Brother Garrison," *Christian Evangelist,* Feb. 7, 1895, p. 88.

FCMS, was not as enthusiastic over Azbill's plan as was first thought.[25] Loos feared that Azbill's volunteer band would entail dividing available mission funds from the churches between the societies and Azbill. If Azbill continued it would ultimately mean fewer funds for the already under-financed missionary societies. In answer, Azbill reiterated that he planned to raise funds only from non-society churches and, therefore, would not cut into the funds designated for the societies. While Azbill surmounted these initial difficulties, he was not destined to overcome the next opposition that now faced him in making his mission ideas successful.

After returning from Japan in 1892, Azbill set about raising adequate support for his groups of volunteers, which now included Eugene Snodgrass and his family.[26] However, he found the task much more difficult than he had anticipated: non-society churches were not all that willing to support his volunteers after all. In fact, he soon exhausted the non-society churches where he could speak to raise funds and, unable to secure speaking dates elsewhere, was reduced to traveling at random, showing up first at one congregation then another hoping to speak.[27] His travels, unfortunately, led him more and more to pro-society churches where he began to get a hearing — and support — for his mission. I say "unfortunate," because it was at this time that society officials cried "foul" and rushed in to protect their sources of income from Azbill. For example, Archibald McLean, President of

25. W. K. Azbill, "I Stand Corrected," *Christian Standard,* Dec. 31, 1891, p. 844.

26. "Some Facts and Comments on Them," *Christian Standard,* Dec. 17, 1892, pp. 1058-1059.

27. W. K. Azbill, "In Opinion and Method Liberty," *Christian Evangelist,* Jan. 14, 1894, p. 37.

the FCMS, wrote in response to an inquirer on this matter these caustic words of Azbill's effort to raise funds.

If the anti-missionary people are supporting any missionaries in the foreign fields I do not know who they are: Mr. Azbill took some people to Japan a year or so ago, but these workers are supported chiefly by personal friends. As I understand it, most of their support comes from churches that are contributing regularly to our missionary societies. Mr. Azbill appeals in all our papers for help. He does not confine his appeals to those churches or persons who are opposed to organized work. I know of no work done by the missionary people exclusively. The fact is, they are spending most of their strength in opposing the work, rather than demonstrating the superiority of their plea by showing larger and better' results from their own so-called Lord's plan.

Eugene Snodgrass got hold of the letter and sent it, along with appropriate comments, for publication in the *Gospel Advocate*.[28] Among his comments, Snodgrass said that McLean showed his "inexcusable ignorance" of J. M. McCaleb and others in Japan who were then working exclusively independent of the society.

Despite such resistance from powerful society leaders, Azbill was able to receive some support from pro-society sources. But, while this success eased somewhat the financial problems for his volunteers, it served also to aggravate a more serious problem which was inherent in his band of volunteers from the beginning. J. M. McCaleb, upon hearing of Azbill's success with pro-society money sources, withdrew and became independent of Azbill's band.[29] The

---

28. Eugene Snodgrass, "A. McLean and the FCMS," *Gospel Advocate*, Feb. 7, 1895, p. 83.

29. J. M. McCaleb, "Notes from Japan," *Gospel Advocate*, Feb. 23, 1893, p. 126.

specific instance which caused McCaleb to withdraw was a pledge of support ($25 each quarter) which Azbill had received from a Young People Christian Endeavor Society from a church in Ohio. The fact that the money was from a Christian Endeavor Society (sic), in McCaleb's thinking, was the same as receiving money from the big missionary society. McCaleb also claimed that this violated an agreement Azbill made with him before going to Japan, namely "no money whatsoever may be received or channeled through the missionary society for their work."[30] Whether Azbill understood his original agreement with McCaleb in exactly this manner is not clear,[31] but it is certain that Azbill saw nothing inconsistent at least in channeling money through a society since, in his thinking, the proper role of a society (whether missionary or otherwise) was to act as a forwarding agent for churches and individuals to transfer funds to the foreign mission field. In commenting on the split, the *Gospel Advocate* said in an editorial,

> Brother McCaleb and Brother Azbill disagreed as to whether funds should be received from a Christian Endeavor Society. We are truly glad Brother McCaleb refused to receive aid from any association or organization save the Church of Christ. But I wrote him before he went with Brother Azbill that Azbill was still latitudinarian on the subject of societies and organs, but was disposed to work in a Scriptural direction.[32]

---

30. J. M. McCaleb, "As to that Public Announcement," *Gospel Advocate,* May 25, 1893, p. 334.

31. "Azbill Explains," *Gospel Advocate,* Sept. 26, 1893, p. 617. Azbill explained that the money from the Christian Endeavor Society was pledged to Carmie Hostetter, and not to McCaleb. Consequently, he had no authority to deny Miss Hostetter the money. Presumably, therefore, although Azbill did not state it, if the pledge had been made for McCaleb, he would have had the authority to refuse.

32. "Azbill and McCaleb," *Gospel Advocate,* May 25, 1893, p. 322.

In addition to the *Gospel Advocate*, the *Christian Evangelist* also commented — but, from a different perspective — on the Azbill-McCaleb split. Azbill answered, and the ensuing correspondence which involved editorial comment and counter-comment quickly led to a deep and irrevocable hostility between J. H. Garrison, editor of the *Christian Evangelist*, and Azbill. Garrison in his editorial comments was unduly harsh on Azbill, and was all too willing to point out weaknesses in Azbill's mission program. Azbill, however, was equal to the task and answered Garrison's criticism each time in admirable fashion. What is of even more significance is that in his answers to Garrison, Azbill spelled out for the first time his ideas on the proper relationship between the local congregation and the para-church missionary organization in fulfilling the Great Commission. These ideas appeared in four major articles (two of which were in reaction to editorial comments by Garrison) which were printed in 1894 in the *Christian Evangelist*.[33] Azbill's ideas bear summarizing here, for in many respects they foreshadowed ideas propounded later in the Direct-Support missionary movement. Azbill's ideas may be summarized under four headings:

-*On the Role of the Congregation in Missions.* Azbill advocated that the supreme duty of a congregation is the spread of the Gospel and the development of the Kingdom around the world. All other duties which are required of a congregation pale in significance in the light of this one duty. To fulfill this duty, congregations should put forth and commend to the grace of God these who desire to do the work of evangelism. Furthermore, these congregations should

---

33. "In Explanation," *Christian Evangelist*, Oct. 19, 1893, p. 665; "Original Contributions," *Christian Evangelist*, Mar. 8, 1894, p. 150; "As to the Prerogatives of Mission Boards and Societies," *Christian Evangelist*, May 24, 1894, p. 326; "An Ideal Convention," *Christian Evangelist*, June 24, 1894, p. 406.

maintain an immediate and close relationship with the evangelists they have commissioned. Para-church missionary organizations were legitimate, but whenever possible each congregation should select, send and support its own missionary. To Azbill, the latter was a more excellent way!

-On Church-Para-Church Relationship. Azbill needed financial support from pro-society sources for his Japan mission project, but he ran into resistance from the societies on this point. He rightly interpreted this resistance as an indication of the amount of power—especially power to control which missionaries would get money from the churches!—that the societies held over the churches. Consequently Azbill asserted that "no person, corporation or association should presume to acquire rights to the whole attention, interest and benefit of the churches." That is, all missionaries (including his volunteers), whose highest allegiance under Christ is to the churches which support them morally and financially, must be left absolutely free from all authority except that of the congregations to which they are accredited. Mission Boards have no right to intervene between the missionary seeking support and the congregation desiring to give support. Therefore, it was wrong for the missionary societies to crystalize the Disciples missions into one method, that of the para-church organization.

-On the Role of the Missionary Society. If the various missionary societies had no authority to intervene, between church and missionary, and it was the duty of the church to select and support missionaries, then what was the role of the society in the churches' task of fulfilling the Great Commission? According to Azbill, "the societies must content themselves with being more accountants, forwarding agents and friendly advisors of those whose efforts (the churches')

they would facilitate." A congregation, after commissioning a missionary, may utilize a society as an agent to forward funds to the missionary on a foreign field.[34] In other words, a society had no role in selecting missionaries for the churches to support, and, once a church had selected a missionary to support, was duty bound, if the church so desire, to act as the church's agent in forwarding funds.

-Role of the Missionary Convention. The General Convention of the American Christian Missionary Society was the main convention during Azbill's time. However, there was a marked tendency to report on, and transact business of, only the mission work of the missionary societies. As a result, the General Convention had assumed a degree of power over what mission work of the Restoration Movement would be presented to the brotherhood. But ideally, Azbill contended, all missions (society or independent) should be allowed to report during the convention. Moreover, reports should be only on evangelistic outreach and not on the business activities of the missions. To prevent undue power from accruing to the convention, Azbill recommended that a preconvention committee meet to appoint the convention officers who would serve only for the duration of the convention. Azbill also recommended that a Board of Advisors be appointed by the convention to advise the missionary societies in their role as accountants and forwarding agents for the churches. However, there was one task that a general missionary convention could legitimately perform in behalf of the churches: if a missionary denied the divinity of

---

34. Azbill, as an illustration of this role, cited the example of the churches in Des Moines, Iowa in sending out Miss Carmile Werick and Mr. & Mrs. H. H. Guy to Japan and using the good offices of the FCMS to transmit funds to them. This arrangement was continued for several years until the FCMS assimilated both Miss Werick's and Mr. Guy's support into its budget.

Christ or taught others to disregard baptism in the plan of salvation, then the convention should make such facts known to the churches for final judgment and dismissal if needed. The convention itself would have no authority to dismiss such a missionary (this was the church's prerogative) or even to pass on information of any other type (only these two doctrinal items were serious enough for transmission).

As to be expected, Garrison responded critically to Azbill's ideas. Garrison's main objection was that such a sharp distinction between the congregation and the para-church organization (which Azbill's ideas would entail) would ignore the organic unity of the church. Instead of seeking to further delineate the respective roles of the church and missionary society, Garrison argued, brethren should seek to merge them into one organic whole. In other words, instead of promoting unity in the Restoration Movement, Azbill's ideas would increase and heighten the division of roles in the Movement. Garrison went on to argue that the present mission boards were already performing all that Azbill had outlined in his ideas and doing it better. Besides, Garrison opined, these ideas—especially those calling for more direct congregational supervision over the missionary—were too radical to endure the test of time; only the society method of carrying out the Great Commission would survive the passage of the years.

The climax of the controversy between Garrison and Azbill occurred at the close of 1894 when both happened to meet each other on a Texas train trip.[35] Azbill was traveling among the churches of Texas hoping to raise funds for his next trip to Japan. Azbill evidently was encountering difficult

---

35. "Notes of Travel—Closing Words," *Christian Evangelist*, Dec. 27, 1874, p. 820.

times in raising funds from the churches, for he mentioned to Garrison that the brotherhood had misunderstood him in his mission project. After this meeting on the train, Garrison caustically commented in an editorial that Azbill's real difficulty lay not in brotherhood misunderstanding but in the fact that his plan had failed to rally the anti-society churches to his support; so he was having to promote his project among pro-society churches. Yet by promoting an essentially anti-society plan among pro-society churches, Azbill was only alienating his pro-society brethren. This, then, accounted for his feelings of isolation in the brotherhood. So if Azbill wanted support for his mission plan, it was implied, he should give up his independent ways and rejoin the ranks of the society.

Azbill reacted sharply to Garrison's editorial on their chance meeting in Texas.[36] In a letter to Garrison he vehemently denied he was disappointed in his efforts to mobilize anti-society churches to support his plan. Indeed, Azbill wrote he had succeeded in rallying fifty such churches into giving $100 a year to independent mission work, which stood in favorable contrast to the forty churches that were giving similar amounts to the FCMS. Moreover, David Lipscomb, a staunch anti-society leader, gave over $20,000 to missions the previous year, an amount that probably no pro-society leader could match. Therefore, what disappointment he was experiencing was in reality over the way pro-society individuals and churches were ignoring him and his mission project. But, in spite of this problem, which he was encountering in the midwest, churches and brethren in California were enthusiastic supporters of his mission.

---

36. W. K. Azbill, "Open Letter to Brother Garrison," *Christian Evangelist*, Feb. 7, 1895, p. 88.

After this final exchange of letters and comments with Garrison, Azbill returned to Japan in the latter part of 1895. He wrote only two short reports of his second term in Japan which were printed in the *Christian Evangelist,* the last one appearing in the March 12, 1896, issue of the journal. Neither did he report on his work after this through the pages of the *Christian Standard.* He continued to send in reports to the *Gospel Advocate,* but only rarely; in his place Eugene Snodgrass and J. M. McCaleb assumed the major part of the task of reporting. Both reported through the *Gospel Advocate,* and after Snodgrass died in 1907, McCaleb began reporting once more through the *Christian Standard.* He continued to report on his mission work in Japan until 1917.[37] Azbill himself continued to do mission work. After serving a second term in Japan he went on to serve three years in Hawaii. After this Azbill returned to the mainland where he preached for churches in California, Kentucky and Ohio. He also wrote a book on Apologetics titled *Science and Faith* which was widely acclaimed by conservative Disciples throughout the brotherhood.

An Unsung Hero

How should we evaluate Azbill's efforts in "bucking the system" by introducing an alternative to the para-church missionary society for the fulfillment of the Great Commission by churches of the Restoration Movement? Such an evaluation is made difficult by two facts of history. First,

---

37. In 1916, McCaleb announced the arrival of another independent missionary, Miss Sarah Andrews of Dickson, Tenn., to help in his work in Japan. (*Christian Standard,* Feb. 26, 1916, p. 767.)

after 1896 Azbill himself took on a much lower profile in the Restoration Movement and for all practical purposes dropped out of sight. No doubt the controversies with J. M. McCaleb over contributions from para-church organizations (in which the *Gospel Advocate* sided with McCaleb) and with J. H. Garrison of the *Christian Evangelist,* plus the coolness of the *Christian Standard* toward his volunteer missionary plan, discouraged him from actively promoting any further his ideas on mission strategy in the Restoration Movement. Consequently we have little material today, written by Azbill in the years immediately following 1896 on which to gauge the progress of his ideas. A second reason which makes evaluation difficult is the fact that historians in the Restoration Movement have all but ignored Azbill. As just mentioned, the three major journals of the Restoration Movement of that time had their own respective reasons for ignoring Azbill. And as was mentioned earlier in this chapter, the historians of the missionary societies and modern day Disciples of Christ historians have their all too obvious reasons for ignoring Azbill. Perhaps the main reason why historians of the Direct-Support missionary movement have overlooked Azbill is that in the Direct-Support movement there has been lacking an historical perspective of where this mission method stands in relation to all else in the Restoration Movement. This is an unfortunate oversight, for, as we shall see in Chapter Six, several dynamics which are to this day operating in the Direct-Support missionary movement owe their origin to Azbill and his attempt to inaugurate a new mission method in the Restoration Movement. Whatever the respective reasons for ignoring Azbill are, it all adds up to the fact that Azbill was effectively "read out of history" by the three main segments of the Restoration Movement. This is one of the more inexcusable oversights in chronicling the progress of the Restoration Movement.

Even though Azbill largely dropped out of sight after 1896, it did not mean the end of his volunteer missionary project. Quite the contrary, for two of his disciples, J. M. McCaleb and Eugene Snodgrass, now assumed the leadership in making the volunteer missionary idea a success in the Restoration Movement. McCaleb, of course, over the years became more closely identified with the Churches of Christ (non-instrumental) and by the 1920's had become a recognized missionary figure in that segment of the Restoration Movement.[38] He served 42 years in Japan and his work became the basis of a successful missionary outreach into Japan by the Churches of Christ in later years.[39] Of more significance, though, is the fact that this success in Japan, as well as the missionary outreach into other parts of the world by the Churches of Christ, was built on ideas first promoted by W. K. Azbill.

Of equal importance to McCaleb's work in Japan, but from a different perspective, was Eugene Snodgrass' leadership in advancing Azbill's ideas on mission methodology to raise the missionary consciousness of that segment of the Restoration Movement which up to that time had been antagonistic to missions. To be sure, the reason for this antagonism was stated as being due to the utilization of para-church organizations, instead of the local congregation, for accomplishing the missionary outreach of the church; but regardless of the stated reason, the outcome of it was still

---

38. For a list of some of his publications and lectures on mission, see *An Author Catalog of Disciples of Christ and Related Religious Groups* (Disciples of Christ Historical Society, 1946).

39. James DeForest Murch, *Christians Only* (Cincinnati: Standard Publishing, 1962), pp. 316-340.

an extremely low interest in missions—almost an anti-mission bias, in fact—in a great number of churches in the Restoration Movement. It was Azbill's hope to overcome this bias by promoting a less objectionable plan for doing mission work. But while Azbill failed to realize this hope of his,[40] Snodgrass was able to. Soon after returning from Japan in 1894 (he became independent of the FCMS in 1893 while still in Japan), Snodgrass was invited by the editors of the *Gospel Advocate* to become the missionary editor of the journal. This was a significant advance for the Advocate, for with but a couple of exceptions[41] the journal had done nothing in missions but to condemn the missionary societies as "human innovations" to be avoided by the true church. Consequently Snodgrass initiated the Foreign Missionary Column in the *Gospel Advocate*, which first appeared in the July 15, 1895 issue of the journal. In his first column Snodgrass struck a positive note.

The opening of this column in the *Gospel Advocate* means that the work of the churches and brethren in the regions beyond has, in the judgment of the editors, reached that state of growth which can be helped on better by regularly presenting in a special column news items concerning it . . . It will be the aim of this column to present practical and accurate information concerning the mission fields.

Direct missionary work of the churches is hardly four years old. It is remarkable the rapidity with which the independent missionary work has grown.[42]

---

40. This failure was due in large measure to the *Gospel Advocate*'s siding with J. M. McCaleb in the controversy over funds received from a Young People Christian Endeavor Society. After this (about 1893), Azbill had little influence among anti-society churches.

41. The *Gospel Advocate* did promote the work of Jules DeLaunay, who went to Paris, France in 1880, and the work of Azariah Paul who went to Turkey in 1889 (See *Christians Only*, p. 516).

42. "Foreign Missionary Column," *Gospel Advocate*, July 25, 1895, p. 471.

In fact, Snodgrass wrote two separate columns for that issue of the *Advocate*. In his second column, he listed and named the "direct" missionaries being supported by local churches in the States.[43] There were twenty-one such missionaries in 1895:

- M/M D. F. Jones who had two years earlier converted from the Christian Connection Church (a denomination resulting from the restoration work of Abner Jones and Elias Smith) and were then serving in China.
- M/M J. M. McCaleb
- M/M W. K. Azbill
- Mr. Smith (an Englishman serving independently in Japan)
- Miss Alice Miller
- Miss Lucia Scott
- Miss Carmie Hostetter
- Miss L. J. Wirick
- Mr. Ishikawa (a Japanese national supported by churches in the States)
- M/M Yoshikawa (Japanese nationals supported by churches in the States)
- M/M R. L. Pruett (new missionaries for Japan, recruited by Snodgrass while on furlough)
- M/M T. D. Garvin (independent missionaries to Hawaii)
- Miss Calla Harrison (independent missionary to Hawaii)
- M/M Eugene Snodgrass
- Mr. S. M. Cook (an independent missionary serving in Lagos, West Africa)

To this list Azbill would probably also had added M/M H. H. Guy, who were supported, as Miss Wirick was, by a special and direct relationship with churches in Des Moines, Iowa.

---

43. "Foreign Missionary Column," *Gospel Advocate*, July 25, 1895, p. 474.

The funds for both Guy and Wirick were channeled through the FCMS, however, a fact which Guy did not find objectionable (perhaps why Snodgrass omitted him from his list) but which Wirick did (probably why she was included). The FCMS refused to allow Wirick's support to by-pass its control, even at her request, and be channeled directly to her on the field. Miss Wirick in the end succumbed to the pressure of this refusal and made a new arrangement with the FCMS to support her completely.[44]

In that first year of writing the Foreign Missionary Column for the *Gospel Advocate,* Snodgrass wrote a total of fifteen articles. In these articles he reported the news of the above independent missionaries, gave background information on the political and religious conditions of mission fields, and appealed for funds. On this latter matter, Snodgrass gave some thought on how, in a mission method that sought to avoid "human innovation," funds should be collected for the support of missionaries, especially since there was no Scriptural precedent for just such a case.

> The interest awakened in the salvation of the natives beyond has led brethren to enquire about the needs of this work, and to desire to aid it regularly. It seems to those who have given thought to the matter that one of the regular Lord's day collections in the month should be devoted to the foreign work. Some churches are doing this, and find it easier and more efficient than to undertake a special offering. It soon becomes an easy service to send this once a month to your missionary on the field.[45]

In these columns, Snodgrass also never missed an opportunity to "twit" the missionary societies, no doubt to the delight of the readers of the *Gospel Advocate.*

---

44. See "New Arrangement," *Christian Evangelist,* July 23, 1896, p. 478; "How not to Manage Missions," *Christian Standard,* April 14, 1914, p. 581.
45. "Foreign Missionary Column," *Gospel Advocate,* July 25, 1895, p. 471.

In any evaluation of Azbill's mission efforts, especially since Snodgrass listed him in the *Gospel Advocate*, we must lay to rest the idea that many in the Direct-Support movement today have, namely that he joined ranks with the anti-organ (i.e., anti-society) segment of the Restoration Movement. Such is implied by James DeForest Murch when he stated that Azbill after having begun, "defected from the anti's to the Disciples, largely because they were more missionary minded."[46] However, from reading the relevant material on Azbill from the *Christian Evangelist*, the *Christian Standard* and the *Gospel Advocate*, it is difficult to see where Azbill ever considered himself as being a member of the anti's, and, more crucially that the anti's ever considered him a fellow-traveler in good standing. All that we can deduct from these journals is that Azbill was mainly concerned about enlisting anti-society churches in the support of missions in the Restoration Movement. This, of course, inevitably brought him into conflict with the powerful societies, but even after this he continued to preach for Disciple of Christ churches. For example, his name appears in the 1914 Disciples of Christ Yearbook as the minister of the Dunham Avenue Church in Cleveland, Ohio, and in the 1920 Yearbook as the minister of the Christian Church in Escondido, California. In short, we must conclude that, even though the results of his volunteer missionary result were eventually absorbed into the Churches of Christ (by way of McCaleb and Snodgrass), Azbill himself never did become an "anti."

If Azbill did not join ranks with the anti's, then how did the idea that he did arise among Direct-Support historians? The answer, I believe, is simply this. Since both the *Christian*

---

46. Murch, *Christians Only*, p. 316.

Evangelist and the *Christian Standard*—which lie closer to the historical identity of the Direct-Support Missionary movement than the *Gospel Advocate*—were essentially unenthusiastic toward Azbill's "para-society" missionary band, there was no place for him to go at the time but to the anti's. In other words, he was forced over to the anti-society segment of the Restoration Movement.[47] Unfortunately the forced association "stuck," and when he stayed with the Disciples of Christ after his missionary days were over, it was erroniously interpreted as a "defection." As in the words of a Disciple contemporary of Azbill, he was the "victim of some misunderstanding" among the Disciples.[48] It is time that this misunderstanding be permanently put to rest and Azbill's contribution, which in many respects foreshadowed the Direct-Support missionary movement, be fully recognized. Again, in the words of the same contemporary just mentioned, Azbill "is the missing-link between cooperative and noncooperative (missionary) forces."

Due to the turmoil that occurred between 1920 and 1926, turmoil which resulted in the Direct-Support missionary movement, it is clear that Wilson Kendrick Azbill was born and lived before his time. There is no clearer proof of this than when in 1914 the *Christian Standard* "resurrected" Azbill enlisting him in its fight of protesting the turning of the General Missionary Convention into a delegate convention

---

47. Eugene Snodgrass found himself in the same predicament. After being forced to resign from the FCMS in 1893 and remaining independent in Japan, the *Christian Standard* informed him that he could not solicit funds through its pages. ("To the Editor of the Christian Standard," by Eugene Snodgrass, *Christian Standard*, Dec. 12, 1896, p. 1608). From this time onward the Standard branded Snodgrass as an "anti." ("Eugene Disturbed," *Christian Standard*, Dec. 12, 1896, p. 1592.

48. Claris Yerrell, "W. K. Azbill," *Christian Standard*, April 18, 1914, p. 679.

for the Disciples of Christ. In fact, Azbill had delivered a speech against the proposed delegate convention during the 1914 General Convention, and because of that was invited by the *Christian Standard* to write on the subject for publication in the journal which, a quarter of a century earlier, had all but snubbed him. But times had changed for the *Christian Standard!*

In 1914 Azbill was 66 years old, and was physically unable to carry on the battle that was about to erupt in the brotherhood over the faithfulness of the missionary societies. Yet despite his age Azbill still had plenty of fire left in his writing. Between January and May of 1914, he wrote fifteen articles which were published in the *Christian Standard.*[49] Titles which Azbill used include "The Menace of Centralization," "How to do Cooperative Christian Union," "How not to Manage Missions," "Wrong Attitudes of Boards," and "The Beast in the Jungle." In these articles Azbill recounted his own sad experience of battling the societies for recognition of his own missionary efforts, a battle which he lost when he was not given a place on the program of the General Convention in the early 1890's to report on the work of his volunteer band in Japan. Even J. W. McGarvey, his former teacher, refused recognition by not letting him present his mission work at the Transylvania Bible College.

While Azbill mostly recounted the history of his controversies with the missionary societies in these articles, he also wrote briefly on his ideas of how missions should be conducted.[50] There was really nothing in these articles to add to

---

49. Most of these articles were also simultaneously published in several journals of the Churches of Christ.

50. Strangely enough, in an editorial comment, the Standard still thought some of these ideas were "Open to criticism." ("A Series of Articles from W. K. Azbill," *Christian Standard,* Jan. 31, 1914, p. 173.

what he wrote in his controversy with J. H. Garrison of the *Christian Evangelist* in 1894 and 1895. Rather they were elaborations of his earlier ideas presented in the controversy. Nevertheless, these elaborations are worth summarizing here, for, like his earlier ideas, these too have become standard doctrines in and for the Direct-Support missionary movement of today. They may be summarized under three headings.

- On Authority in Missions: Azbill ran into roadblock after roadblock erected by society officials in trying to promote his volunteer mission project through the General Convention and the missionary journals of the brotherhood. He saw from this that officials of the various missionary societies had too much power in the brotherhood and that they too often misused that power by exercising authority over the missionary in matters where only God had authority. But in missions of the Biblical order, Azbill argued, the will of God and the Lordship of Christ are the dominant elements, and the guidance of the Holy Spirit is indispensable. In fact, the Holy Spirit has an active role in missions as the promised *paraclete* in its legal sense, i.e., the Holy Spirit serves as the legal advisor and monitor to the church. Consequently the mission of the church is likewise under the monitorship of the Holy Spirit. To Azbill's understanding of the matter, this excluded any para-church missionary official from exercising a similar role in place of the Holy Spirit over the individual missionary.

- On Officers in Christ's Church: To further show that society officials should not have the authority which they were exercising, Azbill referred to Ephesians 4:11 and the gifts that Christ gave to the church—apostles, prophets, evangelists, pastors and teachers. Azbill stated that these

are the only executive ministers which the Holy Spirit in His legal role of paraclete established for the church for all time. Moreover, these offices are limited by Scriptural instruction as to: 1. personal fitness (must be members of Christ's body), 2. function (each officer is limited to the office named), and 3. field of work (each officer is limited to types of work entailed in the name of the office). These are the only officers ordained by the Holy Spirit, but this does not necessarily preclude the right to establish other executive officers for specific functions. It does, however, preclude these additional officers from assuming authority over the officers established by the Holy Spirit Himself. More specifically, regarding the missionary societies of the Disciples, the society official, which is not a function established by the Holy Spirit, may not exercise authority over the evangelist (re: missionary) who is a church official ordained by the Holy Spirit.

 -*On Church-Missionary Relation:* If the society official holds an office which is not ordained by the Holy Spirit, then such an official has no authority to intervene between the missionary and the local congregation. The relationship between the missionary and the congregation is therefore direct and unbroken. This is a much better arrangement, Azbill claimed, than to have the missionary under the authority of a Board, for a missionary on the field knows much better what to do and how to do it than a mission board which is located thousands of miles away on another continent. In addition to this, the missionary on the field is more worthy of trust than a mission board and, therefore, should be completely trusted by the congregation which sent him. Whenever a board steps in between the missionary and the church, in order to supervise the missionary and his work on the field, the results are often chaotic and harmful to the work which the missionary is trying to do.

After writing these articles for the *Christian Standard* in 1914, Azbill again dropped out of sight. He lived another fifteen years, dying in 1929 in California. As far as I know, no record is preserved of what he thought about the battle over the International Convention, the United Christian Missionary and open membership which divided the Disciples of Christ in 1926. But there is no doubt that, had he been born later (e.g. he was 76 years old in 1926), and had he been younger during those tumultuous years, he would have been in the forefront of the battle urging conservative Disciples to consider, even before they got around to it, the independent missionary organization. But, of course, he was not, and because of that Wilson Kendrick Azbill remains among us an unsung hero of missions and missionaries supported directly by local congregations.

J. P. Hieronymous

C. B. Titus

Jesse R. Kellems

Carrie and Leslie Wolfe
1936

Mr. and Mrs. W. D. Cunningham

Enrique T. Westrup

Chapter Five

FROM THE INCIDENTAL TO MODEL

Even though W. K. Azbill went into eclipse as an independent missionary among the Disciples of Christ, it wasn't long before other independent missionaries rose up to take his place. These later independents, in spite of the division which was about to take place between the Disciples of Christ and Churches of Christ over the legitimacy of missionary societies, remained closely identified with the Disciples of Christ even after the division became a sad reality. The reason for this, however, was still due to the pioneering work of Azbill in independent missions. Azbill's early efforts along this line demonstrated two points. First, in spite of the patterns and precedent for mission work established through the para-church organizations, independent mission projects could still be initiated and carried out. Second, in spite of the power of the societies throughout the Disciple brotherhood, there was still a sympathy for independent missions in many pro-society congregations and among many individuals. In other words, without Azbill neither of these points would have been known, and we can only speculate about what would otherwise have been the course leading up to the emergence of Direct-Support Missions among the Disciples of Christ. But with the example of Azbill to follow, it remained only for enterprising Disciples to exploit this precedent and advance the cause of independent missions.

These early mission enterprises, while independent of any society, were only incidental to the bulk of Disciples of Christ mission work which, of course, was carried on first through the various societies and later through the United Christian Missionary Society. Consequently conservative Disciples, during the years of turmoil and debate over liberal theology and open membership on the mission field, did not look to these independent missions as viable alternative models of mission work for conservative Disciple missions; the goal during those years was still reform of the missionary societies and the salvage of foreign mission work, especially that performed by the UCMS, for New Testament Christianity. Not until all hopes for reformation had dissipated and Leslie Wolfe had returned to the Philippines independently of the UCMS did people notice that these earlier Disciple missions were likewise independent, and unknown to them, were all the while forging a new strategy which at last would allow churches of the Restoration Movement to maintain both their congregational supremacy and fulfill the Great Commission of discipling the nations to a significant and substantive degree.

W. C. Cunningham and the Yotsuya Mission

As Azbill was advertising plans for his volunteer band to Japan in the Fall of 1891, William D. Cunningham was entering Bethany College to study for the ministry. No record exists of Cunningham's taking note through reading the *Christian Evangelist* and other brotherhood journals about Azbill's volunteer band of independent missionaries, but there is no doubt that he did, because he was a student greatly interested in missions.[1] And no doubt he kept in the back

---

1. Mrs. E. D. Cunningham and Mrs. Owen Still, *The Flaming Torch, Life Story of W. C. Cunningham* (Tokyo: The Yotsuya Mission, 1939), pp. 16-17. "He always preached missions. During his student days he not only preached mission, — (he) talked missions — he studied missions. And every step forward he took in missionary interest brought him one step nearer to God's plan for his own life." (Unless otherwise noted, material for this section is taken from this biography on Cunningham.)

of his mind Azbill's success and the methods Azbill used in achieving that success, in promoting and financing his independent mission project in an environment totally dominated by missionary societies. For Cunningham it was to pay off in later years!

W. C. Cunningham was born July 19, 1864, in Dawson, Pennsylvania. He was not a strong lad, so it was decided that he should become a teacher. After gaining a Certificate in Teaching in 1881, he taught school for the next eight years, at which time he entered Bethany College. After graduating from Bethany in 1894, he accepted an invitation to preach in St. Thomas, Ontario, Canada. It was a missionary situation, and this no doubt led Cunningham to accept this call over an invitation to serve two churches in his home state. During his first year in Canada, he baptized 139 people. He had an effective ministry with the youth which in time led him in helping to establish the College of the Disciples, a school where the young people of eastern Canada could receive College level training in the Scriptures. He also taught in the college and traveled extensively in raising funds for its operation. In four years of missionary service in Canada, he baptized 750 people.[2]

Cunningham's experience in Canada, however, left him unsatisfied; he soon realized that what he really wanted was to become a missionary outside the North American continent. At the same time, he was corresponding with Emily Boyd of California, Pennsylvania, and was about to ask her to be his wife. So, having made up his mind to be a missionary, he proposed to Miss Boyd by asking her to accompany him to whatever foreign field God would lead

---

2. *Tokyo Christian*, Feb. 1903, p. 1.

them. She accepted, and they were married in June of 1898. They immediately applied to the Foreign Christian Missionary Society and, upon passing the medical examination, they were accepted. The FCMS requested that they go to Japan to work with C.E. Garst. The Cunninghams accepted and began immediately to plan for Japan.

By August of 1898, they had shipped their personal belongings to Japan and were making their farewell visits with friends and family. But on August 19, W. C. Cunningham took ill with what was thought to be a cold. Instead of getting better he quickly lapsed into semi-consciousness. He regained consciousness but for seven weeks lay in bed an invalid, his left side paralyzed. The illness, diagnosed later, was infantile paralysis. Fortunately, he recovered, and several months later, after regaining his strength, he returned to FCMS headquarters in Cincinnati, Ohio to be examined again for mission work in Japan. He was advised to wait a year to see if he had truly recovered. Agreeing to the recommendation he accepted an invitation to return to Ontario, Canada to resume his ministry there.

The year passed, and he traveled once more to FCMS headquarters to be examined. His left side, however, was still greatly affected by his bout with infantile paralysis, and the doctor recommended that the FCMS not allow him to serve in Japan. Disappointed, he accepted an invitation to preach at the California, Pennsylvania, Church. The following year, 1900, he applied to the FCMS once more in hope that this time the society would finally accept him. Several doctors, including two specialists, pronounced him recovered and recommended that the Foreign Society accept him; even F.M. Rains, President of the FCMS, was in favor of Cunningham now being accepted.[3] However, the FCMS

---

3. *Tokyo Christian*, Feb. 1906, p. 4.

Board rejected his application, feeling that his history of infantile paralysis could still prove to be a barrier to effective mission work in Japan. This time the disappointment that Cunningham felt was nearly too much to bear, because he still felt God's call to serve in Japan; but all avenues of service had been closed to him, first by his illness and now by the recalcitrance of a missionary society. But at this moment of greatest despair,

> his mind leaped to a great truth: God and the Missionary Society were not identical. Since God called, he could answer, depending on God, who is more powerful than any society. He would go to Japan. He would go at once. He would answer God's call. He need wait no longer.[4]

Cunningham approached his wife about going to Japan on faith, and she agreed. He resigned his ministry in June of 1901, and on September 12 of that same year sailed with his family from San Francisco for Japan. Taken among his belongings was a small printing press, a piece of equipment destined to play an important role both in his ministry in Japan and in making his independent mission project a success.

A comparison between Cunningham and Azbill at this point is unavoidable. There are certain similarities between the two with respect to their mission projects, but they are more apparent than real. To begin with, Cunningham went to Japan with little if any promotion to raise funds. Naturally, after announcing their intention to go to Japan, the Cunninghams received several gifts, and in the few weeks before they left they received enough money to travel to Japan.

---

4. Cunningham and Still, *The Flaming Torch, Life Story of W.C. Cunningham*, p. 28.

But even at this point it was nothing comparable to what Azbill did. Azbill systematically advertized and promoted his plan for several months before leaving for Japan. Furthermore, Azbill utilized extensively brotherhood journals, such as the *Christian Evangelist,* the *Christian Standard,* and the *Gospel Advocate,* to keep his project and financial needs before the public eye. Cunningham, on the other hand, did not announce his intention through any brotherhood journal; indeed, Cunningham didn't bother to publish anything about his mission work through a brotherhood journal until nearly six months after his arrival in Japan.[5]

It is of interest here to take notice of a conspicuous absence in Cunningham's use of brotherhood journals to promote his mission work. During his first year as an independent missionary in Japan, Cunningham issued only three reports through the *Christian Evangelist.* The absence is made all the more conspicuous due to his extensive use of the *Christian Standard,* once he became settled on the field, in reporting on his work to the brotherhood; for example, between 1902 and 1908, during his first term in Japan, Cunningham published 16 reports through the *Christian Standard.* We can only speculate about the reason why Cunningham did not use the *Christian Evangelist* anymore than he did to promote his work. It may have been that he remembered Azbill's controversy with J. H. Garrison, editor of the *Christian Evangelist,* and how Garrison became very critical of Azbill's fund raising among pro-society churches. This led to a parting of the ways between the two, a division which, for a while at least, pushed Azbill into the camp of the antis. Wishing to avoid this turn of events, Cunningham probably thought

---

5. *Christian Standard,* April 5, 1902, p. 507.

it best not to report through the *Christian Evangelist.* But there is a deeper reason why Cunningham probably did not wish to use this journal. Sensing that the *Christian Evangelist* was committed to the teleological development of the para-church organizations of the Disciples of Christ, and having come to the conclusion that God and the missionary society were not identical, Cunningham undoubtedly felt uncomfortable in using the *Christian Evangelist* to report his work. The *Christian Standard,* though a strong advocate of missionary societies, was nevertheless still pragmatic on the method of doing missionary work. Cunningham was probably much more comfortable with this position, and for this reason used mainly the *Standard* in reporting on his work to the brotherhood in general.

After becoming settled in Tokyo, Cunningham's first priority was to find a job. He had received promise of financial support from a few friends before he left the States, but he had decided to use these funds only for his mission work. Money for living—rent, food, clothing, etc.—would come from whatever occupation he could find. His first job was teaching English in Tokyo, and, as it turned out, was the beginning of a career that not only provided for his temporal needs but also opened up many opportunities for evangelism and church planting. After finding a job, Cunningham's next move was to establish an English Bible Class for young men. He opened his first class in the Hongo mission and it quickly grew from five students to forty-two.[6]

The following year, 1903, Alice Miller, who had come to Japan with W. K. Azbill in 1895, asked Cunningham to take charge of the Yotsuya Mission, which she had managed for

---

6. W. D. Cunningham, "My Japenese Bible-Class." *Christian Standard,* April 5, 1902, p. 507.

eleven years in the middle of Tokyo.[7] Miss Miller was operating a school but had no one to follow up the evangelistic
opportunities arising through the school. Since the Yotsuya
Mission was located on a large lot, Cunningham assumed
the lease on part of the lot on which to carry out his evangelistic
work. The lot was strategically located right next to a well
known college where the nobles and upper class of Tokyo
attended and where Cunningham was soon to become an
instructor in English, a position which he held for several
years and which proved influential in his evangelistic outreach in Japan. Down the street from the college and the
Yotsuya Mission was the Crown Prince's Palace. Cunningham immediately set about raising funds to build a house
and church building on the lot. He raised the funds, by writing to friends in the states and selling English phonograph
records in Japan. The buildings were soon finished, and
Cunningham moved both his family and Bible Class to the
new location. From this time onward, the Yotsuya Mission
was known as the Cunningham Mission.[8]

Of equal importance to the type of mission work Cunningham conducted in Tokyo were his innovations in promoting
the progress and needs of his work. Not being a member of
the Foreign Christian Missionary Society, he of course lacked
an organizational representative in the States to promote
his work among the churches. But with the printing press

---

7. *Tokyo Christian,* February 1903, p. 2.

8. Archibald McLean, *The Foreign Christian Missionary Society,* pp. 220-
222. Of W. D. Cunningham and the Yotsuya Mission, Archibald McLean
comments: "But, according to Mr. Azbill it should never be forgotten, that the
first essential work in the founding of that Mission—the winning of the respect
and confidence of the people on behalf of Christianity—was done by Miss
Scott and Miss Miller during the first eleven years of its existence. They laid
the foundation, and Mr. Cunningham builded thereon."

which he had brought to Japan, Cunningham was able to compensate for this lack. In one month after arriving in Japan, Cunningham published the first issue of the *Tokyo Christian* (November, 1901), a monthly newsletter which he continued to publish for over 30 years.[9] He printed 3000 copies of the first issue and sent them in bundles to friends in the States for distribution. For the *Tokyo Christian* he designed an attractive format and employed a good journalistic style of pithy sentences and short paragaphs. He reported news and trivia of his work and of the work of the FCMS missionaries in Japan. Perhaps the most significant feature of his paper, especially for the progress of his mission work, was this: he took the space to print the name of anyone who did, wrote or contributed something or anything in behalf of his mission work. In other words, Cunningham capitalized upon the human foible that people like to see their names in print! As a consequence, the *Tokyo Christian* quickly became popular with many people throughout the brotherhood, and it was from this popularity — including the mailing list it generated! — that Cunningham was able to successfully promote and raise funds for his mission work in the years that followed.

It was in the context of raising funds through the *Tokyo Christian* that Cunningham ran afoul for the first and only time with the Foreign Christian Mission Society. After a year of being in Japan and publishing the *Tokyo Christian*, it

---

9. At this point, we must draw a distinction between *reporting* (which Cunningham did through the *Christian Standard*) and *promotion* (for which he mainly relied upon the *Tokyo Christian*). Printing and distributing one's own promotional newsletter, as Cunningham so effectively did, was an innovation that has become a common practice in Direct-Support Mission today.

appeared to many brethren in the States that they would like to designate at least part of their March offering to W. D. Cunningham. The March offering, which churches of the brotherhood participating in, was the major source of yearly income for the missionary societies. Realizing that some brethren now wanted their share of the March offering be given to him, Cunningham began to specify through the *Tokyo Christian* how they could do it.[10] For congregations which wanted all their offerings to go to him, he recommended that the money be sent to FCMS headquarters in Cincinnati, Ohio with the request that it be forwarded to him in Japan. For individuals, he recommended that they send their March offering not through the FCMS but to him directly. At the same time, he reported through the *Christian Evangelist* on the program of building a house and chapel on the lot he had leased in Tokyo.[11] A balance of $1650 was due before the building could be completed and paid for. Hopefully, Cunningham added, "our share of the March offering will . . . provide the balance."

The March offering came and went. However, no money was ever forwarded by the FCMS to Cunningham. Moreover, the people who had designated funds through the FCMS for Cunningham but had received no acknowledgment from Cunningham, wrote asking if he had received their money. Since he had not, Cunningham complained through the *Tokyo Christian* that, based on those who had written that they had given, the FCMS had upwards to $300 of his which the society had not forwarded.[12] This brought forth a sharp rebuke from Archibald McLean and F. M. Rains,

---

10. "Our March Offering," *Tokyo Christian*, Feb. 1903, p. 4.

11. "Note From Japan," *Christian Evangelist*, Feb. 12, 1903, p. 128.

12. W. D. Cunningham, "A Card," *Christian Standard*, March 5, 1904, p. 332.

President and Financial Secretary respectively of the FCMS.[13] They stated that churches and individuals had been led astray by Cunningham in advertising that the society "would be agreeable" to forward such funds to him. It was not agreeable, of course, and so the FCMS refused to play the part of being a forwarding agent for an independent missionary!

It is of interest to speculate here where Cunningham got the idea that the Foreign Christian Missionary Society would ever consent to serve as his forwarding agent. It is possible that he thought up the idea himself, but it is more likely that he borrowed the idea from W. K. Azbill. In his controversy with J. H. Garrison of the *Christian Evangelist* in 1894 and 1895, Azbill advanced the thesis that the only role a missionary society could probably play was that of forwarding agent for churches. Knowing this idea and being closely associated with Azbill's work in Tokyo, it was natural for Cunningham to put it into operation for the first time. Unfortunately, Cunningham failed to realize the full significance of the controversy between Azbill and Garrison over this thesis (and other ideas which Azbill presented). Specifically if Garrison was highly critical of the idea, the FCMS would in like manner be highly critical of the practice. If indeed Cunningham did borrow the idea of a forwarding agent from Azbill, as seems likely, Cunningham did not give Azbill the credit. Perhaps it is just as well, since the idea "bombed." After this Cunningham instructed that donations in the form of checks or Postal Money Orders, be sent directly to him in Japan.

The fiasco with the FCMS over forwarding designated funds fortunately did not hinder the progress of the Yotsuya

---

13. W. D. Cunningham, "A Card," *Christian Standard*, Dec. 31, 1903, p. 842.

Mission. In fact, Cunningham had already devised, and was then using, a unique system of "Rope Holders." The term "rope holders," in Cunningham's vision, referred to people who by their contributions had taken hold of the rope to help pull along the work to success. Cunningham actively recruited individuals to become rope holders of his mission work. To facilitate the flow of contributions from individual rope holders Cunningham appointed "Forwarding Secretaries." An individual, instead of sending money directly to Japan, could send it to a Forwarding Secretary, who in turn would collect all such monies and forward one check to Cunningham each month. The first Forwarding Secretary Cunningham appointed was Robert Moffett, a well-known evangelist of the American Christian Missionary Society and who had also served briefly with the FCMS. When Mr. Moffett died, J. P. Hieronymus, a banker of Atlanta, Illinois, was asked to serve as Forwarding Secretary.[14]

Each month in the Tokyo Christian a list of rope holders, i.e., names of people who had given money during the previous month, was published. This monthly listing proved highly effective; not only were people delighted to see their names and their amount given in print, but it also showed who in the brotherhood were contributing. And since prominent individuals were contributing to Cunningham's mission, it became a point of pride to see one's name listed with the names of such brotherhood celebrities as Gen. F. M. Drake (of Drake College), J. H. Mohorter (of the National Benevolent Association) or W. P. Hanna (FCMS missionary to the Philippines). The concept of rope holder proved so

---

14. J. P. Hieronymus is a great-grandfather of Professor Lynn Hieronymus of Lincoln Christian College, Lincoln, Illinois.

popular that by 1907, near the end of his first missionary term in Japan, Cunningham was receiving sufficient funds from individuals and churches in the States[15] to cut back on teaching English and go on half salary from the mission, thus spending more of his time in mission work.[16]

In raising enough outside funds to lease a lot and build a house and a chapel on it, Cunningham had become the sole proprietor of mission property. He realized that, should he die, the property, and the mission work conducted through it, would be lost, since it was legally personal property and not mission property. Consequently, he made a will and deposited it in the American Consul-General in Tokyo. The will named a committee which, in the event of Cunningham's death, would appoint a successor to carry on the work of the Yotsuya Mission.[17] In this way it was assured that the property would be for mission work and not diverted to personal or private use.

In 1908 Cunningham and his family returned on furlough to the United States. Alice Miller was left in charge of the Yotsuya Mission during the furlough.[18] In seven years of mission work, Cunningham had baptized over 150 people and was employing three Japanese evangelists in spreading

---

15. Cunningham also received contributions from Australian brethren. It is interesting to note that such contributions were often forwarded to Cunningham by the Australian Foreign Missionary Committee (cf. *Tokyo Christian.* February 1903, p. 4). Evidently, the Australian missionary society did not object to serving as a forwarding agent for an independent missionary.

16. "Brother Cunningham's Work in Japan," *Christian Standard*, June 1, 1907, p. 937.

17. *Ibid.* Cunningham had the foresight to invite prominent men of the brotherhood to serve on this committee. J. P. Hieronymous was Chairman. E. B. Zollars, President of Phillips University, was a member of the committee, as was J. H. Mohorter of the National Benevolent Association.

18. "Notes of Travel," *Christian Standard*, June 6, 1908, p. 989.

the Word throughout Tokyo. The Cunninghams returned home to a warm welcome from brethren and leaders in the brotherhood. He was asked to speak in several prominent congregations of the Disciples of Christ, and over the course of the year won many friends to the cause of his independent mission. Again, we cannot help speculating why Cunningham succeeded in this regard while Azbill failed. Several reasons account for this. To begin with, since Cunningham walked through the door that Azbill opened he had a much better chance to succeed. A more important factor, however, in this matter was the evident personal charisma of Cunningham, a charisma that Azbill lacked. Azbill was technically correct in promoting his ideas on independent missions, but Cunningham had the personal dynamism to make those ideas a success. Furthermore, Cunningham was the true embodiment of the great American Horatio Alger legend, of a person struck down by personal handicaps but who by virtue of his own strength and initiative overcomes his handicap, confounds his critics and rises to the top. It was the David versus Goliath theme played out again, and as the story would have it to end, David won. In fulfilling these themes of overcoming handicaps imposed upon him by his illness and the big missionary society, Cunningham was assured of success in a way that Azbill could not hope to match.

Independency Spreads — And Becomes an Ideology!

W. D. Cunningham and his family returned to Japan late in 1909. He resumed managing the Yotsuya Mission from Alice Miller who returned to direct her kindergarten and vocational school for the poor. The mission continued to grow under Cunningham's leadership. In 1911, Cunningham issued his tenth annual report.[19] Among the accomplishments of the first ten years in Japan, he listed:

- Mission property leased for 999 years;
- 200 people baptized (about three-fourths of them men);
- Six nationals employed as evangelists;
- Five preaching points, including Bible schools with a total of 400 children;
- Two churches organized;
- Literature translated and published in the Japanese language.

A Japanese monthly, the counterpart to the *Tokyo Christian*, was published and distributed. Herbert Moninger's book *Training For Service*, including tracts on baptism and other subjects, was translated and distributed.

But during these ten years of growth something much more significant was developing because of the Yotsuya Mission. The basic dynamics of independent missionary work were at last being established among the Disciples of Christ. Azbill first introduced these dynamics into the Restoration Movement, but they were not accepted by that portion of the Movement which was pro-society. Cunningham, however, was able to achieve this feat, establishing these dynamics as a viable alternative to the para-church missionary organization in the fulfillment of the Great Commission. The *Christian Standard* recognized this—although belatedly so some twenty years after the fact—in a 1910 editorial about Cunningham titled "The Open Field."[20] In a statement more prophetic in a manner than what the *Standard* could foresee at the time, the editorial exclaimed:

19. "Yotsuya Mission," *Christian Standard*, March 4, 1911, p. 382.
20. "The Open Field," *Christian Standard*, March 19, 1910, p. 488.

The open field for independent enterprises will yet prove, if we mistake not, our greatest asset. Our people occupy the richest portion of the continent. Wealth is increasing marvelously among us. The devotion of means to God's service is certain to become more and more common. Among no other people can the varied activities of healing, teaching and preaching be launched as freely and as safely without need of official supervision or oversight.

The editorial went on to outline and discuss the various benefits of independent missions for the Disciples of Christ. There were four such benefits.

Perhaps the best feature . . . is that by the open-field system each enterprise must rest on its own merit. If, in a given case, an agency is seen to serve profitably, it will win needed support. If in course of time it ceases to "function serviceably," it can be laid by as one might discard a garment. . . . By this arrangement, government is absolutely with the people themselves. No representative or centralized board of control is needed or could be effectively operative, for in the end, the folks that furnish the funds determine the status of an organization by increasing their gifts when an open economic policy prevails, or by withholding them when a contrary condition obtains.

The open field is most favorable to the development of individual ability. But for it, W. D. Cunningham would have been worth as little to the cause as are some of the rest of us, and Yotsuya Mission would never have been.

Such a plan places the balances of power where it belongs — with the membership of the churches. These, and the ministers who lead them are the safest guardians of the plea that makes all our operations significant. . . . Even a board of directors will often be half-blinded to the larger work of which their concern can not hope to be more than a small part — one agency among many.

151

Independence is not only a constant stimulus to merit, but it is the guarantee of safety from harm. . . . With a coalition of our various agencies, disasters, unwisdom or a misstep by one cannot but damage the whole lot.

With the basic dynamics underlying independency established, and more importantly recognized by a major journal of the Disciples of Christ, it wasn't long before other Disciples joined the ranks of independent missionaries. Just before his second furlough in 1916, for example, Cunningham was able to recruit M/M Jay F. Messenger to join the Yotsuya Mission. Jay Messenger was a 1915 graduate of the Phillips Bible Institute of Canton, Ohio. He raised funds from several churches and left for Japan in August of that same year. He directed the Yotsuya Mission while Cunningham was on furlough. The Messengers stayed in Japan until 1920 at which time they returned permanently to the States.

In 1919, M/M M. B. Madden returned to Japan, this time as independent missionaries. The Maddens had first gone to Japan in 1895 as missionaries under the Foreign Christian Missionary Society where Mr. Madden was soon recognized as a "tireless evangelist" and Mrs. Madden as "a woman of rare gifts."[21] They continued as missionaries with the FCMS until 1914 when they resigned for reasons that were never made clear by either the FCMS or the Maddens.[22] They returned to the States where Mr. Madden continued to work for the FCMS in the Men and Millions Movement. The Men and Millions Movement was begun by Abram E. Cory, then Secretary of the FCMS, in 1913 and was designed

---

21. McLean, *The Foreign Christian Missionary Society,* pp. 206, 207.

22. "A Good Man—A Good Work," *Christian Standard.* June 26, 1920, p. 967. "I need not go into details, but say that when the commission of which Professor Bowers of Transylvania College was a member, was here in Japan, because of their autocratic actions and because of their failure to back a policy of self-support among the Japanese Churches, I resigned."

to raise six million dollars for the mission work of the Disciples of Christ. Madden worked for three years in this project. Upon resigning from the Movement, he was immediately offered the job of teaching English at the Osaka (Japan) Higher Commercial School.[23] After working for a while in a grocery store in Seattle, Washington, and receiving funds from friends and churches that had formerly supported him, he and his family were able to raise enough money to book passage for Japan. Both M/M Madden taught English in Osaka from which they were able to make a living. For their mission work they rented two buildings in which they began a Bible school and kindergarten. From this small beginning there was soon to grow a large independent mission work in Osaka.

The next Disciple who went to Japan as independent missionaries were M/M Harold Beatty. They arrived in Tokyo early in 1921 to work with Cunningham in the Yotsuya Mission.[24] They worked with Cunningham until 1927 when they joined M. B. Madden at Osaka. In 1922 Frank L. Lappin went to Japan as an independent Disciples missionary, but returned home the same year.[25] In quick succession Miss Lean Gilbert, a school teacher from Texas, came and went (1923-1924),[26] followed by M/M R. W. Isaacson.[27] The Isaacsons worked with the Yotsuya Mission until 1928, at which time they returned to the States. Lastly,

---

23. *Ibid.*
24. Cunningham and Still, *The Flaming Torch, Life Story of W. C. Cunningham, p. 77.*
25. *Ibid.,* p. 79.
26. *Ibid.,* p. 81.
27. *Ibid.,* p. 83.

in 1925, Miss Grace Farnham arrived in Japan to work with Cunningham.[28]

During the same period of time that the number of independent missionaries was increasing for the work in Japan, the idea of independency was spreading to other mission fields. But there was a different character about these other independent missions than was present in the Japan independent missions. In Japan, under the leadership of Cunningham, the independent missionaries remained on amicable terms with the FCMS; they were viewed as another alternative to the society in fulfilling the Great Commission. When independency emerged in other mission fields, it was not in terms of friendly competition with the missionary societies. It was in reaction to them and their policy of comity agreements with denominational church bodies and the introduction of open membership. In a real sense, this was the final dynamic to be established in independent missions, a dynamic which in a short time would turn the incidental nature of independent missions among the Disciples of Christ to that of a full-fledged model for missions by which churches could carry out the Great Commission of evangelizing the nations of the world.

The first reaction came in Mexico, a mission field which the Christian Woman's Board of Mission entered in 1895.[29] The mission work of the CWBM quickly became centered in Monterey, in the northern part of Mexico. The work grew slowly, but by 1914 there were nine Disciple churches in and

---

28. *Ibid.*, p. 85. During this period the non-instrumental Churches of Christ were also sending direct-support missionaries to Japan. For example, Cunningham reported in 1919 that M/M Orvill Bixler and Miss Bessie Wheeler were soon to arrive in Japan to work with J. M. McCaleb (*Christian*, Jan. 1919, p. 1).

29. Ida Withers Harrison, *Forty Years of Service* (St. Louis: Christian Board of Publication, 1915), p. 55.

around Monterey plus sixteen outstations or preaching points. A mission school was also established along with a preacher-training program. It was at this point, however, that the CWBM made a crucial decision regarding its mission work in northern Mexico. During the Congress on Christian Work in Latin America, which was held in 1916 in Panama, the CWBM met with various denominational mission boards also working in Latin America to draw up comity agreements for the evangelization of Central and South America.[30] Since both the CWBM and Methodists had mission work in Mexico, an agreement was made with the Methodists to divide up Mexico so that the country could be better served, without overlap of missionaries, by the two mission boards. The CWBM agreed to pull out its missionaries from Monterey and relocate them in central Mexico. The mission property — the church buildings, the school, land — which the CWBM had purchased and accumulated over the years was to be sold or given to the Methodist mission in northern Mexico. Mexican members of the Disciples of Christ churches in Monterey were told to join forces with the Methodists.

When the decision became final to turn CWBM missions in northern Mexico over to the Methodists and Disciples of

---

30. The Panama Congress was an outgrowth of the Edinburgh 1910 missionaries conference. Edinburgh inspired many missionaries and mission boards to rethink their strategy for preaching the Gospel to the whole world. As a result many saw there was duplication of mission activity in one area by several mission boards while other areas remain untouched by any Christian witness. To remedy such imbalances conferences and congresses were held after 1910 to plan better coordination of missionaries so every area of the world would have an opportunity to hear the Gospel. The missionary societies of the Disciples of Christ participated in these conferences and agreed to do their part in leaving areas where the Gospel had been preached and work in areas where the Gospel had never been proclaimed.

Christ missionaries began to move away, a reaction immediately set in among the Mexican Disciples of Christ. The reaction was led by Enrique T. Westrup, a national who over several years of Christian service had accumulated a unique blend of experience and commitment to the Restoration Movement. Westrup was born in 1879 in Mexico and for a short time attended public school in Austin, Texas.[31] His father was a Baptist preacher, and accordingly Enrique Westrup followed in his father's footsteps by studying for the Baptist ministry at Southern Baptist University in Jackson, Tennessee. About this time, however, his father became dissatisfied with the Baptist mission in northern Mexico. He resigned from his Baptist pastorate, and in 1902 led his family, including his son Enrique, into the Disciples of Christ in Monterey.[32] Because of his extensive education in English, Enrique Westrup obtained a position teaching English at the State Civil College in Monterey. It was not long before he also obtained a leading position among the Disciples of Christ churches in northern Mexico. So it was no surprise that when the CWBM decided to turn these churches over to the care of the Methodists, Enrique Westrup opposed the decision.

To save these congregations from being submerged into the Methodists, Westrup organized in 1919 the Mexican Society for Christian Missions and appealed to Disciples of Christ in the U.S.A. for financial support.[33] The *Christian*

31. J. H. Fuller, "Our Leader in Mexico," *Restoration Herald,* July 1926, pp. 3-4.

32. "At that time the mission was much strengthened by the addition of Thomas M. Westrup, a veteran Baptist missionary and hymn writer, and his accomplished family. His perfect acquaintance with the language and the people and his literary ability made him of great value to the work. He edited *La Via De Paz,* and eight-page weekly with a circulation of one thousand copies, and translated valuable religious literature into Spanish." (*Forty years of Service,* p. 56.)

33. "A New Mission in Mexico," *Christian Standard,* May 31, 1914, p. 851.

Standard took up Westrup's cause and urged the brotherhood to support him. The *Standard* also announced that it would be happy to forward funds to Monterey.[34] Later in that year, Westrup traveled to Cincinnati, Ohio to attend the Restoration Congress which was sponsored by the *Christian Standard* to protest the International Convention and the coming merger of the various missionary societies into the United Christian Missionary Society. After his appearance at the Congress, the *Standard* in an editorial entitled "To the Rescue of the Mexican Mission" wrote:

> The time has come when we should pull together, and when churches and individuals should encourage one another by letting their intentions be known. The columns of the Standard will be open to churches, Bible schools, CWBM auxiliaries [sic], and other mission bands that may wish to have their future policy announced to the brotherhood.[35]

It was a public call for churches, individuals and groups—including CWBM auxiliaries!—to openly break with the CWBM and rush their offerings to Westrup.

Under Westrup's leadership, seven Disciples of Christ churches in the Monterey area were able to retain their identity with the Restoration Movement.[36] With the funds that came in from the States the Mexican Society for Christian Mission was able to support five national evangelists who traveled in three circuits to serve the seven churches. The Christian Institute, which the CWBM had allowed to die, was reopened with 70 children.[37] At first, Westrup had

---

34. "E.T. Westrup, President Mexican Society for Christian Mission," *Christian Standard*, June 21, 1949, p. 928.

35. *Christian Standard*, Nov. 1, 1919, p. 119.

36. "Plans for Mexican Work" *Christian Standard*, Sept. 17, 1919, p. 1298.

37. "Wreck of the Christian Institute, Monterey, Mexico," *Christian Standard*, Sept. 20, 1919, p. 1253.

hoped to use the CWBM building where the old Institute was held but was refused. After two days of holding classes in the building, a CWBM official showed up ordering Westrup and his students out, after which the door was locked and the building delivered to the Methodists. Westrup also tried to obtain the church property which the CWBM had purchased for the congregations in Monterey, but the only offer he received from the mission Board was an opportunity to buy a portion of one lot on which he could build a church building; otherwise, all mission property was to be turned over or sold to the Methodists.[38] Yet, despite the unsympathetic response from the CWBM, Westrup was still able to rally his Mexican brethren to remain firm and grow in their commitment to the Restoration Movement.[39]

Not two years after Enrique T. Westrup had successfully salvaged and reorganized the Disciples of Christ mission work in northern Mexico, the *Christian Standard* announced in a lead article that Thomas Bambes Kalane was ready to return to South Africa as a missionary.[40] The story of Thomas Kalane, who was a black student from Africa in America at the time, is a remarkable one.[41] His conversion here in America to the plea of the Restoration Movement is just as remarkable. Kalane (pronounced ka-la-ne) was born in what is now in east Africa, the son of a tribal chief. When a

---

38. "CWBM Officials Should Answer a Question," *Christian Standard*, Sept. 13, 1919, p. 1849.

39. For a brief history of the Restoration Movement in Mexico and a critique of the Mexican Society for Christian Missions, see Francisco H. Villa, *The Restoration Movement in Mexico*, unpublished M.A. thesis, Lincoln Christian Seminary, 1979.

40. "A New Light-House in the Dark Continent." *Christian Standard*, Sept. 13, 1919, p. 1231.

41. W. H. Book, "The Remarkable Story of Thomas Kalane," *Christian Standard*, Jan. 25, 1917, p. 107.

teenager, in 1899, he decided to walk to South Africa to work in the mines. It took him three months to walk the 1000 miles to South Africa, during which he was captured by Arab slave traders but escaped. Soon after arriving in South Africa he learned English, and converted to Christianity, joining a Methodist mission church. Reading about the United States, he decided to go to America to study. He saved his money for passage and, taking a letter of introduction with him, sailed for New York. In New York he was told by a Methodist clergyman that he should travel on to Ohio to study at Wilberforce University.

In 1913, Kalane, while on a speaking tour giving lectures about Africa by chance met W. H. Book, who was then the well-known minister of the Tabernacle Church at Columbus, Indiana.[42] He told Book he had studied Greek for four years at Wilberforce. Book asked him what the Greek word *baptizo* meant. After understanding that the word meant immersion, Kalane asked to be immersed. He returned to Wilberforce University to finish his education.

Seven years later, in 1920,[43] Kalane announced his decision to return to South Africa to preach the message of the Restoration Movement to the Black population of that country. The Tabernacle Church of Columbus, Indiana, promised to underwrite his full support. On his way back to South Africa, he stopped in his home country to visit his family — it had been over twenty years since he had seen any of his family. There he found only one sister who was still alive. He traveled on to South Africa and set up his first mission among a tribe

---

42. W. H. Book, "A Man Sees The Light," *Christian Standard*, Sept. 20, 1913, pp. 15, 16; W. H. Book, "Thomas B. Kalane," *Christian Standard*, Oct. 11, 1913, p. 1659.

43. Max Ward Randall, *We Would Do It Again*, Kempton, Ind., Mission Services, 1965, p. 87.

located close to the city of Kimberly. His immediate objectives were to start a school for tribal children and to establish a church. From this small beginning, Kalane's mission work quickly grew in size and influence. Within two years, he had succeeded in leading some 3000 people into the Restoration Movement. More than fifty stations, many of them functioning churches, were in operation.[44] To shepherd these Christians and churches, Kalane employed nearly fifty tribal evangelists. His success, however, attracted the attention of the British colonial government and certain denominational authorities. The British arrested Kalane because, as a Black, he was not allowed to head the mission; only a white person could legally be the director of a mission in South Africa. Consequently he was charged with being a seditious person, an accusation thought to be inspired more by jealous denominational leaders than by government concern. Kalane was subsequently cleared of the charge and released, but was told to request from the U.S. a white missionary to be the director of his mission work.[45]

W. H. Book, in response to the British requirement, recruited O. E. Payne, a well-known evangelist, to go to South Africa to assume the directorship of Kalane's work. Book appealed for funds to support Payne, requesting that monies be sent to W. B. Treadway of Columbus, Indiana for forwarding. Payne was scheduled to leave for South Africa in August of 1923, but before he arrived in the country Kalane died. The circumstances surrounding this unfortunate death are not known, but upon arrival in South Africa Payne found that "the last days of Kalane had left a trail of scandal and

---

44. "Wonderful News From South Africa," *Christian Standard*, January 19, 1924, p. 393.

45. "Helpers For Kalane," *Christian Standard*, Sept. 1, 1923, p. 1384.

unrest."[46] Some have even privately speculated that tribal rivalry and jealousy, due to Kalane's success, could very well have led to his untimely death.

In spite of this set back, Payne began immediately to reorganize Kalane's work. He formalized the mission structure by establishing and registering with the colonial government the African Christian Missionary Society. He next sifted through the fifty tribal evangelists which Kalane had employed and dismissed over forty of them. For the remainder, he appealed to the States for additional funds to support them. From this beginning, Payne's work grew rapidly, He made contact with several indigenous restoration movements in South Africa and was able to lead many of their adherents to associate with the Church of Christ. In one year's time, he had built the force of tribal evangelists back up to more than fifty. To support these evangelists and to keep alive his contacts with South African restoration movements, he appealed to churches in America for $12.50 a month for each of his evangelists:

> Given this amount, Africa will surpass all other missions . . . and will escape the shoals upon which most missions have foundered and at a fourth of the cost. Most of the work is by natives who if thus trained, can do the work better and cheaper.[47]

In addition to tribal evangelism, Payne also laid plans to evangelize the white population of South Africa. He called for evangelistic teams from America to come to South Africa and establish churches in the leading cities of the nation.[48]

---

46. "Another Life For Africa," *Christian Standard*, May 23, 1725, p. 805.

47. O. E. Payne, "An Urgent Message to America," *Christian Standard*, August 23, 1924, p. 1167.

48. "South African Mission Gathers in Conference," *Christian Standard*, June 28, 1924, p. 975.

Unfortunately the work of reorganizing Kalane's work, tribal evangelism, and the concern for the white population of South Africa took its toll on Payne. Payne succumbed to exhaustion in May of 1925 and lay sick in bed for two weeks attended only by his wife.[49] Instead of responding to rest, though, he grew weaker and finally died on May 15, 1925. He was buried in Kimberly, South Africa. Another call went out to America for a new missionary.

W. H. Book, who began the mission enterprise in South Africa, knew just the man to take up the fallen mantle. He was Charles Buttz Titus of New Castle, Indiana, an experienced but controversial formal missionary to China under the Foreign Christian Missionary Society.[50] Titus first went to China in 1900 and was stationed in Nanking to work in literature distribution and evangelism.[51] However, being in Nanking, he was able to observe first hand the comity agreements that the FCMS was making with various denominational groups. Alarmed, he began to write articles for the *Christian Standard* recounting what was taking place. For example, when the FCMS made such an agreement with the Friends mission board, with the provision that FCMS mission property worth $3000 be given to the Friends, Titus asked

> Would it now seem from this . . . that such "new or federated" policy may be helpful to the "Quakers" but a practical failure to undenominational Christianity?[52]

---

49. "Modern Missionaries Heroes," *Christian Standard*, May 15, 1925, p. 979.

50. "A Successor Ready," *Christian Standard*, July 11, 1925, p. 979.

51. C. B. Titus, "Among the Chinese," *Christian Standard*, Jan. 9, 1909, p. 82.

52. C. B. Titus, "The 'Tried and True' vs. The 'New,'" *Christian Standard*, Jan. 15, 1910, p. 122.

Titus also witnessed the merger of $20,000 worth of FCMS mission property, this time a Bible training school, in with Nanking University, a union school ran by the Methodist and Presbyterian mission boards.[53] When he complained to the FCMS Board of Directors about the merger, he was rebuffed.[54]

Titus now became sarcastic in his reporting through the *Christian Standard* on what the FCMS was doing. In his reports he repeatedly complained about "a certain missionary" who was a Disciples of Christ professor at the union university and who was teaching not the true Gospel but liberal theology. The missionary was not named, but there was no doubt that Titus was referring to Guy W. Sarvis, a controversial liberal Disciple whom the FCMS appointed in 1910 for the teaching position at Nanking University. The exposés, and the sarcastic way in which they were written, angered the FCMS leadership as well as many of Titus' fellow missionaries in the Foreign Society. So in 1911, missionaries voted to have him recalled from the mission field, a decision which the FCMS leadership in Cincinnati, Ohio was all too happy to follow.[55] When Titus received the notice that he was fired from the FCMS, he wrote one last article to the *Christian Standard,* charging that the FCMS had compromised the message of the Restoration Movement by favoring

---

53. C. B. Titus, "What Are We Here For?," *Christian Standard,* June 11, 1910, p. 998.

54. C. B. Titus, "The Machinery of Mission Government," *Christian Standard,* March 12, 1910, p. 438.

55. C. B. Titus, "Out of Harmony with FCMS Officials," *Christian Standard,* January 20, 1912, p. 84. Titus recall caused only a minor stir among the Standard's readers in 1911. (cf. M. P. Hayden, "The Facts in the Case," *Christian Standard,* Dec. 30, 1911, p. 2172). There was nowhere the outpouring of indignation as when Leslie Wolfe was similarly recalled by the UCMS fifteen years later.

union and not unity, and by not insisting on the name Christian over the use of sectarian names.[56] A more serious charge, however, was the accusation that the FCMS was not training Chinese leaders to carry on the Restoration Movement in China: in fact, all the Restoration Movement had in this regard was a one-third interest in a union university!

Titus left China in October of 1911.[57] He stopped in Japan and visited the independent mission work of W. D. Cunningham at Yotsuya, in the heart of Tokyo. The visit undoubtedly left a lasting impression upon Titus, for in 1920 he wrote in the *Christian Standard* an article entitled "Direct Evangelism" in which he offered a suggested improvement in world evangelization: Leave the indirect and take up the direct way.[58] By "indirect" he meant the support of missionaries and mission work indirectly through the missionary society. By "direct" he meant for churches to bypass the society and support direct the missionary as in the case of W. D. Cunningham. Unfortunately, Titus lamented, the indirect mission work was then the popular method. Yet it was not long before Titus would personally see his suggested improvement —i.e. direct mission support—at last implemented.

The very week that Titus received a telegram from W. H. Book to go to South Africa, Titus' wife died.[59] But instead of letting this tragedy drag him down into remorse, he vowed to spend the rest of his life in foreign mission work. He accepted the call and immediately left for South Africa in September

---

56. C. B. Titus, "What Do We More Than Others," *Christian Standard*, Sept. 16, 1911, p. 1502.

57. C. B. Titus, "Nearing the Home Land," *Christian Standard*, Nov. 11, 1911, p. 1886.

58. C. B. Titus, "Direct Evangelization," *Christian Standard*, Oct. 16, 1920, p. 1372.

59. James B. Carr, *The Foreign Missionary Work of the Christian Church*, privately published, 1946, p. 1190.

of 1925. Upon arrival he found a mission work, which had been begun by Thomas Kalane and continued by O. E. Payne, consisting of 22 stations, 60 outposts, 2493 members, and some 50 tribal evangelists which Payne had under his employment.[60] Titus quickly sifted through the evangelists and reduced their number to eight whom he found of sufficient moral character to continue under employment as preachers. He next initiated a thirty-day Preacher Training Program to train new and more faithful preachers to preach among the various stations and outposts. Before long, the number of tribal preachers supported by mission funds was back up to fifty.

After Titus had completed reorganizing the mission work among the tribal people, the Thomas Evangelistic team arrived in South Africa.[61] The team came in response to O. E. Payne's concern for the whole population and cities of the British colony. The team consisted of Jesse Randolph Kellems, a flamboyant preacher who had just received a Ph.D. degree in theology from the University of Edinburgh, Scotland,[62] and Charles H. Richard who was to serve as the song evangelist. The coming of the team had been heavily advertised throughout South Africa for weeks, so when they arrived in Johannesburg and rented a large hall for their evangelistic meetings, a large crowd was soon attending.[63] During the first week after his arrival, Kellems saw in a newspaper a notice about a lecture to be given by a Zionist in support of the rights to the world's Jews to reinhabit the land of Palestine. Sensing the publicity value that such an

---

60. C. B. Titus, "State of Cause Among Natives in South Africa," *Christian Standard*, Dec. 19, 1925, p. 2140.
61. Idem. The term was sponsored by Mike Thomas of Dallas, Texas. "Take South Africa For Christ," *Christian Standard*, Aug. 28, 1926, p. 826.
62. "Au Revoir to Kellems," *Christian Standard*, May 15, 1926, p. 470.
63. "First Week in Johannesburg," *Christian Standard*, July 17, 1926, p. 687.

event would generate for his evangelistic meetings, Kellems immediately challenged the lecturer to a public debate over the issue of Zionism. His challenge and the fact that he had a Ph.D. from a prestigious British University quickly attracted the attention of the press. With his flowery speech, arguing that theologically the Jews no longer had any *divine* right to Palestine, Kellems outtalked the Zionist. The report of the debate in the newspaper causes a sensation throughout Johannesburg, and even larger crowds began to attend the evangelistic meetings. The press also attended and ran nightly coverage of the meetings and Kellem's sermons.

The Johannesburg meeting ran for 107 nights, longer, Kellems claimed, than any other protracted meeting in the history of the Restoration Movement.[64] There had been an average of *ten confessions of faith every night for ten weeks,* resulting in 386 baptisms.[65] The small Disciples of Christ church, which had been in existence in Johannesburg since 1903, grew from 17 to 617 members. At the close of the meeting, church attendance was running over 400, making it the largest church in Johannesburg. Eugene Farrow of Eugene, Oregon was called to serve as the minister.[66] The team went on to Pretoria, Durban and Cape Town to hold other evangelistic meetings in South Africa. At the end of these meetings in early 1927 there was reported a total of 740 baptisms.

The Early Independents — Their Contributions to the Model

In thirty-five years, from W. K. Azbill in Japan (1891) to C. B. Titus in South Africa (1926) independent missions

---

64. T. R. Kellems, "Fruitage of Johannesburg," *Christian Standard,* Oct. 23, 1926, p. 507.

65. "Amazing Harvest of Johannesburg," *Christian Standard,* Sept. 18, 1926, p. 398.

66. "Johannesburg Welcomes First Minister," *Christian Standard,* October 23, 1962, p. 522.

among the Disciples of Christ had developed from an incidental method of world evangelism to that of a model whereby congregations and individuals could fulfill the Great Commission in a significant manner. Moreover, it was an accumulative development, where contributions were made by different people at various times throughout the thirty-five years. What were the contributions that these early independents made which, from 1926 onward, formed the model for missions for Christian Churches and Churches of Christ? There were four such contributions and their significance for present day Direct-Support missions cannot be over-estimated. As seen below, each of the four revolved around the individual missionary as compared with the missionary society.

The Missionary As Mission Executive: The first contribution that the early independents made was that the individual missionary could function as the executive of a mission enterprise as well as any society official. This was perhaps the most important contributions made during the time period, for there had grown up in association with the missionary societies the assumption that leadership in the missionary outreach of the Restoration Movement should be restricted to those in executive positions; indeed, until the emergence of independent missionaries, it was thought that it could not be otherwise. In one respect, when Azbill initiated his program of volunteer missionaries for Japan, this assumption was not in reality challenged, for he had been a mission executive with the Christian Woman's Board of Missions and the Foreign Christian Missionary Society.[67] And when

---

67. In 1883, Azbill was appointed, without pay, as the superintendent of the proposed FCMS mission in Panama. As it turned out, there were no funds for the mission, so the project was abandoned. (McLean, *The Foreign Christian Missionary Society*, p. 435.)

he outlined his plan for recruiting, supervising and raising funds for his band of volunteers, he was functioning no differently than he had when working as an official with the missionary society. Nevertheless, the fact that Azbill performed these executive duties outside the purview of the societies opened the way for another person without previous executive enterprise to head a mission enterprise.

Such, of course, was the significance of W. D. Cunningham. Cunningham, to be sure, had demonstrated executive ability in his work in Canada, but it went unrecognized by the Foreign Society because of his illness; all that the FCMS could foresee was the possibility of a recurrence of the illness on the mission field. Fortunately this shortsightedness of the FCMS worked to the eventual benefit of Direct-Support missions. It allowed Cunningham not only to demonstrate but also initiate an important dynamic in independent missions, namely the individual missionary is just as capable as anyone else to administer the missionary outreach of the Restoration Movement. This lesson was not lost on W. H. Book when he recruited first O. E. Payne, then C. D. Titus, both without previous experience as mission executives, to supervise the work in South Africa. Nor was the *Christian Standard* impervious to the lesson as it changed over the years from a staunch advocate of the missionary societies to a strong agitator for individual initiative in missions. As a further development along this line, the *Standard* was willing to recognize that even a foreign national, as in the case of E. T. Westrup, could just as well administer the foreign mission work of the brotherhood. In other words, by the time Leslie Wolfe was ready to work separately from the United Christian Missionary Society in 1926, there had already been laid a foundation for accepting the individual missionary in the role as his own mission executive over the work he was performing.

The Missionary as Promotional Representative: The second contribution which the early independents made to the Direct-Support model of missions among the Disciples of Christ was that the individual missionary could serve as his own promotional representative before the brotherhood. To be sure, all missionaries did promotional work, but such work was designed mainly to emphasize what the societies were doing and accomplishing. Nevertheless as in the case of Azbill during his days with the CWBM and FCMS, the major promotional work for missions in the brotherhood was reserved for society officials. Even M. B. Madden, after resigning from the field, returned to work as a fund raiser in the Men and Millions Movement.

Yet in spite of such precedents, Cunningham broke away from it and spent a great deal of his time in promoting his own mission work. More significantly, however, was the fact that many in the brotherhood thoroughly enjoyed his promotion, a development that set a precedent for the independents who followed. Such personal promotion throughout the brotherhood of one's mission work was also made possible by the consistent policy of the *Christian Standard* of reporting on *all* mission activity of the Disciples of Christ. Again, such acceptance of individual promotion in the brotherhood paved the way for the success of Leslie Wolfe's independent efforts in the Philippines. The precedents thus established allowed missionaries in the years immediately following 1926 to effectively and directly mobilize a significant segment of the Disciples of Christ for the cause of Direct-Support missions.

The Missionary as Final Judge Regarding Field Policy and Strategy: With the establishment of societies and boards

169

in the Restoration Movement, there came into existence mission executives, based in the United States, and the field missionary. With this division of labor in the missionary outreach of the church, there were also the inevitable conflicts and tensions between what the mission executives ordered done versus what the missionary on the field thought should be done. In all instances the decision of the mission executive prevailed. Such a conflict was the reason Eugene Snodgrass' salary was cut off by FCMS in 1892, causing him to stay on and work independently in Japan. A similar conflict laid behind C. B. Titus recall from China in 1912, for he thought that the FCMS leadership should not merge the work of the Disciples of Christ with the denominationalists. M. B. Madden resigned from the FCMS, first in Japan and later from the Men and Millions Movement, for the same reason. According to Dean E. Walker (in personal communication) Madden disagreed with the FCMS officials when they ordered — from Cincinnati, Ohio! — him to carry on a mission work among the uneducated masses of Japan. Madden thought that, if Christianity was to have an impact in Japan, the educated Japanese must be evangelized. Since he was disposed to reach this level of Japanese society, but was forbidden to do so, he had no alternative but to resign.

In these cases of conflict between the mission executive and the missionary on the field, it was the missionary and not the mission executive who proved to be right: Snodgrass received the independent support to stay on in Japan, Titus' warning of liberalism in China proved true, and Madden's return to Japan to work among the educated proved fruitful. Consequently when Leslie Wolfe refused to follow the Philippine comity plan which emanated from UCMS headquarters in the States, a large segment of the Disciples of

Christ was more disposed to listen to him, because he was, after all, the missionary on the field. More importantly, this segment was willing to entrust to Wolfe, from 1926 onward, the management of the Philippine mission, a task at which he proved more than adequate in performing.

The Missionary's Message as the Only Proper Basis for Unity: The various societies and boards of Disciples of Christ were joined together as a means of achieving a greater unity of the brotherhood and as a means of speaking with one voice in negotiating a broader organizational union with religious bodies. Such negotiations proceeded much faster and further on the mission field than in the States. However, a few Disciple missionaries opposed these negotiations, claiming that the message, or Plea, of the Restoration Movement was the only proper basis for unity among the sects on the mission field. At first the protests of these few missionaries were barely audible, but by 1920 a loud chorus of protests was being heard throughout the brotherhood. The chorus grew louder until in 1925 a great number of Disciples demanded that missionaries not believing in the Restoration Plea as the basis of Christian Unity be dismissed from the UCMS. When this demand was not obeyed, these Disciples concluded that union of mission organizations, whether within the Restoration Movement or along denominational lines, was ultimately a false unity. If true Biblical unity is to be achieved, it was now thought, then it must be along the lines of Biblical faith.

From this perspective the growth of independent Disciple missions in the first three decades of this century is significant theologically, because their growth in popularity also signaled a growing repudiation of one interpretation of unity. In other words, the Unity for which Jesus prayed was no longer perceived in terms of organic connections among autonomous

171

units, but in terms of a fellowship around a central core of faith and practice as set forth in the New Testament. Wherever such fellowship is found, there is unity. Many Disciples of this period, of course, failed to grasp this ramification of the independent missionary movement. J. H. Garrison, for example, thought the movement would not last long, and no doubt many other Disciples dismissed independent missions as only a temporary aberration in the missionary outreach of the Disciples of Christ. On the contrary independent missions and missionaries did not fade away but increased, and as a result they laid a foundation for a more Biblical view of unity among the Disciples of Christ.

In short, when it came time for Leslie Wolfe to consider staying on in the Philippines, even after he had been fired from the UCMS, the dynamics for operating an independent mission among the Disciples of Christ had already been tested for thirty-five years and more importantly found productive as a strategy in fulfilling the Great Commission. There remained only the implementation of these dynamics on a broad scale in the brotherhood. From 1926 onward, through the concerted effort of both brethren in the States and independent missionaries on the field, this was done. Over the next fifty years these dynamics of independent missions became known as the Direct-Support Missionary Movement.

Part III

THE FIRST FIFTY YEARS

(1926-1976)

Mr. and Mrs. Harry Schaefer, Sr.
and family - 1928

J. Russell Morse, Sr. - 1925
(in native costume)

R. Tibbs, Maxey Sr. and family in 1922

J. D. Murch

Dr. Rothermel

Dorthy Sterling

Chapter Six

SHARPENING THE FOCUS

As was pointed out in the Introduction, Direct-Support missions among Christian Churches and Churches of Christ did not suddenly "crop up." There were pecedents in the history of the Restoration Movement which set the stage for the emergence of Direct-Support missions and missionaries. Up to this point it has been the purpose of this book to detail these reasons — more properly, tensions — in order to understand the problems of the Restoration Movement which the Direct-Support Missionary Movement was and still is trying to solve. These problems revolve around the question of what is the proper strategy for the church, in a movement to restore the primacy of the church, to evangelize all the world. There developed in short order within the Restoration Movement, two streams or approaches of solving these problems: first, the para-church organizational approach with its inevitable reaction by those who thought that such organizations were nothing more than human innovations; and, second, a more direct approach in which congregations and individuals could bypass the organization and support the missionary directly. At the risk of over simplifying history, these two streams in the Restoration Movement are displayed in the schema of Figure 1.

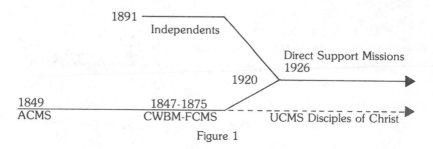

Figure 1

The dates in the schema are the respective years in which the various societies began and which independent missions began. It was in 1926 that the independent Disciples and those reacting to the missionary societies—a reaction which reached fever pitch in 1920 with the creation of the United Christian Missionary Society—consolidated to begin the Direct-Support missionary movement. The schema is incomplete as far as all the Restoration Movement is concerned, for it does not show the development of mission strategy among the Churches of Christ (non-instrumental). But, as was mentioned at the end of Chapter One, this development, while interesting in its own right is outside the scope of this book. Our concern here, especially from this point onward, is to trace the development of the Direct-Support missionary movement.

For the purpose of this book we count the beginning of Direct-Support missions with the dismissal of Leslie Wolfe from the United Christian Missionary Society, which was formally accomplished on April 30, 1926. One reason, as was mentioned in the previous chapter, was the incidental nature of earlier ventures. With Leslie Wolfe, however, it was a whole new "ball game," it was now "sink or swim," not only for Leslie Wolfe, but for all other conservative Disciples of Christ missionaries whose belief and understanding of the Scriptures would not allow them to conscientiously accept and practice open membership and comity agreements. Moreover, for many Disciples of Christ congregations, it was no longer an incidental matter of supporting an independent missionary as W. D. Cunningham; rather it was now a matter of faithfulness to the Scriptures, for to support the UCMS was tantamount to supporting false doctrine and practice. Earlier independent missions symbolized nothing beyond individual efforts in the midst of organizational missions, and for this reason there was often fellowship between the two.[1] After 1926, however independency and direct support became highly symbolic of fidelity to the original plea of the Restoration Movement; from this time onward, to many conservative Disciples, the UCMS became the test of fellowship. To support the UCMS was apostasy, to support directly independent missionaries was to "seek . . . first the Kingdom of God and His righteousness." In short, independency and direct support were no longer incidental, it was now "for real," a viable and necessary alternate strategy for Christian Churches in carrying out the Great Commission to make disciples of all nations.

1926-1933 The Christian Restoration Association

With the steady deterioration of the Restoration plea under the management of the United Christian Missionary Society, a sense of urgency about the present and future prospects for the plea invaded the hearts of many brethren. Conservative Disciples began to look elsewhere for ways and means to preserve the message of the plea and to assure its faithful proclamation to the world. In their search for ways other than the UCMS, these brethren began to take notice of the independent missionaries already operating and saw in them the hope and salvation of evangelical missions for the Disciples of Christ. Several therefore began to promote these missions and urge conservative brethren to support them. At this point, however, these brethren ran into a practical problem, namely, how to transfer money from concerned brethren and churches in the States to the independent missionary on the foreign field. Ordinarily money

---

1. James B. Carr, *The Foreign Missionary Work of the Christian Church* (privately published, 1946), p. 137.

would be sent through the central organization, the UCMS, but this was now thought inadvisable as many Disciples now claimed that the UCMS was inefficient, even mismanaging the church's missionary dollar. On the other hand, money could not be easily transferred without some type of organization serving the churches by receiving funds and serving the missionary by forwarding the funds to the field.

As conservative Disciples began to consider independent missions as possible alternatives to the UCMS, they also began to tackle the problem of transferring mission contributions without the organizational structure of a mission society or board to foreign countries. The concept of direct-support, as practiced today, and even though existing in an incipient form at the time, had not emerged as a full-fledged dynamic. Consequently, conservative Disciples were still thinking in terms of some type of central organizational structure to step in the breach between congregation and missionary to function as an agency in transferring funds. It was from this frame of reference that some Disciples organized the Christian Restoration Association in Cincinnati, Ohio on September 1, 1925.[2]

The Christian Restoration Association, or CRA, was not exactly a new organization; it was a continuation of what was originally known as the Clarke Estate.[3] In 1871, Sidney S. Clarke, who was moderately rich, wrote in his will that what remained of his estate after the death of his wife should be used to establish new churches in America.[4] The remainder of the estate amounted to $50,000, and with interest

---

2. James DeForest Murch, *Christians Only* (Cincinnati: Standard Publishing, 1962), p. 250.

3. *Ibid.*

4. A more extensive account of the Clarke Estate, and the work it did, appears in Chapter VIII on Home Missions.

it soon grew to $70,000. The additional money was placed in a new fund, named the Clarke Fund, in 1921.[5] With the need to solve the practical problem of forwarding funds to independent missionaries it was thought advisable in 1925 to reorganize so that the Fund could finance the necessary apparatus to perform this service.[6] With this reorganization, the Clarke Fund was broadened to include the whole world as its field of evangelistic labor. James DeForest Murch, editor of the *Lookout* at the time, resigned from the Standard Publishing Company to become the President of the CRA and the editor of its monthly publication, *The Restoration Herald.*

A major function of the Christian Restoration Association was to serve as a "clearing house" for missions, missionaries and other church agencies that were "free," i.e. independent, of the UCMS.

. . . A second factor in the situation calling for the establishment of the CRA is the demand, quite universal among the brethren, for some sort of clearing house through which two services could be obtained: (1) The forwarding of contributions to the many free agencies; (2) the publication of missionary literature for use of local groups supporting the free agencies. Hearing this demand and realizing that it is unwise to form yet another agency, the trustees offered to perform these two services of a "clearing house."

A. That the Clarke Fund is anxious to reorganize its work upon a larger basis, and

---

5. J. D. Murch, "A Group Evangelism Sending Station," *Christian Standard,* Jan. 22, 1921, p. 1787.

6. "Plan Undenominational Missionary Service," *Christian Standard,* Jan. 3, 1925, p. 346.

B. That it is willing to become a clearing-house for our free missionary and benevolent agencies, with the understanding that these free agencies do not thereby become subservient to the Clarke Fund.

By the term "clearing-house" we mean an agency for two purposes: (1) To receive and forward contributions for any free agencies for which the organization may agree to perform such service. (2) To act as publicity agent for such free agencies.[7]

Moreover, many conservative Disciples hoped that by establishing the CRA, the era of confrontation against the UCMS could now pass into a more constructive stage.

It is the belief of the Promoters [of the CRA] that the era of destructive criticism of the brotherhood must pass, and that an era of construction upon sure foundations must come in.[8]

The journal of the CRA, the *Restoration Herald*,[9] was billed by the *Christian Standard* as a "New Missionary Journal."

. . . The first issue will contain thirty-two pages of stories, essays, mission programs, etc. covering every phase of the Church's task — evangelism, missions, benevolence, education, fellowship, spiritual growth, etc.

As a missionary and educational journal, it will be pushed everywhere among the brethren. Already a circulation well into the tens of thousands seems assured.

---

7. *Christian Standard,* January 3, 1925, p. 346.

8. *Christian Standard,* July 18, 1925, p. 1001.

9. The *Restoration Herald* continued a previous publication called *Facts*. Consequently, the *Restoration Herald* did not begin publication with volume one but with volune four (1925).

Independent missionary societies have wanted such a paper for years, and loyal preachers, elders, and deacons will welcome it as an ally long desired. [10]

The *Restoration Herald* lived up to its billing. From the beginning there were reports on and by Enrique T. Westrup in Mexico, African Christian Missionary Association, Osaka Mission, and stateside work as Cincinnati Bible Seminary, Christian Old People's Home of St. Louis and others. Each month there was a two-page spread entitled Monthly Missionary Program of the W. M. S., a program designed and written for the women's missionary society of local congregations for use in the study and promotion of missions. [11] In fact, during the early days of the *Restoration Herald,* a full two-thirds, and often more, of the journal were taken up with mission reports and lessons for the study of missions in the local church. Figure 2, taken from the March, 1926, issue of the *Restoration Herald,* gives a "bird's-eye view" of the "Associated Free Agencies" (thirteen in all), which the *Restoration Herald* regularly reported on, as well as the money received and forwarded to them.

When it became evident that Leslie Wolfe in the Philippines would soon be dismissed from the United Christian Missionary Society (April 30, 1926), the Christian Restoration Association under the leadership of James DeForest

---

10. *Ibid.*

11. The promotion of the women's missionary society in the *Restoration Herald* was a carry-over from the Christian Woman's Board of Mission. In mobilizing the women of the Restoration Movement to underwrite foreign missions, the CWBM was unsurpassed. CWBM women in local church auxiliaries proved a popular outlet for women's talents and energy in the church. It was a tribute to the CWBM that James DeForest Murch recognized this popularity and sought to preserve the women's auxiliary as a dynamic for the Direct-Support Missionary Movement.

Murch, promised to underwrite Leslie Wolfe's support if he would stay in the Philippines as an independent missionary. The Philippines Christian Mission, comprising of Mr. & Mrs. Wolfe, was from that time listed in the *Restoration Herald* as another Associated Free Agency.

The ANNUAL REPORTS of the
Associated Free Agencies

A BIRD'S-EYE VIEW of the REPORTS

RECEIPTS.		ASSETS.	
African Christian Missionary Board	$ 9,913.01	African Christian Missionary Board	$ ---------------
Christian Bible College of Colorado	ᵉ10,000.00	Christian Bible College of Colorado	---------------
Christian Normal Institute	12,895.09	Christian Normal Institute	122,000.00
Christian Restoration Association	42,194.09	Christian Witness to Israel	ᵉ10,000.00
Christian Witness to Israel	10,454.74	Christian Woman's Benevolent Association	850,000.00
Christian Woman's Benevolent Association	207,287.06	Eugene Bible University	860,800.00
Eugene Bible University	115,141.27	International Bible Mission	503,700.00
International Bible Mission	77,396.46	Mexican Society for Christian Missions	10,400.00
Mexican Society for Christian Missions	6,000.00	National Home-finding Society	ᵉ75,000.00
National Home-finding Society	ᵉ20,000.00	Osaka Mission	1,200.00
Osaka Mission	3,951.50	Southwest Virginia Evangelizing Board	---------------
Southwest Virginia Evangelizing Board	ᵉ3,000.00	Yotsuya Mission	150,000.00
Yotsuya Mission	62,514.62	Christian Restoration Association	60,000.00
COMBINED RECEIPTS	$580,747.84	COMBINED ASSETS	$2,641,900.00

e — Estimated.

Figure 2

It is for this reason that the beginning of Direct-Support Missions is dated from 1926, for this offer of being a "clearing house" to receive the forward funds to Leslie Wolfe set the

182

pattern for other conservative Disciples of Christ missionaries to follow. It was not long after this that several missionaries resigned to serve independently of the UCMS and to appeal for supporting funds from churches through the Christian Restoration Association. In each case, report of another "Free Agency" was published in the pages of the *Restoration Herald.*

The first of these additions was Sterling Gould Rothermel and his wife, Dr. Zoena Rothermel, who first went to India under the Christian Woman's Board of Missions in 1914.[12] However, after the CWBM merged with the other societies to become the UCMS, a disagreement arose between the Rothermels and the UCMS over the direction which the Disciples of Christ mission in India was taking. S. G. Rothermel wanted a more conservative and evangelistic approach while the UCMS favored a federated approach involving associations with denominations not practicing immersion. As a result the Rothermels, after returning to the States on furlough in 1921, were not invited by the UCMS to return to India.[13] They remained for four years in the States where Mr. Rothermel attended the graduate school of the University of Chicago and led in the establishment of a new church (for the Clarke Fund) at Kenosha, Wisconsin. In December of 1926, with the help of the Christian Restoration Association, they sailed to India to work independently of the UCMS.[14] Two years later, however, Mr. Rothermel died in

---

12. Carr, *The Foreign Missionary Work of the Christian Church,* p. 123.

13. S. C. Rothermel, "A Judgment at Work." *Christian Standard,* Feb. 18, 1928, p. 182. "Our failure to compromise with modernisn and denominationalism, and our stand against the indirect conduct of a certain fellow-missionary, are at the root of the refusal of the UCMS to return us to India."

14. *Restoration Herald,* Sept. 1927.

India from scarlet fever.[15] His wife, Dr. Zoener Rothermel, continued to serve as a medical missionary in India until 1965.

Soon after the departure of the Rothermels in 1926, there appeared in the April, 1927, issue of the *Restoration Herald* an article with the following title and subtitle:

> "A Venture of Faith in the Forbidden Land. Christian Restoration Association underwrites Russell Morse in establishment of mission station on highest point in the world occupied by a Herald of the Gospel."

J. Russell Morse and his wife, with a baby son, were appointed in 1921 by the UCMS to serve in Batang in Western China. They went to work with the famed UCMS medical-evangelist, Dr. A. G. Shelton,[16] but soon after their arrival Dr. Shelton was murdered by Chinese bandits. The tragic death caused such a great outpouring of grief among churches in America that a memorial fund of $100,000 was raised to establish a new mission station on the China-Tibet border, an area where Dr. Shelton had hoped to preach the Gospel before he was killed. However, when new UCMS missionaries arrived in Batang in preparation to open the new station, a bitter controversy arose in the UCMS mission. Older missionaries, it turned out, were not in favor of the new station and sought to prevent its establishment. The new missionaries fought back in behalf of the new station, but to no avail. At this point, J. Russell Morse stepped in to help mediate the controversy only to gain the ill will of both old and new missionaries. A UCMS official arrived in Batang to settle the dissension but was likewise unsuccessful. In fact, the

---

15. "Sterling G. Rothermel," *Christian Standard,* Sept. 29, 1928, p. 993.

16. E. R. Errett, "Obeying the Great Commission," *Christian Standard,* March 12, 1927, p. 245.

official seemed to favor the older missionaries in the controversy, at which time the new missionaries left in disgust to
return to the States.

J. Russell Morse was also disgusted, since it meant that
the UCMS was not interested in evangelistic outreach into
the China-Tibet border area. Since preaching the Gospel in
this area was uppermost in Morse's mind, he resigned in
January, 1926, from the UCMS, hoping to become immediately free to evangelize in western China where the
Gospel had not been preached. But his resignation was not
immediately accepted until March of that year, and because
of civil turmoil in China at the time Morse was unable to
leave Batang until September. The last salary from the UCMS
was given to them in October.[17] From Batang the Morses
moved to the China-Tibet border to begin their work.

During the summer of 1926, James DeForest Murch of
the CRA wrote to urge the Morse family, as Leslie Wolfe,
to stay on as independent missionaries with the help of funds
raised by the CRA. The letter did not reach J. Russell Morse
until after he had left UCMS employment in October of that
year. In January, 1927, Murch received a letter from Morse
stating agreement . . . "to an arrangement by which the
Christian Restoration Association will assume the task of
raising the necessary funds for his support."[18] The CRA sent
funds to a Shanghai bank account, but Morse, located in
western China, was unable to use them. Civil turmoil continued in China to the point of endangering the lives of J.
Russell Morse and his family. In September of 1927, the

---

17. *Restoration Herald*, April, 1927, pp. 3-4. Morse also stated that the
UCMS attempted to prevent his supporting church in Enid, Oklahoma from
sending support to him after October of 1926. At this, his mother wrote to
Christian Standard exposing what UCMS officials were doing.

18. *Ibid.*

Morses were forced to flee from western China through unexplored mountains into Burma. They arrived in Burma destitute, at which time a U.S. Consulate cabled UCMS headquarters in St. Louis, Missouri for emergency repatriation funds to help them travel on to America. This request started a rumor that J. Russell Morse had denounced independent mission as a failure and had given up the work in Tibet.[19] The UCMS supporters tried to capitalize on this in order to show the weakness of independent missions.[20] This caused still more confusion about Morse and his relation to independent missions.

On returning to the States, J. Russell Morse dispelled any notion that he was rejoining the UCMS. He also disagreed with the interpretation that the necessity for using UCMS emergency funds in this case signaled any weakness in the independent mission method, for, according to Morse, it amounted to what the UCMS had already promised to them as returning missionaries.

> That missionary society faithfully carried out its agreement to pay our travel expenses to America, as it always has done for those who have left its employ. — Even if the other society had failed to carry out its agreement, there would have been sufficient funds (in a Shanghai bank) for our passage to America.[21]

The money was subsequently repaid to the UCMS. Late in 1929 the Morse family returned to the Tibetan border to resume mission work independently of the UCMS.

Before J. Russell Morse returned to China, however, Harry Schaefer and family had returned to India to work

---

19. "About Russell Morse," *Restoration Herald*, Sept. 1927, p. 2.
20. "In Perils of Unfriendly Brethren," *Christian Standard*, Sept. 24, 1927, p. 715.
21. J. Russell Morse, "Our Return to Tibet," *Restoration Herald*, Feb. 1928, pp. 3-4.

independently of the UCMS. Like the Rothermels, Mr. & Mrs. Schaefer were missionaries under the Christian Woman's Board of Missions and had first gone to India in 1913.[22] Mr. Schaefer likewise opposed the federated plans of the UCMS,[23] and thus was deemed incompatible by many of his UCMS colleagues. He had also opened on the side a small furniture factory which brought in a private income outside of his mission salary. This was an infraction of UCMS policy which prohibited such enterprises. Consequently, while on furlough in the States in 1926-1927 the UCMS and Harry Schaefer came to a mutual understanding over their dispute.

> [Schaefer] came to the United Society's headquarters, then in St. Louis and talked the matter over. When informed that the Society could not send him back to India, against the advice of his fellow missionaries, he said he would return as an independent missionary. He was asked not to locate in one of our own centers, but to take a new field where there would be no competition or controversy. He promised to do that.[24]

In 1928, the Schaefers sailed for India to serve independently of the UCMS.[25]

The aggressive promotion by the Christian Restoration Association of missionary work operated independently of the UCMS opened the way not only for conservative UCMS missionaries to continue their work but also for new

---

22. Carr, *The Foreign Missionary Work of the Christian Church*, p. 127.
23. "Comity by Coercion," *Christian Standard*, Dec. 22, 1928, p. 1296.
24. Stephen J. Corey, *Fifty Years of Attack and Controversy*. The Committee of Publication of the Corey Manuscript, 1953, p. 140. Corey (page 139) also claims that Harry Schaefer was an earlier advocate of receiving unimmersed persons into church membership. Whatever the truth of the matter is, Harry Schaefer returned to India, as an independent missionary, not advocating open membership.
25. *Restoration Herald*, May 28, 1928.

missionaries to go for the first time to the mission field independent of the UCMS. In 1926 John T. Chase went to work with W. D. Cunningham in Japan; Ruth Schoonover and Vivian Lemmon also joined the Cunningham work.[26] After M. B. Madden returned to Japan in 1928, his daughter, Mrs. Grace Bradey along with Ray Sawyer and Cicile Harding joined the Madden mission work.[27] In 1930 Fred Smith joined the Rothermels in India.[28]

In 1927 Carl A. Roy Lewis arrived in South Africa to help C. B. Titus. A year later, however, he resigned because he discovered members in mission churches who had not been immersed, a situation which he claimed was no different than open membership in the UCMS.[29] Lewis also charged the CRA with breach of contract and sent in his resignation. The CRA had promised Lewis that, when he was ready to return, the organization would provide passage money to America. When he resigned, he requested this money, but because of certain delays which the CRA experienced in booking passage on a ship for Lewis, he went ahead and borrowed money on his own to return. Since he booked more expensive passage than what the CRA allowed, the CRA refused to pay the difference. On returning to the States, Lewis published a pamphlet titled "The Christian Restoration Association Self-Impeached," charging the CRA with condoning open membership in South Africa and with heavy-handed administration at home. The CRA responded to these charges by explaining that the instances of open

---

26. Carr, *The Foreign Missionary Work of the Christian Church*, p. 138.
27. *Ibid.*, p. 141.
28. Lora Banks Harrison, *The Church Abroad*, (San Antonio, Texas: Southern Christian Press, 1960), p. 188.
29. "The Situation in the South African Mission to Negroes," *Christian Standard*, March 15, 1930, p. 263.

membership occurred in congregations of black restoration movements which had only recently become associated with the South African Mission.[30] There were nonimmersed members in these churches, of course, but they were being taught and immersed, and those not willing to be immersed after being taught were no longer counted on the church roll. With regard to passage money back to America, the CRA countered that it was the policy for all CRA missionairies to travel by freighter as an economy measure.

Despite such misunderstanding in the South Africa work, the *Restoration Herald* of April, 1931, reported thirty (independent) missionaries at work around the world, 156 native workers, 40,000 Christians in foreign countries, eight mission benevolent institutions treating 3,000 people annually, and seven mission educational institutions serving 600 students. In the annual report of that year it was reported that 3,000 new Christians, both in the States and abroad, had been added to the church through the outreach of the Christian Restoration Association.[31] After 1931, moreover, more new missionaries entered independent mission work. In 1933 Dr. Norton Bare and Vernon Newland joined the J. Russell Morse work in China.[32] In 1937 Edgar Nichols, Harold Taylor, Gladys Schwake, Isabell Maxey and Melba Palmer also joined J. Russell Morse in China.[33]

The importance of the pivotal role which the Christian Restoration Association played in the formation of Direct-Support Missions between the years of 1925 and 1931 cannot be overestimated. (The CRA) is "the 'keystone of the

---

30. *Restoration Herald*, April 1928; "The Reply of the Christian Restoration Association," *Christian Standard*, March 15, 1930, p. 263.

31. "The Sun Never Sets on (CRA) Labors," *Restoration Herald*, June, 1931.

32. Carr, *The Foreign Missionary Work of the Christian Church*, p. 134.

33. *Ibid.*, p. 137.

arch' of our loyal missionary, benevolent and educational work," stated an editorial in the *Christian Standard* in 1930.[34] Under the leadership of James DeForest Murch the CRA consolidated what was only incidental and incipient in the missionary work of the Disciples of Christ—the independent missionaries and conservative missionaries resigning from the UCMS—and gave them a form and essence which individuals and churches could readily recognize in contrast with the UCMS: they were now "Free Agencies." By aggressively promoting these Free Agencies through the pages of the *Restoration Herald,* James DeForest Murch, more than anyone else, launched independent missions making them a missionary movement within the Disciples of Christ brotherhood. In other words, out of his energy and genius James DeForest Murch launched a dynamic which, since its beginnings, has swept up both individuals and congregations for the cause of fulfilling the Great Commission of making disciples of the nations. Christian Churches and Churches of Christ, and especially every Direct-Support missionary who has ever served, owe much to this tireless administrator, editor and writer.

There was another aspect to the pivotal role that the Christian Restoration Association and James DeForest Murch played in giving substance to independent missionary work. This aspect was a sense of urgency in the task of evangelizing the world. Because of liberal theology and the ever increasing emphasis on institutional development in the UCMS, making and baptizing disciples among the ethnic groups of the world were being neglected. Since so much

---

34. *Christian Standard,* August 9, 1930, p. 774.

190

time had been lost, and so much that had been gained through evangelism was being lost, and because of devoting so much energy to interdenominational federation, there was now much to recoup. The CRA led the way in regrouping Christ's Church for evangelism by urging Christians to support independent missionaries who were free of any cumbersome bureaucracy or society, i.e. to "redeem the time" in preaching the gospel to the world.

Perhaps the greatest debt which we owe James DeForest Murch is the formulation of the Biblical principles — principles which were lost during the development of the missionary societies — which must underlie the establishment and use of para-congregational organizations for carrying out the church's commission from our Lord of evangelizing the world. In an earlier chapter (Chapter Two) it was noted that early conservative Disciples neglected to construct a theology clarifying the proper Biblical role of the missionary societies in contrast with the congregations, thus leaving by default the development of the societies to liberal Disciples. In a series of editorials printed in the *Restoration Herald* in the first half of 1926, James DeForest Murch stepped in the breach to spell out those principles which must govern the relationship between the para-church missionary organiztion and the local congregation. There were seven of these principles:

Free Agency Principles

I. Church and Society Different in Kind
The New Testament church, or the Church of Christ, is a divine institution or organization, societies or associations, whether missionary, educational or benevolent, are human expediences; hence, being different in kind,

191

there must of necessity be no organic relation between the two and no attempt on the part of the one to dominate or control the other.[35]

II. Individual Freedom in Giving and Serving

Churches of Christ and individual disciples of Christ are and must be left free to serve or give in the way that they deem wise and proper.[36]

III. The Credentials of Agencies

The Field of Christian service is and must remain open. The only credentials that may be required of any agency are (1) loyalty to Christ and (2) efficiency in service. The only human recognition possible, or that should be desired by any agency is that of patronage extended on merit.[37]

IV. Monopoly in Christian Service is Undesirable

Monopoly in Christian service is undesirable. The appearance or organization of any missionary or educational society in the very nature of the church presupposes that no human agency has a right to exclusive authority or prerogatives in any field.[38]

V. Freedom to Meet Changing Conditions

The best method of co-operative Christian service may not hitherto, or even more, have been discovered. The Churches should have at their disposal a variety of means and methods of work so that the best may survive and be improved to meet the changed conditions, and the obsolete, outworn or disloyal be superseded.[39]

---

35. *Restoration Herald,* January, 1926.
36. *Restoration Herald,* February, 1926.
37. *Restoration Herald,* March, 1926.
38. *Restoration Herald,* April, 1926.
39. *Restoration Herald,* May, 1926.

VI. Variety of Methods

Variety of methods is especially desirable among the great Restoration plea for the unity of God's people, the divine inspiration and supreme authority of the Holy Scriptures, the sovereignty of the Lord Jesus Christ, and the autonomy of the local congregation.[40]

VII. Agencies are Merely Expediencies

The missionary, benevolent or educational agency is an expediency merely. The formation of new associations, therefore, or the affiliation of agencies in any form, cannot truthfully be construed as unchristian or unscriptural. Different local churches of Christ may make use of different agencies, or a local church may make use of several agencies, without in any way disturbing the status of the church, or of such groups of its members as may give to this or that agency, or to no agency. In this way we accept and recognize the New Testament teaching of the personal rights of the individual Christian and the autonomy of the local churches of Christ. The denial or violation of these plain Scriptural principles will tend toward a centralized ecclesiasticism and the ultimate overthrow of the Restoration plea.[41]

These principles effectively solved the Cambellian dilemma which was mentioned at the beginning of this book, viz. without creating para-congregational organizations the church finds it difficult if not impossible to carry out the Great Commission, but if such organizations are created they tend to supersede the congregation in power and importance. But

---

40. *Restoration Herald,* June, 1926.
41. *Restoration Herald,* July, 1926.

now, by following these principles, the local church could both maintain its own power and importance *and* create agencies to perform specialized tasks as foreign missionary work, for it is within the church's right to create a *variety* of organizations, choose which and which not to support, and to *abolish* those which are no longer useful. In essence, a basic principle was proposed through these principles to solve the dilemma: There must be plurality of, and competition between, agencies. As long as there were several organizations competing with each other in appealing for available funds from churches, there could be no supra-organization which would overshadow the church. Direct-Support Missions have followed this metaprinciple until this day by proliferating and competing for funds from local congregations throughout America. Regardless of what the reader may think of proliferation of missionary agencies and the use of competition in fulfilling the Great Commission, such have nevertheless allowed Christian Churches/Churches of Christ to effectively avoid the two horns of the dilemma which in effect have plagued the other two segments of the Restoration Movement: the stifling of evangelism in the Disciples of Christ because of an overemphasis on bureaucratic development, and the weak showing in missions and benevolent work (until recently at least) among the non-instrumental Churches of Christ because of the fear that creating the organizations to accomplish these tasks were not Scripturally legitimate.

1933-1945 Refining the Dynamic

James DeForest Murch resigned from the Christian Restoration Association in 1933 to return to the Standard Publishing

Company. Under new leadership the CRA, in order to avoid charges of pursuing an authoritative status in missions, changed focus, and the formative role of the CRA exercised in mission work gradually diminished. But this development did not negate the earlier and most important accomplishments of the CRA, viz. *the re-establishment of the first principles for governing the relationship between the local congregation and the para-congregational organization.* Murch, writing in later years,[42] expressed that the *Restoration Herald* (and by extension the Christian Restoration Association) never received its due for the contribution that it made to independent missions in those early years. While this is regretably true — and certainly recognition from the brotherhood is long overdue — a major part of the reason no doubt lies in the extreme independency that developed among the churches in reaction to the United Christian Missionary Society. For even though the CRA had done much to launch independent missions, it was, nevertheless, a para-congregational organization and as such it was still suspect.[43] Consequently, both churches and missionaries began to bypass the CRA in search for a more direct way of fulfilling the Great Commission. The *Restoration Herald* continued to carry appeals for funds in behalf of the pioneers of the independent missionary movement, e.g. Leslie Wolfe, J. Russell Morse, Enrique Westrup, etc., and the CRA forwarded these funds on to their respective fields. The *Christian Standard* likewise performed this service in behalf of independent missionaries. But by this time World War II had

---

42. Murch, *Christians Only*, p. 253.
43. *Ibid.*

come and gone, both the *Restoration Herald* and the *Christian Standard* had largely turned to other issues, leaving missions and missionaries to carry on the dynamic on their own.

Even though the Christian Restoration Association grew less significant in the missionary outreach of the Christian Churches in the years immediately following 1933, this did not mean that missions operating independently of the UCMS suffered correspondingly. On the contrary, independent missionaries held their own financially during these years of depression and attracted new workers for the mission field. And with the declining importance of the CRA as an intermediary between the church and missionary, missionaries looked more directly to local churches for financial support, and local churches responded in kind by sending funds directly to the missionaries. To strengthen this relationship between congregation and missionary, and to expedite the fruits of such, independent missionaries revived and developed even further two concepts which were first introduced and promoted among Christian Churches at the close of the 19th Century. Those two concepts were the Living Link church and the Forwarding Agent.

The Living Link Church

W. K. Azbill claimed to have been the originator of the living link church concept while serving as an elder in the Central Christian Church of Indianapolis, Indiana in 1890.[44] The church offered to be the living link of C. E. Garst, a missionary under appointment to Japan. However, Azbill

---

44. W. K. Azbill, "Wrong Attitudes of Boards," *Christian Standard*, April 11, 1914, p. 628.

alleged, The Foreign Christian Missionary Society refused such a relationship for Garst insisting that he was a missionary sent out by the society and not by the church. It was not long before the FCMS changed its mind, for in 1894 the Central Christian Church of Des Moines, Iowa, agreed to become the living link church for Harvey H. Guy, an FCMS missionary to Japan. From this time onward, the FCMS promoted the concept as a means of raising more money to send missionaries abroad. Archibald McLean, President of the FCMS from 1900 to 1919, in writing the history of the FCMS, stated that

> A third device for increasing the amount of financial support was entitled the Living Link. A church that gave enough to support a missionary was listed as a Living Link church. The missionary thus supported was a living link between the field and the church . . . The man on the field is as dear to the congregation as the man in the pulpit, and the church would no more think of failing to support one than the other.[45]

By 1919 McLean reported that there were 189 living-link churches supporting missionaries.[46]

The living-link church, however, was only one of several devices employed by the FCMS to raise mission funds. Other devices of the time were county-wide crusades to enlist new churches and individuals to send contributions to the FCMS, sales of Christian literature, special recognition to those churches which gave (and gave beyond what was expected), and the employment of financial agents by the FCMS to

---

45. Archibald McLean, *The Foreign Christian Missionary Society* (New York: Fleming H. Revell Co., 1919), p. 366.
46. *Ibid.*

travel full time speaking and raising funds for the Society.[47] The most profitable method, though, for raising mission funds was the March offerings. Not long after the FCMS was established, it was suggested that one Sunday in March be set aside by all the churches of the brotherhood during which a special offering be collected for foreign missions. The offerings immediately became popular and remained the major supply of funds for the FCMS, and the later UCMS, for many years thereafter.

It is no wonder that the concept of the living link church, originally a minor device for raising funds compared to more popular methods, was never really developed in the day of the missionary societies. To be sure the concept was promoted from time to time in the brotherhood. For example, during the 1907 meeting of the Foreign Christian Missionary Society, L. E. Sellers delivered an address entitled *The Living Link Idea*. The address was also published in the *Christian-Evangelist* of that same year.[48] In the article Sellers stated that the main problem of Christendom "is the Christianization of her wealth," of inspiring Christians to give more and more of their wealth for preaching the Gospel in other lands. The Living Link Idea, he claimed, provides inspiration and incentive for giving more.

> It is the unanimous judgment of those who have measured its benefits and shared its blessings that our effective means of enlisting the churches and advancing the work is through the Living Link plan. It is a Living Link. The interest centers about a person and the special field in which he works. Facts,

---

47. *Ibid.*, pp. 365-367.
48. *Christian Evangelist*, November 21, 1907, p. 1483.

not theories, begat conviction and enthusiasm. . . . Produce
a man—a living, equipped, spirit-filled man; a man who
has the love and coverage of a martyr. Ask that he be sent
to China, to a particular field in China, and immediately the
theory of missions fades out before the concrete reality of
China's needs and how they are to be met. From that
moment the burden of that man's work is upon the heart of
the church that supports him. His name is a household word,
and is mentioned with a love and reverence as though of
kindred flesh and blood. And in many a prayer, rising on
wings of faith, this servant is remembered in tenderest
petition before the throne of grace. And when the people
assemble for worship, prayer, sermons, and letters from
the field easily keep fresh and vigorous the interest of the
entire church in their missionary and his work. This is a simple
interpretation of the great commission. It kindles in the conscience of the church the sense of divine fellowship.[49]

Sellers recounted how the Living Link Idea in support of
missions gradually emerged among the churches.

At the first, small gifts came from a few individuals. Then,
other individuals joined their contributions. Next the basket
was passed with due apologies. Then the basket was passed
without the apology. Finally the basket was passed with an
appeal. Following this, the work of systematic information
was pursued and offerings were taken for this cause as though
it were important. This was a great advance. Later a church
of groups of churches determined to provide the support of
a missionary. This created a new standard and a new name. It
was the beginning of the Living Link movement among us.[50]

---

49. *Ibid.*
50. *Ibid.*

The blessings rising from Living Link arrangements between missionary and congregation are manifold, Sellers continued:

> . . . one living link missionary will bring more blessings to a congregation than the highest salaried choir in the brotherhood.[51]

Moreover, the Living Link concept

> . . . puts the responsibility where it belongs. The local congregation is the unit of power and support. It is the base of supplies.[52]

If the Living Link idea would be widely adopted, it would relieve the FCMS from worry about the support of many missionaries. Rather the FCMS could count on such support as assured amounts that would be given yearly.

> The Congregation very quickly comes to think of the missionary's support as being as much a part of its financial obligation as the support of its pastor. . . . The hit and miss policy in vogue in many congregations is unknown in the Living Link church. . . . It insures the FCMS of a stream of money, the total amount of which may be estimated in advance. . . . Broaden the base of supplies, increase the number of churches who stand for definite contributions to the work, and the hazard of the hit and miss plan is mightily reduced.[53]

Sellers ended the article with a stirring call for the FCMS to enlist as many Living Link Churches as possible.

> No better step could be taken in this convention than the determination to advance as many churches as possible to the Living Link class. We ought to have 500 congregations

---

51. *Ibid.*
52. *Ibid.*
53. *Ibid.*

enjoying this spiritual fellowship. The favor of God would rest upon us as never before. It is a reasonable service which we should gladly render. The work demands it; the doors invite it; the Lord expects it; your own heart prompts it. Shall it come to pass.[54]

The Christian Standard was also a promoter of the Living Link concept. In a 1905 news item entitled "Ministers of New Link Church of the Foreign Christian Missionary Society," the *Christian Standard* editorialized:

The relation of the churches to the missionaries whom they support is most intimate and vital. The missionaries report directly to their perspective churches at least once per quarter. They speak of their difficulties, the problems of the work, give fresh and direct reports of victories won, and the signs of promise for the future. This is a most valuable means of educating the churches and holding their warmest interest. On the other hand, the churches in the home land think of their respective missionaries in a special way. Each is the object of constant prayer, and each missionary becomes a household word with every member. They know exactly where the missionary is located. This creates intelligent interest. The field, its geography, its people, its various religions, its deep degradation, all become common information throughout the church. The supporting church watches the growth of the infant congregation on heathen soil with tender solicitude. This larger plan is helping to reproduce the spirit of Acts of Apostles.[55]

Despite the promotion of the Living Link idea in both the *Christian Evangelist* and *Christian Standard,* the concept did not become a popular method for generating mission

---

54. *Ibid.*
55. *Christian Standard,* April 1, 1905, p. 544.

funds among the Disciples of Christ in the first two decades of this century. How minor a method it really was can be seen in a quote from Seller's article above where he called for 500 churches to be enlisted as Living Link churches. This number was not reached (in 1919 there were only 189 Living Link Churches),[56] but even if it had been—or even some number close to 500—it would still have represented only a small percent of Disciple congregations joining the ranks of Living Link churches, for the same issue of the *Christian-Evangelist* reported an astonishing 11,301 congregations of the Disciples of Christ in 1902.[57] The percentage, moreover, would not be appreciably increased even if we subtract several hundred of these congregations because— as was happening during that time—they disassociated from the Disciples of Christ and aligned themselves with the non-instrumental Churches of Christ. Several of these churches were still being counted, even after the 1906 formal announcement of division, by officials of the Disciples of Christ and it was only after a few years that these churches were eliminated from any Disciple listing.[58] Most Disciples of Christ congregations preferred to support foreign mission work not directly to the missionary but through the offices of the missionary societies.

The main reason, however, that the Living Link idea did not gain any more popularity than it did in the early 1900's was the drive toward unification—which was likewise being promoted during the same years—of the various foreign and state missionary societies (the ACMS, CWBM, FCMS, etc.) into one large organization (the UCMS). Plans for unifying all these diverse missionary, evangelistic and benevolent

---

56. McLean, *The Foreign Christian Missionary Society*, p. 366.
57. *Christian-Evangelist*, November 21, 1907, p. 1499.
58. *Ibid.*

agencies called not only for centralizing the organizational structures for greater efficiency of operation but also for closer coordination of the methods of raising and disbursing funds for greater economy in financing the missionary enterprises of the Disciples of Christ. Under the methods current then, all the various societies and agencies overlapped each other in personnel and procedures for raising funds, thus creating inefficiencies by having redundant personnel and operations. Unification would, therefore, eliminate such organizational redundancy which in turn would release more funds for actual mission work. Plans for unifying the brotherhood agencies were promulgated in the General Convention, and, to create a climate favorable for unification, editorials and articles written by leading Disciples in favor for unification were published in the *Christian-Evangelist*. Officials of the various societies and agencies were in favor of unification. Thus momentum for consolidation of a structurally diverse ecclesiastical system was created in the brotherhood, a momentum which in a short time captured the energies and devotion of brotherhood leaders and overshadowed other developments for the promotion and support of missions. Naturally one development which was overshadowed was the Living Link idea, because while this concept of supporting missionaries was entirely compatible with a brotherhood composed of a fellowship of autonomous congregations, it was antithetical to the organizational concept of unification as envisioned by many Disciple leaders. Consequently, the Living Link idea, so eloquently promoted by L. E. Sellers in speech and print, did not receive the attention it deserved and remained in embryonic form underdeveloped as a missionary support dynamic within the missionary program of the Disciples of Christ.

Another reason why the Living Link idea never was developed in the early missionary societies was the Men and Millions Movement. The Men and Millions Movement, begun in 1913, was a project to raise $6,000,000 for the missionary benevolent and educational causes of the brotherhood. According to Loren E. Lair, the inauguration of the Movement created pressure from within the brotherhood for unification. Moreover

> Its success demonstrated the value of unified endeavor and gave evidence of what might happen if the total work of the churches could be supported by all the churches and all the members of the churches.[59]

The Living Link concept, as noted above, did not lend itself to centralization, since it was based on the concept that an individual congregation could independently and voluntarily make a contract to underwrite the support of a missionary. The Men and Millions Movement, on the other hand, was amenable to the unification scheme being proposed at that time. In fact the Movement itself quickly took on the characteristic of a para-church organization. Funds were given in behalf of and through the Movement, and recipients of these funds (the missionary societies, educational institutions, etc.) came more and more to look upon the Movement, and not the churches, as the source of funds. Because of its success the concept embodied in the Men and Millions Movement and not the Living Link concept, was adopted as the primary model for raising funds to underwrite the

---

59. Loren E. Lair, *The Christian Churches and Their Work* (St. Louis: Bethany Press, 1963), p. 149.

missionary, educational and benevolent enterprises of the Disciples of Christ.[60]

The first missionaries who worked independently of the societies, however, early discovered that the living link church was the key to financial survival in an atmosphere of the near total dominance by the para-church organization. For example, Alice Miller, in 1895, was able to go to Japan and work for many years because of a living link relationship with a church in Los Angeles.[61] Indeed, early independent missionaries were enthusiastic supporters of the living link concept as a mission dynamic in its own right. Calla J. Harrison, writing in a 1909 *Christian Standard* editorial, exclaimed:

> God speed the day when every church will be a living link and send on its own responsibility its noblest most consecrated servants to the front, and leave them to work there, untrammeled by organizations other than the church itself.[62]

Moreover, the churches recognized that a Living Link arrangement with a missionary was theologically compatible with the doctrine of the autonomous church, allowing a congregation to both maintain its supremacy and fulfill its obligation in evangelizing the world. Seeing that there could be a direct relationship — i.e. without the need of an intermediate organization — between church and missionary, the Living Link idea quickly developed into a missionary dynamic for Christian Churches.

There were two ways in which the Living Link idea was developed by the early Direct-Support missionaries. The

---

60. That the Living Link idea was conducive to the local, autonomous church concept and that the Men and Millions Movement was more conducive to unification no doubt underlay the *Christian Standard's* support of the former and qualified support of the latter. (cf. *Christian Standard*, Oct. 18, 1919, p. 57).

61. *Christian Standard*, April 16, 1910, p. 655.

62. Calla J. Harrison, "Independent Mission Work," *Christian Standard*, Jan. 16, 1909, p. 106.

first way, in keeping with the original idea, was for a church to underwrite all the support of a missionary, his family and work. However, most churches were unable, or unwilling, to commit their resources to this extent. Consequently the Living Link idea underwent a second development. Independent missionaries sought several congregations to support their work, each congregation providing Living Link support for a specific and different project, e.g. a congregation could underwrite the funds needed to build a school building while another congregation could underwrite the monthly Living Link support of one of the missionary's children. Thus a missionary could have several Living Link churches contributing to his support and work. However, this development carried one disadvantage: contrary to the original plan, having a number of Living Links destroyed the special relationship between the congregation and missionary, a relationship that was at the same time both a strength and blessing of the original idea. This defect was to be partially corrected later with the addition of the Service Link. With this addition, Living Link became restricted to personal and family living expenses encountered in preaching and performing other types of mission work. This latter refinement now enables a missionary to build up significant personal relationships, on the basis of Living Link, with a congregation while allowing him to raise other funds (Service Link) which the Living Link church perhaps cannot provide.

The Forwarding Agent

The establishment of more direct relationships between church and missionary through the re-emergence of the Living Link concept favored over the "clearing house" concept promoted by the Christian Restoration Association, produced the same problem. This problem was how to transfer funds form the congregation to the missionary in the foreign field. In the case of UCMS, the organization was the intermediate agency which transferred American funds to the foreign mission field, and the CRA along with the *Christian Standard* performed this type of service for the early independent missionaries. The Living Link concept, however, required a different solution to this practical problem, a solution which was more compatible with the underlying dynamic of the living link concept than a more centralized concept.

The solution which was instituted was the Forwarding Agent. As with the Living Link idea. W. K. Azbill was the first to introduce the term Forwarding Agent, a term he first used in 1894.[63] Azbill was not referring to a person functioning in this capacity but to the role which the para-church society should play in the missionary outreach of the brotherhood. The missionary societies of the time were not content to be mere forwarding agents for foreign missionaries, so the term was not heard of again for many years. W. D. Cunningham, on the other hand, selected Forwarding Secretaries, whom we can justly claim as the forerunner or proto-type of the Forwarding Agents now in use in Direct-Support missions. C. B. Titus appointed a stateside treasurer to receive funds from contributors. Of more interest, perhaps, is the term the *Christian Standard* used for itself in collecting funds for the J. R. Kellems evangelistic party to South Africa: the *Standard* requested that contributions be sent to the "volunteer forwarding agent" in behalf of the Kellems party.[64]

---

63. *Christian-Evangelist,* March 8, 1894, p. 150.

64. "Kellems Homeward Bound," *Christian Standard,* Sept. 10, 1927, p. 875.

A Forwarding Agent, as the term suggests, was a personal agent of the missionary to receive funds and then forward these funds to the missionary on the foreign field. The first record of a person serving under the term Forwarding Agent for an independent missionary was in 1933 when Dr. Norton Bare, missionary to China and Tibet had Mrs. W. E. Sipple of Los Angeles, California, serve in this capacity; later in 1938, C. W. Nichols of Seminole, Oklahoma served as Forwarding Agent for Dr. Bare.[65] Harry Schaefer, Jr. and Robert Morse (in personal communication) reported that after World War II they likewise employed the use of volunteer Forwarding Agents in place of the Christian Restoration Association and the *Christian Standard*.

Employment of Forwarding Agents on a volunteer basis within independent missions signaled a subtle yet profound shift in emphasis within Christian Churches on how the Great Commission was to be carried out. This shift in emphasis is still very much a part of the dynamics of Direct-Support Missions today and is essential in order to properly understand Direct-Support Missions. Previously, it was thought in the Restoration Movement, foreign mission work had to be carried out through para-congregational *agencies* or organizations, e.g. the Foreign Christian Missionary Society. The Christian Restoration Association did not significantly alter this pattern of thought, for it was still a "clearing house" for the *free agencies*. But, with the emergence of the Forwarding Agent as the intermediary between church and missionary, the shift in emphasis was from that of *agency* to *agent*. That is to say, the Christian Churches no longer carried out the Great Commission by means of (impersonal)

---

65. *Christian Standard,* July 30, 1938, p. 753.

agencies or organizations but by means of (personal) agents, whether on the mission field in the person of the Direct-Support missionary or on the home front in the person of the Forwarding Agent. Direct-Support Missions are *person-oriented*, relying on the genius and energy of the individual — not the solvency and continuity of the para-church missionary society — to carry the Gospel to the uttermost parts of the earth. To be sure, the individual missionary may create an organization to expedite the execution of his missionary calling and others may even join him in his organization, yet the emphasis is still on the person of the individual missionary as the driving force in fulfilling the Great Commission.

The years 1933-1945 presented two formidable barriers to mission work, the Great Depression and later World War II. Both barriers, however, were surmounted by Direct-Support Missionaries. In spite of the Great Depression, which was world-wide, funds from the churches were forthcoming and missionaries, including new missionaries, returned to missions fields in the Far East, Africa and Latin America. World War II, however, did seriously affect the work of Direct-Support Missionaries. Vernon Newland, who had already served in Tibet as a missionary from 1933 to 1939, attempted to return to that country in 1941 but was prevented because of the war which had already begun on the Asian mainland. As a result, Newland stopped in the Philippines to join the mission work being done by Leslie Wolfe, only to be incarcerated with all other missionaries when the Japanese invaded and captured the Philippines in 1942. Vernon Newland survived four years of concentration camp but Leslie Wolfe died soon after liberation by Allied Forces in 1945. He was buried in the Philippines. In India, Harry Schaefer and family found it impossible to leave and so stayed in that country throughout the war. J. Russell Morse and others in China and Tibet made their way into Burma where that country borders India and Tibet and so were safe from the Japanese who controlled China. In 1944, Dorothy Sterling was able to reach India and flew by the United States Air Force plane over the Himilayan Mountains into this area of Burma to join the mission work of J. Russell Morse.[66]

In 1945, independent missions and mission Churches were still operating in India, Burma, Mexico, South Africa, Jamaica, the Philippines, and Alaska. Groups of Christians, the product of independent missions, also existed in Japan, China and Korea. Some sixty independent missionaries were serving in foreign countries at that time and, according to James Carr, were reporting over 3,000 baptisms annually.[67] In short, Direct-Support Missions survived the Depression and World War II. More importantly, though, a missionary dynamic had been consolidated and refined during these years, and because of that Direct-Support Missions at the end of World War II were prepared to resume operation in areas where the war had prevented and to enter new fields where previously Direct-Support missionairies had never labored.

---

66. David Filbeck, "A Missionary for all Tribes and Tongues," *Christian Standard*, Jan. 7, 1973, pp. 7-8.

67. Carr, *The Foreign Missionary Work of the Christian Church*, p. 158. According to McGilvrey, (Horizons) there were 90 independent missionaries in 1945. The difference between the two is probably accounted for by the inclusion of home missionaries in McGilvrey's count.

John Pemberton

Mr. and Mrs. Mark Maxey
and family

Tibbs Maxey

W. H. Book

Woodrow Phillips

Dr. David Grubbs, Archie Walters and
Dr. Dennis Pruett

Max Ward Randell and Bill Rees

Chapter Seven

A MISSIONARY DYNAMIC AT WORK

At the end of World War II, the Direct-Support Mission program of the Christian Churches/Churches of Christ entered a period of expansive growth. In fact, the most remarkable feature of Direct-Support Missions since the War has been their ability to attract each year an ever increasing number of new missionaries. From 90 independent missionaries in 1945, the number of Direct-Support missionaries grew to 1,976 by 1976,[1] an astonishing 2,184% increase in the number of missionaries supported by congregations and individual Christians over this 30 year period. Broken down into yearly increases, this 2,184% increase represents an average yearly growth of 72.8% in the missionary force of the Christian Churches. In addition to the growth of the number of missionaries in this period, by 1976, Direct-Support missionaries were serving in over 45 different nations, a 500% increase over the nine nations where independent missionaries were serving 1945. This averages out to more than one new nation per year that Christian Church missionaries entered for the first time. Moreover, besides new nations being entered, new mission stations were being opened in both "old" and "new" nations during this 30 year period. By 1976 there were more than 300 missions in the more than 45 nations being served by Direct-Support missionaries.

---

1. *Horizons*, September 25, 1976. In this section the number of Direct-Support missionaries at any given time is taken from Horizons. There are, of course, problems over how Horizons (and Mission Services) count missionaries. In order to minimize the problems involved, and to arrive at a more accurate picture, I have utilized percentages and rate of growth to describe the growth of Direct-Support Missions after World War II. Problems of statistics —just how many Direct-Support missionaries there really are—are discussed in Chapter Nine.

However, this remarkable growth in Direct-Support missions and missionaries was not as consistent over each of the 30 years as the averaging technique indicates. Indeed, in studying the new trends and developments of Direct-Support missions during this period of 30 years, three distinct stages are discernible, and in comparing the growth patterns of these three stages we discover that the rate of growth was not identical for each stage. From 1946 to 1955, the first stage of this period, the number of Direct-Support missionaries grew from 90 to 450, a whopping 500% increase in only nine years; this averages out to 40 new missionaries added each year. From 1956 to 1962, the second stage, the number of missionaries grew from 450 to 724, a smaller but perhaps still respectable 62% increase, an increase which nevertheless still averages 39 new missionaries for the seven year period. From 1963 to 1976, the last stage, the number of Direct-Support missionaries jumped from 724 to 1,976 a 270% increase for this twelve year period, an increase which averages 100 new missionaries being added each year to the missionary force of the Christian Churches.

The significance of these three stages lies partly in the different rates of growth. As was noted above, after a burst of rapid growth in the number of missionaries in the years immediately after World War II, the rate of growth dropped considerable over the next seven years only to enter once more a new period of rapid growth that has continued even beyond the date of 1976 to the present time. The different rates of growth of these stages are not unrelated but flow in cause-effect fashion from one to another. That is to say, trends and patterns which developed in a preceding stage formed the basis for what occurred in the succeeding stage, and the third stage built on what had developed in the preceding two stages. But there is more to the delineation of

212

these stages than just the differing rates of growth in new missionaries in each stage. The three stages can further be demarcated from each other by significant events which occurred in the years 1955 and 1963 respectively. To be sure, at the time these events appeared inconsequential compared to other happenings occurring at the same time; in retrospect, however, we can now see that they represent important developments in Direct-Support Missions since World War II, and they opened the way for the further expansion of Direct-Support Missions. This is especially true of the year 1956 to 1963, a period which on the surface, because of a greatly decreased rate of growth, would appear to signal the decline of Direct-Support Missions. Yet, as we shall see below, what occurred in 1956 with respect to missions in the Christian Church set in motion new trends and patterns that allowed Direct-Support Missions to grow at a much accelerated rate from 1963 onward.

1946-1955 Forgetting the Past

World War II played both an indirect and direct role in the rapid growth of the number of Direct-Support missionaries during the period spanning 1946-1955. On the one hand, the War years prevented many recruits for the mission field from traveling to foreign nations; but with the end of the War, the accumulation of new missionaries, pent up as in prison by several years of war, burst forth to carry the Gospel once more into the uttermost parts of the world. In a more direct fashion, on the other hand, the War allowed soldiers and chaplains from the Christian Churches to see first hand the spiritual needs of war-ravaged nations and peoples. Consequently many soldiers and chaplains dedicated their lives to return to these same lands with the Gospel of peace and reconciliation after leaving the armed services. Guy Mayfield, who served as an Air Force chaplain in Europe from 1943-1945, returned to Italy as a missionary in 1947. On the other side of the world Mark Maxey and Harold Woodruff who were chaplains during the War in the Pacific dediated their lives to missionary service in Japan and Okinawa respectively.

Missionary now followed missionary into the far corners of the earth — in 1945 Owen Still began a mission work in Hawaii while waiting for permission to re-enter Japan as a missionary (he and his wife had served there before the War); Harry Schaefer, Jr., son of one of the first pioneer independent missionaries, returned to India; and Ruth Smith went to the Philippines. In 1947, Harold Sims went to Japan, and Harland Cary began Colegio Biblico to train workers for Spanish speaking Latin America, and Charles Selby entered the Philippines. In 1948, Lloyd Sanders went to Brazil while Bernel Getter joined missionaries in India, and Andrew Patten traveled to Japan. In 1949, Bertrand Smith went to Chile. That same year, mainland China, because of the Communists gaining control of the government, was closed to mission work, which in turn caused all missionaries in that country to leave. By the following year Direct-Support missionaries who were serving in China had fanned out to serve in other countries of Asia, going even as far as South Africa where a sizeable overseas Chinese population lived. In October of 1950 Max Ward Randall arrived in South Africa. In 1951 Donald Fream and Woodrow Phillips went to Jamaica to renew work begun before the War in that island nation.

And so on it went, and many more names could be added to the above list of those who went to mission fields in the years following World War II. The additions of so many new missionaries and so many new fields being opened up, however, created new strains on brotherhood journals and agencies to publish all the news of a rapidly increasing force of Direct-Support missionaries. Since the Christian Restoration Association and the *Restoration Herald* had moved away from its original missionary orientation into other brotherhood concerns, there were only two brotherhood agencies left to report the happenings of Christian Church missionaries around the world: the North American Christian Convention (NACC) and the *Christian Standard*. It soon became apparent that these two agencies were inadequate platforms from which to report and promote further the rapidly expanding Direct-Support mission program of the Christian Churches. As a result, in order to meet the growing publicity and promotional needs of an expanding missionary force, new agencies and journals were designed to promote the evangelistic and missionary outreach of the Christian Churches.

The first agency created was the National Missionary Convention. Before the formation of this convention, missionaries and others interested in missions would share time at the North American Christian Convention for reports on mission activities. However, certain mission leaders were concerned that more time was needed and so met together to make plans for a missionary convention.

The first meeting was planned as a one-day rally preceding the North American Convention in Springfield, Illinois in April, 1948. Miss Marian Schaefer (daughter of Harry Schaefer), and J. Russell Morse met in the J. T. Chase home in Los Angeles in March, 1948 and announced plans

215

which called the meeting at West Side Church of Christ, Springfield, (Illinois).[2]

A second missionary rally, likewise preceding the NACC, was held two years later at the Englewood Christian Church, Indianapolis, Indiana at which time

. . . two decisions were reached which have served to build a strong (missionary) convention: 1) By popular demand, it was decided to include home missionaries on the program, instead of making it strictly a foreign missions meeting; 2) It was decided to make the meeting a separate convention.[3]

On November 14-17 of that same year, 1950, a missionary convention was held in Webster City, Iowa and was designated as the Third Missionary Convention.[4] The National Missionary Convention has been held annually since and has performed an important function in not only promoting missions but also galvanizing the Direct-Support method of the Christian Churches into a missionary movement.

Another agency created in the years immediately after World War II was Mission Services, an organization begun by Harrold McFarland at his home in Willernie, Minnesota, in 1945. Seven years later he moved Mission Services to Joliet, Illinois.[5] The purpose for establishing Mission Services was twofold: 1) to publish news and reports of missionaries and their work for churches and individuals in the USA; and 2) to serve as a purchasing service for missionaries through which missionaries could buy equipment more cheaply than otherwise. A newsletter, *Among Ourselves,*

---

2. *Horizons,* September 3, 1955, p. 2. See also, "The National Missionary Convention—A History," by Robert E. Lillie, *Christian Standard,* October 6, 1974, p. 905-907.

3. *Ibid.*

4. *Ibid.*

5. "Expanding Mission Service," *Christian Standard,* March 19, 1972, p. 245.

was published by Harrold McFarland until June, 1952, at which time it was combined with *Horizons* to produce a more complete magazine for reporting on all the Direct-Support missionaries of the Christian Churches.[6]

The *Christian Standard* still reported the activities of Direct-Support missionaries, but since several hundred missionaries served around the world in 1952, it was becoming increasingly more difficult to report all the news being sent in. Burris Butler, then editor of the *Christian Standard,* undertook to streamline the format of the weekly paper in respect to these missionary news reports. First, the missionary lesson material, which the *Christian Standard* had printed for many years, was eliminated. Next Harrold McFarland was invited to write a weekly news column, "carrying boiled-down, brief, news items about the missionaries."[7] This latter arrangement, however, lasted only until the end of 1954 when, as Harrold McFarland sarcastically wrote,

> Without fanfare or previous preparatory announcement, "Christian Standard" dropped the column "World Wide Evangelism" beginning with the issue of the magazine dated December 11th. Editor Burris Butler in that issue editorialized on the problems of "independent missions," published the story of two ministers who have just completed a year of "missionary-evangelistic meetings," and chopped the only regular news coverage the weekly church paper has *carried since it began this policy in an announcement in the issue of June 14, 1952.*[8]

---

6. *Horizons,* September, 1952, p. 2.
7. *Christian Standard,* June 14, 1952, p. 376.
8. *Horizons,* January 1, 1955, p. 1, (italics mine).

In other words, Burris Butler had succeeded in changing the *Christian Standard's* orientation from worldwide evangelism, an orientation which the journal had had for nearly one hundred years, to that of being only a magazine of "local church evangelism."[9] To take up the slack left by the *Christian Standard, Horizons* was expanded in 1955 into an 8-page missionary magazine to report on the ever-growing missionary outreach of the Christian Churches.

During this period, and in part as a result of the above change from an orientation to worldwide evangelism, the *Christian Standard* also ceased attacking the United Christian Missionary Society as a matter of general policy. This policy had actually begun in 1915 when, in an editorial titled "A New Mission Policy," the *Standard* moved from a staunch supporter of the missionary societies to that of a watchdog over the activities and tendencies of the societies. This policy reached a climax in the 1920's with the formation of the UCMS and continued unabated until 1950. But in its July 29, 1950, issue, the *Christian Standard* announced that from that date forward its pages would not be devoted to "controversies over issues that won't matter anyway one hundred years from now!" The controversies, of course, referred to the direction which the UCMS and the Disciples of Christ were taking. More significantly, though, the *Standard* announced that in place of these controversies its energies would now be "pledged — to promote New Testament evangelism — a program of soul-winning and evangelism that will build the Kingdom of God by building the local church." This represented another radical change in direction for the

---

9. Quoted by Harrold McFarland as a personal communication from Burris Butler (*Horizons*, June, 1953, p. 3).

paper, yet, unlike the change mentioned above, it was a wise change, one with far reaching ramifications for a brotherhood of Christian Churches not affiliated with the Disciples of Christ.[10] It meant that the raison d'etre of this brotherhood from this point on would be not in reaction to the Disciples of Christ but to present a positive and aggressive program of proclaiming the plea of the Restoration Movement in the world. Of course, the change was not completed immediately for there was still a great deal of antagonism in the brotherhood against the Disciples of Christ and especially against the UCMS: many Direct-Support missionaries still looked upon themselves as independent missionaries (i.e. Christian Church missionaries serving independently of UCMS). Nevertheless, the change had been set in motion for a future generation of missionaries to complete.

Oddly enough, however, just as the *Christian Standard* and the brotherhood were at last moving on to a more positive program of promoting evangelism, some prominent leaders among the Disciples of Christ decided to take the offensive and go on the attack against those who had, in their estimation, caused all the trouble. Early in 1950, Loren E. Lair, state secretary of the Iowa Christian Missionary Society, brought a $25,000 libel suit against Robert E. Elmore and the Christian Restoration Association alleging defamation of character.[11] The suit was immediately moved

10. From this point on *brotherhood* will refer to Christian Churches and Churches of Christ that are not affiliated with the Disciples of Christ (Christian Church). This separation was made formal when the Disciples of Christ underwent restructure in the 1960's. During this decade the Disciples' congregations were formed into a denominational structure.

11. "Corey Manuscript LXXIV," *Restoration Herald*, Nov. 1960. The *Restoration Herald* also speculated that the reason why the *Christian Standard* changed from attacking the UCMS to a positive policy of evangelism was the possibility of being drawn in as a co-defendent with the CRA in Lair's libel suit. By announcing such a change, a few weeks after Lair's lawsuit, the *Restoration Herald* alleged, the *Standard* left the CRA "holding the bag" to fight the suit alone.

to a Federal Court where the suit was increased to $50,000. Lair argued that he was defamed by Elmore's writings in the *Restoration Herald*. [12] The jury, however, composed of people from various Protestant denominations, returned a verdict that Elmore did not defame Lair or the United Christian Missionary Society. Lair appealed the verdict but to no avail: the appeal courts could discover nothing wrong, either technically or in substance with the conduct of the trial or the verdict. When Lair failed to meet the deadline for appealing to the U.S. Supreme Court the suit was finally dropped. Of more significance than winning the suit, moreover, was what the trial substantiated from a legal viewpoint, namely that open membership and interdenominational federation, which the UCMS advocated, were indeed contrary to the historic position of the Disciples of Christ and that any opposition to such no matter how vigorous was doctrinal in character and not defamatory.

Before Lair's lawsuit against the Christian Restoration Association was concluded, Stephen J. Corey published *Fifty Years of Attack and Controversy*. Corey had had an illustrious career in missions for the Disciples of Christ, first with the Foreign Christian Missionary Society and later as President of the United Christians Missionary Society. In these positions he had been instrumental in negotiating for the Disciples of Christ comity agreements on several mission fields and as a consequence had been a prime target of attack by the *Christian Standard* and the *Restoration Herald* down through the years. Corey charged that

> Repeated attacks on the organized and cooperative agencies and leaders of the brotherhood, led by certain periodicals,

---

12. Stephen J. Corey, *Fifty Years of Attack and Controversy* (St. Louis: Christian Board of Publication, 1953), p. 253.

have disrupted the harmony and thought of this indigenous American Protestant body [re: Disciples of Christ].[13]

The beginning of disruption, according to Corey, began in 1900 when the *Christian Standard* voiced opposition to a federated plan of evangelism favored by the American Christian Missionary Society. By tracing this opposition in his book from this point onward to 1950, Corey provides what can justly be considered as the Disciples of Christ interpretation of the tumultuous events that led to the emergence of Direct-Support Missions among the Disciples of Christ. Naturally, his interpretation differs from what has been given here. One main difference, outside the doctrinal issues of open membership and denominationalism, was that Corey failed to detect and understand the various other dynamics at work in the Restoration Movement which ultimately led to the emergence of the Direct-Support missionary movement and which in turn made the movement a success story in the Restoration Movement. This failure led Corey, in closing his book, to ignore the growth of Direct-Support missions since 1926 and exult only in the growth of the cooperative work of the Disciples of Christ.

Corey's book did not go unanswered. As soon as it was published, Edwin Hayden, then a professor at Ozark Bible College, published a small pamphlet titled "Fifty Years of Digression and Disturbances," which asserted that it was S. J. Corey and his kind who were the real troublemakers over the previous fifty years. In other words, the true problem was not the attacks led by the *Christian Standard,* the *Restoration Herald* and others, but the digression from the historic position of the Restoration Movement.

The *Restoration Herald* also answered S. J. Corey's book. In a remarkable series of articles, that ran for 75 consecutive

---

13. *Ibid.*, p. v.

issues—from "Corey Manuscript I" to "Corey Manuscript LXXV"—the *Restoration Herald* over a period of *seven* years (January 1954 to December 1960) critically reviewed Corey's charges of fifty years of attack and controversies. For each point or event which Corey raised as proof of his accusations, the *Restoration Herald* provided extensive answers to show that the real problem was digression, first by the various missionary societies and then by the UCMS, from the historic position of the Restoration Movement. If such digression had not occurred, as it did for example, in the Guy W. Sarvis case (1911) or in the Leslie Wolfe case (1926), it was argued, there would have been no controversy, much less any attack, by conservative brethren or journals like the *Christian Standard* or *Restoration Herald*. These articles are an excellent collection of facts and documentation concerning the issues and the personalities who figured prominently in the emergence among the Disciples of Christ of the Direct-Support missionary movement.

There was one missionary agency, established soon after World War II, which deserves special mention before leaving this section. That agency was the Christian Missionary Fellowship (CMF), and it deserves special mention because of the controversy its establishment created in the Direct-Support missionary movement. The CMF was incorporated in the State of Kansas in 1949 under the leadership of O. D. Johnson, who had at one time served as a missionary in India.[14] Its purpose was to evangelize non-Christian peoples in the order, manner and fashion of a missionary society. After its formation the CMF applied to the International Convention for permission to present a yearly report, along with the UCMS, of its missionary activities. Hopefully, it

---

14. James DeForest Murch, *Christians Only* (Cincinnati: Standard Publishing, 1964), p. 304.

was argued by its supporters, the presence of a conservative missionary society would be a moderating influence within the International Convention and perhaps would prevent the division between the "cooperatives" (UCMS) and the "independents" from growing any wider. The request to be a reporting agency in the International Convention was not without precedent. Interestingly enough, during these same years of turmoil and de facto division between the Disciples of Christ and "independents," there were two missionary agencies which regularly reported to the International Convention of the Disciples of Christ. One agency was the Brazil Christian Mission,[15] a mission established by Lloyd Sanders who went to Brazil in 1948; the other agency was the European Evangelistic Society. These precedents notwithstanding, the CMF's application was rejected, and it was not long afterwards that the Internation Convention likewise withdrew recognition from the Brazil Christian Mission. The European Evangelistic Society still reports to the Convention (now The General Assembly of the Disciples of Christ).

The CMF as a conservative missionary agency was not popular with the majority of brethren. In fact, it encountered a great deal of hostility and denunciation from several leaders in the brotherhood.[16] Two reasons lay behind this rejection. One, noted in the purpose of the CMF, was the choice of the term "missionary society" to describe its method of performing missionary work. As it turned out, the choice of "society" was unfortunate, because vivid memories of the apostasy of the United Christian Missionary Society were still fresh in the minds of many brethren. Immediately

---

15. *Horizons*, December, 1951.

16. These arguments against the CMF are put forward in *The Christian Missionary Fellowship, Its First Fifteen Years*, by Mark Maxey (San Clemente, Ca.: "Go Ye" Books, 1965).

upon organization, many brotherhood leaders denounced the CMF as a "new UCMS" and warned the churches not to support it. [17] The second reason for the unpopularity of the CMF was its open commitment to structure and organization in carrying out the Great Commission. However, this commitment was made much too early, if indeed it should have been made at all in a brotherhood than zealously on guard to protect its independency from any external organizational structure! This commitment was definitely out of tune with the missionary dynamic which was still gaining impetus and had yet to crest in the brotherhood, viz. individual missionary establishing living link relationships with congregations from which financial support was forthcoming directly to the missionary in the field. It was also out of tune with what was becoming a desire of the brotherhood to forget the past and forge ahead with a positive program of New Testament evangelism. The CMF, organized in the mold of a missionary society, unfortunately reminded many brethren of a more negative, though necessary, period of controversy with the United Christian Missionary Society.

Yet, even though it did not tap the dynamic of Direct-Support missions, the CMF survived, attracted a few missionaries and sent them off to work in India, Japan, Brazil and later Ethiopa. Survival was not without a struggle, however. The opposition, often intense and cutting from within the brotherhood, took its toll on both the missionaries and leadership of CMF. After twelve years of existence (1950-1965), the organization could claim only fifteen missionairies. [18] While all fifteen were serving overseas in India,

17. "I Do Not Recommend Support of the Christian Missionary Fellowship," by Harrold McFarland, *Horizons,* January 5, 1963, pp. 2-3.

18. Mark Maxey, *The Christian Missionary Fellowship: Its First Fifteen Years,* p. 42.

Brazil, Japan and Ethiopa, this still compared unfavorably with the several hundred other Christian Church missionaries who were likewise serving overseas at the end of the same period.[19] It was not until two decades after its establishment, when the brotherhood had largely put out of its mind the sad memories of the United Christian Missionary Society, that the Christian Missionary Fellowship began to gain a measure of acceptance among Christian Churches and was finally able to realize its goal of evangelizing non-Christian people in the order, manner and fashion of a mission society.

1956-1962 New Developments in Recruitment

The growth in the number of Direct-Support missionaries in the years immediately after World War II was made possible by the existence of Bible Colleges. Several Bible Colleges had been established by 1956, but the majority of missionaries were coming from just four institutions: Johnson Bible College, Northwest Christian College, Minnesota Bible College and Cincinnati Bible Seminary. At Cincinnati Bible Seminary, for example, Isabel Maxey Dittermore, who had served a missionary term in Tibet, established in 1942 the World Missionary Volunteers.[20] Among those who were charter members of this group were C. W. and Lois Calloway, Ralph Harter, Mark and Pauline Maxey, Tibbs and Norma Maxey, William and Jean Roland, Dorothy Sterling, Imogine Williams, and M/M Harland Cary. Other colleges, of course, were producing graduates who chose missionary work as their career, and few of the newer colleges (e.g. Lincoln Bible

---

19. At the end of 1965, *Horizons* reported 461 missionaries serving outside the Continental United States.

20. Isabel Maxey Dittermore, *He Leadeth Me,* Joplin, Mo., College Press, 1978, p. 76.

Institute in Illinois) were beginning to supply new personnel for Direct-Support missions. On the other hand, a number of Bible Colleges had yet to send out their first graduates to the mission fields. Ozark Bible College of Joplin, Missouri, was one such school, and it was a matter of concern for Don Earl Boatman, President of the College. His solution was to invite a missionary to come and teach at OBC.

In August of 1956 Woodrow Phillips, who had been serving as a missionary in Jamaica, went to Ozark Bible College as Professor of Missions. This addition of another faculty member to a small Bible College—the total enrollment at OBC that year did not exceed 200 students—did not appear particularly auspicious at the time much less a crucial turning point in the development of Direct-Support Missions. There were hopes, of course, that the additioin of a mission professor for the first time in the short history of the school would expand the school's program for that of training only leaders for churches in America to include also the training of missionaries to preach the gospel in other countries. That these hopes would be realized to the point of becoming a pattern for Direct-Support missions as a whole were not perceived at the time. Yet they were realized in just this way and, as it shall be pointed out below, the pattern which was thus established formed the foundation for the flood of new missionaries from 1963 onward.

Woodrow Phillips first went to Jamaica in 1951 and, with Donald Fream, established a seminary to train ministers and other leaders for the mission churches of that island nation. However, in 1956, Woodrow Phillips, suffering from ill health, was advised to move back and live in the U.S. to regain and maintain his health.[21] The move was the correct

---

21. *Horizons,* August 4, 1956.

prescription, because Woodrow Phillips brought to OBC and to the whole Direct-Support Mission movement an enthusiasm for world missions that was contagious and has yet to abate as a dynamic in the missionary outreach of the Christian Churches.

While the addition of Woodrow Phillips to the faculty of Ozark Bible College in 1956 is considered a crucial turning point in the development of Direct-Support Mission, no true assessment of his role and subsequent impact in mission can be made without taking into account the 9th National Missionary Convention. The Convention had been slated to be held in association with Ozark Bible College in Joplin before Woodrow Phillips arrived to teach at the school. Both were used of God to set in motion dynamics of missionary recruitment and training without which the Direct-Support Missionary movement would perhaps have stagnated. In retrospect it is doubtful how much impact Woodrow Phillips would have had on Direct-Support Missions without the National Missionary Convention, and it is equally doubtful how much influence the Convention would have in subsequent years in mobilizing the brotherhood for greater missionary outreach without Woodrow Phillips joining the OBC faculty when he did.

The 9th National Missionary Convention left a lasting impact upon the student body at Ozark Bible College, an impact which was to grow in intensity under the leadership of Woodrow Phillips in the years to follow and which other Bible Colleges sought to emulate. On the program of that Convention were Gerald Bowlin, Ray Mings, Elmer Kile, Harvey Bream, Jr., Malcolm Coffey and Robert Morse. However, the most significant development which took place during this convention came at the end of a sermon preached by V. Alex Bills, a missionary on furlough from Korea. Since the convention was being held in a city where a Bible College was located, Bills extended an invitation to students at Ozark Bible College to commit their lives to missionary service. To the knowledge of V. Alex Bills, this was the first time that a call for missionary recruits had been issued at the close of a sermon at a National Missionary Convention. Four OBC students responded during the hymn of invitation which followed: Robert Allen, who had already served a missionary internship in Jamaica; David Filbeck, who served over a decade in Thailand; Harvey Bacus, who served in Jamaica; and David Bayless, who went to Brazil as a missionary.[22] Before the convention was over, more OBC students responded to invitations by other speakers, but what was more important than the number of those who responded was the trend that was initiated. It was a trend that was to have far reaching ramifications for the Direct-Support Missionary movement.

What occurred at the 9th National Missionary Convention also had an impact on subsequent conventions. With the invitation issued during this convention to Bible College students to commit their lives to missionary service, the National Missionary Convention assumed a new and greater role: it became a major recruiting agency for new missionaries in the Direct-Support movement. Subsequent to the

---

22. The influence of the sermon and invitation by V. Alex Bills did not end here. Harvey Bacus, after serving in Jamaica became Professor of Missions at Ozark Bible College, and David Filbeck, after spending fifteen years in Thailand, was Professor of Missions at Puget Sound College of the Bible for one year and then joined the faculty of Lincoln Christian Seminary as Professor of Linguistics in the Department of Church Growth and World Missions. In addition to teaching, David Filbeck also serves with the Pioneer Bible Translators.

1956 National Missionary Convention many Bible College students as well as those who were not students of Bible College, made their first commitment to missions at the Missionary Convention. Perhaps the climax of this role came during the 22nd National Missionary Convention, which was held in 1969 at Knoxville, Tennessee and where Johnson Bible College is located. In a moving article titled "Some Came Running,"[23] David Savage recounted how many were wondering how the Knoxville Convention would turn out since at the 1968 Missionary Convention, which was held at San Antonio, Texas, 98 people had answered the invitation to become missionaries. As David Savage told the story there was no need to worry, for at the invitation on the first night of the convention people

> From all over the Civic Auditorium — came down every aisle and from the balcony. Some walked and some came running. Some stepped out slowly with deliberation. Some were crying. Some were elderly, but most were young. All were caught up with a desire to give their lives to Jesus in full-time missionary service. All agreed that the Holy Spirit was acting in their lives. Not everyone that made a public decision for Christ during the convention waited until the last evening. Eighty-one had stepped forward during eight previous invitations making a total of 165 Christians expressing a desire to serve God full time.

Under the impetus which the 9th National Missionary Convention gave to missions at Ozark Bible College, Woodrow Phillips instituted a program of missionary internship at the school. It is uncertain whether this was the first instance

---

23. David Savage, "Some Came Running" mimeograph manuscript (Copeland, Kansas: National Missionary Convention, n.d.).

of missionary internship among the Bible Colleges of the Christian Churches,[24] but it is certain that other Bible Colleges soon came to look upon the Ozark Bible College internship program as the leader in this type of missionary preparation. Moreover, as news of this program became known, it caught the attention of young people who in turn enrolled at OBC for missionary training. A missionary internship, as conceived by Woodrow Phillips, is both a time of testing and introduction for the Bible College student. During the internship, which may last a summer or even longer the student can test his desire to serve as a missionary. If the student decides not to be a missionary, it is better to discover that during an internship than to suffer the agony and embarrassment of discovering it during the first term of missionary service. An internship can also introduce the mission field to a student, revealing to him or her what to expect as a missionary and what further training may be needed. As an introduction to missions, an internship is not a total loss to the student who decides not to become a missionary, because the experience gained during the internship on a mission field often makes the student an enthusiastic supporter of missions for life. But not many who have served missionary internships while Bible College students have failed to return to serve as missionaries. Phillips estimates that three out of four of our current (overseas) missionaries have had some form of internship training. This means that, if this estimation

---

24. Woodrow Phillips, *Internship as a Tool for Recruiting and Selecting Missionaries for Independent Christian Churches*. (Ph.D. dissertation, unpublished). "In our own (Christian) Churches, this concept of internship seems to have begun almost simultaneously in several of our Bible Colleges. In the early 1950's some of our people began to think about how practical it would be to have students spend a summer on an actual mission field."

is true, in 1976 over 400 Direct-Support Missionaries had served internships. Many of these 400 would probably have become missionaries without internship training, but it must still be admitted that this type of training undoubtedly played a major role in the final commitment of these people to serve on the mission field. Since the beginning of missionary internships among the Christian Churches, Woodrow Phillips has noticed that missionaries are staying and working longer than in previous years, a stability which he attributes in part to the missionary internship program.

The home front was not the only area in which Direct-Support Missions were developing during the years 1956-1962. Advances were being made on the mission field as well. By 1956 Max Ward Randall, flying his own airplane from his mission station in South Africa, had surveyed parts of southern Africa still under the control of colonial powers. He found areas in which are now Zimbwabwe-Rhodesia and Zambia where missionaries were needed. In Rhodesia he came into contact with Church of Christ missionaries from New Zealand, who in effect were unable to evangelize all the areas opened to them. They asked Randall to secure missionaries of the Restoration Movement from the United States of America to assume the mission work in the Mashoko area.

The Restoration Movement first reached Rhodesia in 1898 when John Sheriff, a stonemason from New Zealand, settled in that territory, which was then a British Colony, and started a church.[25] The first New Zealand Church of Christ missionaries were Mr. and Mrs. F. L. Hadfield, who arrived in

---

25. Dr. A. C. Watters, "Our Missions in Southern Rhodesia," *Christian Standard*, Nov. 19, 1960, p. 755.

Rhodesia in 1906. Other missionaries from New Zealand as well as from England joined the Rhodesian mission over the years that followed. In 1934, Garfield Todd from New Zealand joined the mission. Todd went on to settle permanently in Rhodesia eventually serving as Rhodesia's Prime Minister from 1953 to 1958. The New Zealand missionaries opened mission stations first in Bulawayo then in Dadys. A third station, Mashoko, was opened in 1920, but it was never adequately supervised. Mashoko was placed under Garfield Todd's supervision, but since his political duties consumed more and more of his time, he began to look for help. He saw in the Direct-Support missionary movement of the United States a source that could provide the help and personnel to take over the Mashoko mission work.[26]

John Pemberton was the first American to answer Garfield Todd's call for help from American churches. Pemberton, along with a fellow student from Kentucky Christian College. Dennis L. Pruett, had already committed himself to missionary service in Rhodesia. While attending the World Convention of the Restoration Movement in 1956, they met with Garfield Todd, who invited them to work with the New Zealand Mashoko mission. Pruett was in medical school at the time, so Pemberton traveled on to Rhodesia, arriving there in September of 1956. On January 1, 1957, the New Zealand brethren turned over the Mashoko work to John Pemberton. Dennis Pruett, now a medical doctor, arrived in 1958 along with three nurses to begin the medical work of the mission.

---

26. The details of the survey and negotiations for the mission fields in Rhodesia and Zambia are told in Randall's book, *We Would Do It Again.* Max Ward Randall, *We Would Do It Again* (Joliet, IL: Missions Service Press, 1957), pp. 194-220.

The mission work of the American Christian Churches in Rhodesia has been, along with the work in the Philippines, one of the most productive in the history of Direct-Support missions. Both institutional methods and evangelism have been used to gather thousands of people into churches. From the beginning, when John Pemberton and Dr. Dennis Pruett entered the country, the advances made in Rhodesia caught the imagination of churches and individuals in America, and from 1958 a large number of missionaries flocked to the mission field to expand the work even further. Of more interest, though, than the excitement aroused in the brotherhood was the enthusiasm which the *Christian Standard* at this point showed toward the Mashoko Hospital project. Not since the days of Leslie Wolfe or J. Russell Morse had the *Standard* lent its *prestige and influence to help* a mission project such as this one get started.

When Dr. Pruett arrived in Rhodesia to begin his mission work, he had to hold his first clinic in a 10 x 12 foot tent. He was soon able to move to a mud house where he continued to treat scores of sick people. Through his acquaintance with Garfield Todd, he began negotiating with the Rhodesian government to build a hospital. The government promised to furnish half the cost of building, so Dr. Pruett designed a 13-bed hospital which would cost $175,000.[27] For his one half of the cost, Dr. Pruett approached leading brethren in the United States, asking them to help him raise the money. He convinced Edwin Hayden, editor of the *Christian Standard,* to help him. In the October 31, 1959 issue of the *Standard* there appeared an article entitled "A Hospital for

---

27. "We Dedicate This Hospital," *Christian Standard*, December 23, 1961, p. 817.

$100,000." The article told of the unusual opportunity which had come available in Rhodesia and the need for immediate action to raise the money for the Mashoko mission hospital. The article also told about prominent preachers and other Christian friends, including the executive editor of Standard Publishing and members of the National Christian Education Convention, who had pledged to back Dr. Pruett to the limit of their ability in raising the needed funds. The article ended with the invitation to readers to send their contributions to the *Standard* for the hospital. Willard Mohorter of Standard Publishing was appointed trustee of these funds.

This article, which was written by Edwin Hayden, also made note of the *Standard's* "bold departure from recent practice" in promoting this particular mission project. In fact, it was such a bold departure that Hayden, under the sensational title "Stop the Presses!," wrote in an accompanying editorial of the same issue a defense for the change in policy. Using the form of a rhetorical question, Hayden began the defense by asking

> Isn't *Christian Standard* breaking rather sharply from its self-chosen practice of recent years in sponsoring a mission project at Mashoko? It is most certainly doing just that, with enthusiasm![28]

The editorial then went on to explain why the *Christian Standard* changed its policy (abruptly made some five years previously) and decided to sponsor this project.

> This is not a competitive project, to make others seem unimportant by comparison, and to draw support from them. It

---

28. Edwin Hayden, "Stop the Presses!," *Christian Standard*, Oct. 31, 1959, p. 604.

is a leading project, well designed to show people everywhere that Christian missions, separately supported from the home churches, each on its own merit, can achieve and have already substantial character, constructive, serving, and capable of rising to the needs and opportunities of the hour. If this project does not result in increased interest and support for faithful missions carrying the plea of the Restoration movement all over the world, we shall be greatly disappointed.[29]

The money was raised in eighteen months, and on August 27, 1961, the Mashoko mission hospital was dedicated debt-free. Edwin Hayden saw in this accomplishment far reaching ramifications for the Direct-Support missionary movement. In an editorial which he wrote a year later, he said of the Mashoko Mission:

This mission is big in concept, big in accomplishment, and practically boundless in possibilities. We have seen well-prepared, capable, and consecrated young people in amazing numbers offering their services in Rhodesia, and now we know why. For too long Christian churches have been content with small projects on mission fields, because we thought that was all we could support. We have done too little in preparing our missionaries and have expected them to work with pitifully inadequate tools.

Dr. Pruett has proved that we can do better![30]

In one respect Edwin Hayden in the editorial was correct in his assessment. Dr. Pruett and others associated with him in the Mashoko mission did indeed prove that Direct-Support missions can do bigger and greater projects. But in another

---

29. *Ibid.*, p. 604.
30. Edwin Hayden, "It Can't Be Done," *Christian Standard*, Oct. 27, 1962, p. 674.

respect Hayden was not entirely correct in his assessment of why Dr. Pruett was able to accomplish all that he did. What Hayden left out in his assessment was this: Dr. Pruett, from the beginning, *enlisting the aid of the Christian Standard in promoting the Mashoko hospital.* In other words, Dr. Pruett tapped into a powerful, historical dynamic of missions in the Restoration Movement, for the *Standard* has always been in the forefront of missions in the Restoration Movement, first through the missionary societies and later in leading the way into the Direct-Support missionary movement. In his assessment Hayden failed to note how powerful a role the *Standard* played in the Mashoko project. Not only did Hayden fail to recognize this role, but he also failed to realize the impact that the *Standard* could have for foreign missions if this role were once again assumed in a more general way in the brotherhood. Great things in foreign missions were accomplished in the past through the pages of the *Christian Standard,* and great things were accomplished in Rhodesia through the *Christian Standard* in 1959.

There was still one other factor that Hayden overlooked in his assessment, and that was the role which he as the editor of the *Christian Standard* played in the successful completion of the Mashoko project. Granted that modesty would prevent him from even mentioning this factor, nevertheless, in agreeing to promote the Mashoko Hospital, Hayden was re-entering the role that editors of the *Christian Standard* — e.g. Isaac Errett during the days of the missionary societies, or Willard Mohorter during the period when Direct-Support missions were beginning — had played in giving the journal its historical orientation in foreign missions. For, without question, the greatest contribution which the editorship of the *Christian Standard* has made in the Restoration Movement has been this basic orientation toward worldwide evangelism. Fortunately this orientation re-emerged during the opening of the Mashoko mission. Unfortunately, after this the *Christian Standard* did not promote, at least to the same extent, other mission projects. If it had, as in times past, we might very well have a greater story to write about in Direct-Support mission from 1963 on.

1963-1976 New Developments in Financing Missions

In the November 9, 1963, issue of the *Christian Standard* there appeared an article written by James Strauss entitled, "A Most Disturbing Little Book."[31] The article reviewed a small paperback with the imposing title of *Triumphant Missionary Ministry in the Local Church,* a book which was later updated and reissued under the title *Faith Promise for World Witness.*[32]

As the latter title states, the paperback was about the Faith Promise concept in raising financial support for missions. The first church to introduce and use the Faith Promise was Park Street Church of Boston, Massachusetts, which was in 1940. However, the concept was not widely adopted until after the book, under its first title, was published in 1960. Since that time many congregations have adopted the Faith Promise program and correspondingly have seen their missionary giving and outreach grow beyond all expectations, as can be seen from this one example given in the book, the Christian Church of Los Gatos, California.

Our Faith Promise story is one of exciting results beyond all expectations. First we read the book, *Triumphant Missionary*

---

31. James Strauss, "A Most Disturbing Little Book," *Christian Standard,* November 9, 1963, p. 769.

32. Norm Lewis, *Faith Promise for World Witness* (Lincoln, NE: Back to the Bible Publication, 1974).

Ministry in the Local Church. Since ours wasn't very triumphant we decided to do everything suggested, just as the book described it.

That was in 1967. Missions giving had been $7,000 and included items not really pertaining to missions. Our first Faith Promise Goal was $10,000. When $27,000 was reached, we were overjoyed![33]

By 1972 this church was giving over $150,000 a year to missions by means of the Faith Promise concept and program.

Paradoxically enough, James Strauss' article on the concept in the *Christian Standard* failed to mention the term Faith Promise. Yet this did not deter the article's influence upon the brotherhood, nor did the oversight prevent the brotherhood from coming in contact with the term and quickly adopting both the term and the program as an exciting new method to support and advance Direct-Support missions. The first Faith Promise in a Christian Church was held that same year, 1963, at the First Christian Church of Fairfield, Illinois. Actually, under the leadership of the minister of that time, Robert E. Reeves, the concept was first discussed and adopted for trial in 1962.[34] When the Faith Promise was finally held in April of the following year, little did the Fairfield congregation and their minister realize that their trial was a turning point in the development of Christian Church missions, not only for themselves but also for the brotherhood as a whole and especially for the Direct-Support missionary movement. From Fairfield the concept spread to the Englewood Christian Church of Jacksonville, Florida and the Palmyra Church of Christ, Fredericktown, Ohio.

---

33. *Ibid.*, p. 82.
34. Nellie Milner, *The First Decade* (privately published by the author; available through the First Christian Church, Fairfield, IL., 1962), p. 1.

From this beginning, hundreds of Christian Churches-Churches of Christ have conducted Faith Promise Missionary Conferences. In nearly every congregation a more vigorous mission program has resulted. In some cases goals have not been met. In others income has failed to equal the Faith Promise. But when comparing the mission programs previous to the Faith Promise conference with that which followed, more is being done for worldwide evangelism than before in the history of the church.[35]

The introduction and adoption of the Faith Promise came none too soon. As noted earlier, the number of Direct-Support missionaries between the years of 1956 and 1962 increased by only 62%, a large drop in the rate of growth compared to the years 1946 to 1955. A major reason for the decrease in the rate of growth no doubt lay in the capacity of the then current methods to raise funds to support all the missionaries it could, viz. the approximately 700 Direct-Support missionaries who were serving at the end of 1962. In other words, without some new and inspiring concept of fund raising, it is doubtful whether the Christian Churches during the 1960's could have exceeded in supporting directly 1,000 missionaries.

There is one more reason why the adoption of the Faith Promise program by Christian Churches/Church of Christ was so timely in 1963. Again, as noted above, even though the rate of growth in the number of new missionaries was decreasing between the years 1956 to 1962, there was, on the other hand, during this same time an upsurge in recruiting new missionaries from among Bible College students, especially through the National Missionary Convention.

---

35. Gene Dulin, *The Faith Promise Missionary Conference* (Indianapolis: TCM International, 1968), p. 20.

According to Mark Maxey,[36] it takes on the average six years for a new missionary recruit to finish his training, raise his support, and reach the mission field. Accepting this average, or even some slightly lower computation, we can see that there was building up such a supply of new missionaries in the six-year period between 1956 and 1962 that by the year 1963 — and for the years following — the Direct-Support method would have been taxed to the limits of its capabilities to support all of them. But the introduction of the Faith Promise program made available new funds to support the many new missionaries who were recruited before as well as the many hundreds of others who came after 1963.

The impact which the Faith Promise concept has had upon the Direct-Support missionary movement cannot be overestimated. It is not known, nor can it be computed, just how much more income for missions has been produced by the adoption of this concept, but, if the example of the Christian Church of Fairfield, Illinois is any true indication, the extra income gathered was beyond all that could be expected or hoped for, since in this congregation alone from $13,378.25 committed in the first Faith Promise in 1963, the amount committed ten years later in 1972 was $56,915.42.[37] This amounts to a 425% increase this one congregation in the amount of funds made available for missions.

This bringing together of recruitment and the Faith Promise concept created a missionary dynamic which in a very short time produced once more accelerated growth in Direct-Support Missions. Figure 1 shows in graphic form the acceleration that took place between 1963 and 1976. The graph

---

36. Mark Maxey, "Statistics," *Horizons*, June 5, 1976, p. 10.

37. Milner, *The First Decade*, p. 47. See also David Savage, "A Second Time Around," *Christian Standard*, May 17, 1969, p. 331.

shows that between 1963 and 1967 there was a steady and fairly steep incline in the rate of new missionaries coming into the Direct-Support movement. The rate leveled off slightly from the previous period. For the total fourteen year period, however, the graph shows an impressive and fairly consistent steep rate of increase in the number of Direct-Support missionaries, a rate of increase made possible in large measure by the new funds generated by Faith Promise programs during this same period of time.

GROWTH IN NUMBER OF DIRECT-SUPPORT MISSIONARIES
SINCE ADOPTION OF FAITH PROMISE PROGRAM

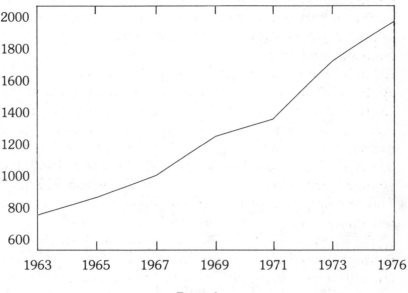

Figure 1

At the same time when so many new missionaries were being recruited new mission fields were opened, and existing mission fields received an influx of new workers. But of more interest than the increase in numbers of new missionaries during this period is the diversity of new works and services which have been initiated under the free and unstructured system of Direct-Support Missions. Without the constraints imposed by a central organizational structure, Direct-Support missionaries have recently initiated a wide range of new mission enterprises both at home and abroad. Since home missions will be discussed in more detail in the next chapter, we will confine our remarks to the diversity that has developed in foreign missions in the Direct-Support movement.

In addition to evangelism and planting congregations after the New Testament pattern, Direct-Support missionaries have instituted a wide variety of services around the world. From the establishment of hospitals in Rhodesia there has arisen the Fellowship of American Medical Evangelists (FAME), an organization dedicated to establishing more hospitals in other mission fields, notably India. Primary and secondary educational institutions have been established in Rhodesia, India, and the Philippines. Missionaries in Zaire, Brazil, Chile, South Africa, among other places, have specialized in translating, printing and distributing Bible study materials. Taking their cue from the Philippines (where five Bible Colleges are in operation), Bible Colleges have been established in India, Ghana, in addition to training centers in several other places. Radio ministries beam the plea of the Restoration Movement into Europe, behind the Iron Curtain and into Asia. Bibles and hymnals are printed and distributed in lands where Christian literature is restricted. In 1972 the International Disaster Emergency Service (IDES) was established to collect funds and distribute emergency supplies to areas hit by natural disasters. During this time, also, the declining state of the Restoration Movement in countries as England, Australia and New Zealand came to the attention of American Christian Churches. Ministers were subsequently recruited to spend time strengthening the churches in these countries. Out of this was established the South Pacific Evangelistic Fellowship, an organization to help Restoration churches in Australia and New Zealand.

In 1974 the Pioneer Bible Translators (PBT) was organized. Actually PBT was the convergence of two separate projects to enlist Christian Churches in the missionary task of translating the Bible into the 2,000-to-3,000 languages of the world which do not yet have the Bible. Al Hamilton, a veteran missionary, first conceived the idea of an organization to recruit from among Christian Churches, especially in Bible Colleges and Campus Ministries, people who would be trained in linguistics and related subjects to translate the Scriptures into these languages of the world.[38] After training, these recruits could then join the Wycliff Bible translators (WBT), a non-sectarian organization. At the same time, Max Ward Randall, Professor of Missions at Lincoln Christian College, began conversations with the Wycliff Bible Translators about Bible College students of the Christian Churches doing the missionary work of Bible translation under the auspices of WBT. At this point, however, both Hamilton and Randall encountered an obstacle: the Wycliff Bible Translators did not wish to have any person brought up in the tradition of the Campbellian Restoration Movement as a member of the

---

38. David Filbeck, "The Pioneer Bible Translators," *Christian Standard*, Dec. 7, 1975, pp. 1108-1110.

WBT organization unless, of course, that person agreed, in a signed statement, to suppress his or her strong commitment to the necessity of immersion for the forgiveness of sin. When a few Bible College graduates, upon applying to WBT for membership, were rejected on the grounds that their doctrinal commitment to immersion is incompatible with the nonsectarian policy of WBT, both Hamilton and Randall merged their efforts and reorganized the Pioneer Bible Translators to become a full-fledged missionary agency of the Christian Churches.

In all this diversity it is interesting to note a development that almost took place within the Direct-Support missionary movement, a development that, had it been realized, would have had a significant impact not only upon Direct-Support missions but upon Christian missions in general as well. In 1961, Donald McGavran, having served several years as a missionary to India under the United Christian Missionary Society, established the School of World Missions at Northwest Christian College, Eugene, Oregon, and began to recruit missionaries and missionary recruits from within the Christian Churches to study missions and church growth principles under him. However, in 1965, McGavran moved his School of World Mission to Fuller Theological Seminary and although McGavran's thinking on missions and church growth has been well received at Fuller, the move nevertheless delayed for some years the dissemination of these ideas in Direct-Support Missions. While the matter is now purely academic, one may still wonder what new trends and patterns —i.e. new dynamics—would have really developed in Direct-Support Missions had McGavran remained at Northwest Christian College or at one of the other Bible Colleges of the Christian Churches.

Out of all the diversity — and by no means is all of it itemized above — that has occurred recently in Direct-Support Missions, there is one development that deserves to be noticed. Direct-Support missions are becoming more structured and organizationally oriented. That is, as Direct-Support Missions increase in the number of missionaries, we can observe a lessening of individual enterprises and the banding together of more individuals in organizations to work together. This recent trend has no doubt been helped along by the survival of the Christian Missionary Fellowship, which underwent some early severe criticism because of its orientation toward organizational structure. But there have been other factors. For example, certain governments in Africa have imposed upon Direct-Support Missions a requirement for entry into their respective countries more organizational structure than what was formerly thought necessary or even legitimate. Nevertheless, in order to enter such nations, organizational structures were created and acted as mission boards, although for particular nations only and not for the brotherhood as a whole. This represented a significant move from the extreme independency of former years and showed that more structure was indeed possible without compromising the emphasis on the importance and primacy of the local church. As a result, several people began to put together organizations comprising both missionaries and staffs of promotional directors, secretaries, printers and other personnel.

There is one consequence from this increased orientation toward organizational structure in missions which should be noted, because it may very well portend a new trend — hence a change in the dynamic — in the Direct-Support missionary movement. The increase in the number of mission agencies has also brought about corresponding reliance upon these agencies to fulfill the church's commission of evangelizing the world. Specifically congregations and individual Christians are more and more transferring their own duties in this regard to para-church agencies. There is nothing unexpected in this: it parallels what has been occurring in American society and churches for some time. Sociologically, for example, we have transferred the job of educating our children to the school and school teacher, of social control to the court or policeman, of entertainment to the television and professional actor, etc. More crucially, we have largely transferred the various tasks of the Church to the religious specialist—the minister, youth minister, children's home director, Bible College professor, etc. It is no wonder then to see the same development taking place in regard to the church's duty of implementing the Great Commission in the world.

One result of this increased reliance on the para-church agency has been a general weakening of the Living Link concept in Direct-Support missions.[39] If it is (sociologically) more convenient to transfer the church's mission of worldwide evangelism to the para-church agency, then it is also more convenient to have the missionary "linked" directly to the agency instead of the local congregation. This has in turn weakened the linkage between the missionary and church. Another factor which has caused the Living Link concept to weaken has been economics. The inflation rate over the past few decades has lessened the meaning which the Living Link relationship entails between a missionary and a church. Traditionally, if a church furnishes $100 a

---

39. David Filbeck, *If You Want To Be A Missionary* (Joplin, MO: College Press, 1977), pp. 28-39.

month support to a missionary, that church was considered as the Living Link for a missionary. Of course, in years past, $100 had more buying power and, consequently, meant more by way of Living Link. But the decrease in buying power of the American dollar in recent years has also brought an accompanying decrease in the symbolic value and importance of the traditional $100 in establishing firm Living Link relationships between missionaries and churches. Fortunately, many churches have offset this weakening effect by increasing the amount given as Living Link to missionaries. It is not uncommon today to hear of a single congregation giving $500 or more as its Living Link to a missionary.

It is essential for the Direct-Support missionary movement that the Living Link concept be kept alive and strong. Its current weakening, I believe, lies behind much of the criticism we hear today of Direct-Support missions. While such criticism is yet minimal, it still represents a desire to hold the para-church agency and not the church accountable for fulfilling the Great Commission. But the bottom line of this accountability is the local church, and any attempt to transfer it to the agency is to invite dissatisfaction and criticism. For a healthy relationship between the church and its mission in the world, there must be a strong linkage between the local congregation and those who are charged with carrying out that mission. When a local church gives up this linkage or weakens it in some way, the Direct-Support missionary movement suffers and, worse still, the missionary outreach of the church often goes unfulfilled. Perhaps the greatest task that lies before us in the Direct-Support missionary movement as we look to the future is to make sure the Living Link concept undergoes no further erosion but rather is strengthened to assure that more and more Christian Churches are enlisted in evangelizing the world.

The trend toward more diversity and para-church structure in Direct-Support missions is evident. Several questions about what this trend means for the future, of course, remain to be answered. For example, will this trend continue and eventually change the character of Direct-Support missions? Do the structural developments we see now taking place represent a changing missionary dynamic for the future? Will all the diversity we have witnessed in Direct-Support missions since 1963 survive, or will some of it (if not most of it) disappear leaving only a core of missionary enterprises for a future generation of missionaries to carry on? It is too early, of course, to assess the diversity, as well as the new structural orientation that has accompanied it and accurately forecast the dynamics of Direct-Support missions in the future. This must be left for future historians.

A. B. McReynolds
and family - 1959

Leland Tureell

Dr. Dennis Pruett and Betty Iddings

In the picture are: Dr. Norton Bare,
Edgar Nichols and J. Russell Morse - 1938-43.

Ashley S. Johnson

Robert M. Lillie

The Vernon Brothers and wives

Chapter Eight

HOME MISSIONS: THE FIRST FIFTY YEARS

Up to this point, our history of the Direct-Support missionary movement has focused only on foreign missions. Nothing has been related concerning the progress of home missions. It is time to dip back into history once more and bring us up to date, this time with regard to missions in the United States which were also supported independently of the various state societies of the Disciples of Christ.

Delaying any accounting of home missions until now is not to say that nothing of significance was taking place in home missions during the years of development in foreign missions. Much was happening on the home front as well; however, home missions were overshadowed by the issues of open membership and (supra) organizational legitimacy in foreign missions. Such issues soon spilled over into home missions also, but by that time precedents for resolving these issues on the foreign mission field had been initiated, and so it was only a matter of implementing similar procedures for home missions as well.

This does not mean that home missions in the Christian Churches have been the younger brother to foreign missions; it means only that the issues involved were livelier and more emotional abroad than in home missions. Quite the contrary has been the case, for as time progressed churches turned more and more attention to home missions and the need for home missionary work until in recent years the number of home missionaries has approached the number of foreign missionaries in the Christian Churches.

1919-1925: The Clarke Fund

Home missions, operating independently of the various national and state missionary societies, received an early

249

boost among the Disciples of Christ by the formation of the Sidney S. Clarke Estate.[1] The Estate was established in 1919 under the supervision of the Elders of the Richmond Street Christian Church of Cincinnati, Ohio. Clarke's will specified that funds from the Estate were to be used to establish new churches in "destitute places," a term which was "interpreted to mean communities where there is no New Testament Church of Christ."[2] Under the direction of a board of trustees established by the elders of the Richmond Street Church, new churches were planted and weak congregations assisted. By 1921, two years after its formation, the Clarke Estate had been used to establish some thirty new congregations in Ohio, Oklahoma, Illinois, Arkansas, Virginia, Michigan and Iowa. In addition, 200 weak congregations in eleven states were assisted. Over 6,000 people had been baptized in the two-year period.

As a result of the above experience, an eight-part plan of work was formulated and adopted by the trustees of the Clarke Estate for the planting of new churches:

1. Survey fields destitute of Churches of Christ.
2. Hold series of evangelistic meetings in an area selected (all expenses guaranteed by the Estate but offerings taken to offset expenses of the meetings).
3. Organize a New Testament Church.
4. Set the Church in order.
5. Provide pastoral care.
6. Survey adjoining areas for the planting of additional churches.

---

1. See Chapter Six above.
2. James DeForest Murch, "A Group Evangelism Sending Station," *Christian Standard*, Jan. 22, 1921, p. 1787.

7. The central church becomes a "mother church" in providing workers to plant "daughter churches" in adjoining areas.

8. All new congregations to send semi-annual reports to the trustees of the Clarke Estate for a period of not less than five years to guarantee oversight of their progress.

To implement the plan in an area, an evangelist was hired by the trustees to enter the area and begin the plan of surveying and planting a church.

In 1921 a new fund was was added to the Clark Estate. A plan was approved by the trustees to allow voluntary contributions from interested individuals and churches to the Estate in order to accumulate more funds for the work of establishing new churches. Accordingly the Estate was divided into two funds: 1) the original Clarke Estate, deriving funds from interest bearing securities and rentals, and 2) the Clarke Fund, obtaining funds from voluntary contributions. The two funds were to be kept as separate accounts under the supervision of the trustees but used according to the provision of the will of Sidney S. Clarke. To further assure that all monies received would be used according to Clarke's will, an advisory board made up of prominent ministers was established to help the trustees in administering the funds. One means of raising funds to supplement the original Clarke Estate was to invite individuals and churches to assume "living link" support of an area which had been surveyed for a new church or for a missionary who would be establishing a new church in a new area.

Four years later, in 1925, under the clouds of controversy with the United Christian Missionary Society over open membership on foreign mission fields, the Clarke Estate/Fund underwent a reorganization.[3] The Fund itself was separated from the Estate and expanded to support foreign missions as well as home missions. At the same time the Fund was removed from the control of the elders of the Richmond Street Church, being placed wholly under the supervision of a self-perpetuating board of trustees. A new name, the Christian Restoration Association, was chosen for the new organization. A major purpose of the new organization was to serve as a "clearing house" for all free missionary and benevolent agencies, both at home and abroad. As a clearing house the Christian Restoration Association would receive funds from contributions and forward them to the missionary or agency so designated. The CRA would in turn act as publicity agent for missionaries and agencies.

However, there was more to this reorganization of the Clarke Fund than just the expansion needed to include foreign missions. There was, at this time, a growing distrust of the capability of local congregations to withstand successfully the incorporating efforts of the UCMS and the state societies. Many congregations were, of course, aligning themselves with the societies and not with the independents. Other congregations were wavering. For many of these latter congregations, their ultimate alignment depended on what type of minister each obtained (e.g. pro-society or pro-independent) or which power-block (pro-society or pro-independent) in the congregation could influence the membership to declare allegiance to one side or the other. Moreover, should such an allegiance be declared, it might only be temporary, since

---

3. "Plan Undenominational Missionary Service," *Christian Standard*, Jan. 3, 1925, p. 346.

ministers moved and power-blocks within congregations changed due to death, change of mind or apathy. In other words, in the minds of many conservatives, the situation in 1925 was too unstable to allow any one congregation to be in control of an important independent agency as the Clarke Fund. There could be no certainty that any such congregation would not in the near or distant future be brought under the control of the UCMS or a state society, at which time the independent agency would be dismantled or even incorporated into the work of the society.

This was the fear of the trustees of the Clarke Fund as they considered the need for reorganization.

> The purpose of the trustee grows, first of all, out of the conviction that a work of such general character as the Clarke Fund ought not to be subject to the vicissitudes of the local congregation. There are always but a limited number of members in any congregation intelligently interested in the larger work. There is always a large element of the congregation that can be easily swayed by any demagogue or schemer who may get into the pulpit, eldership or other place of power. A loyal congregation may be captured very easily by a liberal preacher, especially if he definitely purpose to do so.
>
> Despite the fact that those loyal to the Clarke Fund are definitely and safely in control of the affairs of the Richmond Street Church, they are eager to have the Clarke Fund separated from the church, because recent events have clearly revealed the perils of such a connection, both to the church and to the larger work.[4]

Under the rationale that the larger work (i.e. foreign missions in addition to home missions) required a corresponding

---

4. *Ibid.*

enlargement of counsel (i.e. multi-congregational), the trustees moved to create a self-perpetuating board of trustees of not less than nine members. To assure that the Fund, now renamed the Christian Restoration Association, would be free from vicissitudes of any one congregation in regard to future allegiance, the self-perpetuating board would "choose its own members from year to year with due discretion." It was, in short, a reorganization which turned the Clarke Fund into a non-profit, religious organization, autonomous of any congregation as a free para-church agency.

Realizing that this was the course they were taking, the trustees of the Clarke Fund disavowed any intention of assuming ecclesiastical or authoritative control over congregations or other para-church agencies. For this reason, it was explained that

> . . . we definitely decline the suggestion that our trustees and officers be chosen and our work passed upon in an assembly of loyal brethren. If we had permitted such connection to be made — we should have opened the door to a train of evils, not the least of which would have been the assumption on our part of a position that would at once have placed the others (such as the Yotsuya Mission, the Mexican Mission, the Christian Woman's Benevolent Association, etc.) under a handicap. Brethren would at once have claimed for us some official character. This we distinctively disclaim. We are frankly a free, self-perpetuating board, deserving the support of the brethren only so long as we serve them as they desire.[5]

Incorporated as a non-profit, religious organization, autonomous from any local congregation, the Christian

---

5. *Ibid.*

Restoration Association established a precedent for the initiation and conduct of independent mission enterprises among the Christian Churches. Other missions, both home and foreign, soon followed suite and incorporated themselves as non-profit organizations. It has been a precedent, furthermore, that the vast majority of Direct-Support missions have followed since. Ironically, it must be pointed out, there was no difference legally between what the trustees of the Clarke Fund did to incorporate the CRA from the way that the UCMS or a particular state missionary society was incorporated; both essentially had to follow the same laws and regulations for incorporation. Theologically, however, there was a vast difference and still is between an incorporated mission agency and an ecclesiastical organization such as the UCMS. The Christian Restoration Association hastened to assure the brotherhood that it too knew what the difference was, and was willing to accept the role of being only an agency.

This precedent soon became a dynamic for home missions in the Direct-Support missionary movement. To initiate a home mission project, it was recommended first of all to organize, as this editorial article from a 1935 issue of the *Restoration Herald* illustrates under the appropriate title "Our Organized Work."

> The way to organize is very simple. Years ago in Southern California the writer got thirteen people together and this group elected him President of the Southern California Christian Evangelistic Association. Enough money was pledged and Clayton C. Root was named as evangelist. He began his work by holding a revival during which he planted a New Testament Church. This (organization) continued and in 3 years there were planted fifteen New Testament Churches.

Thus in whatever section you live, call the brethren together who are free and independent in their spiritual make-up.
Organize them and start the fireworks by holding a revival
to establish a New Testament Church.[6]

It is interesting to note that such a dynamic, in contradis-
tinction to what was assumed in Direct-Support missions, in
effect by-passed the local congregation in initiating and
conducting mission projects by creating an organization of
(interested) individuals from several congregations. One
reason for this by-passing of the local congregation was the
initial distrust in the beginning days of the Direct-Support
movement of a congregation's ability to remain free of the
missionary society. By the time that such distrust had at
last been laid to rest in the brotherhood, the precedent was
too well established to change. By this time there was a
more practical reason for by-passing the local congregation
and establishing a para-church agency to initiate a mission
project. Mobilizing individual brethren who were interested
in the project from several congregations into a single non-
profit organization or agency could be achieved much more
quickly than mobilizing a whole congregation. An agency,
in other words, can more quickly initiate and complete a
project. Not only did the nonprofit organization by-pass the
slow acting local congregation, it also allowed interested
individuals to by-pass disinterested or even antagonistic
brethren that might be in control of the local congregation.
Through the nonprofit, religious organization, therefore,
individuals could band themselves together to evangelize
unchurched areas more quickly.

---

6. "Our Organized Work," *Restoration Herald,* Jan. 1935, p. 14.

1926-1945: Regaining Lost Ground

The Clarke Fund, the forerunner of the Christian Restoration Association, had been established to "Cover America with the Plea."[7] This was done by establishing new churches. Meanwhile new church evangelism in America had largely been neglected by the United Christian Missionary Society and its sister organizations, the various state societies. This neglect, according to the 1931 Year Book of the Disciples of Christ, resulted in a loss of 72 churches and 4,924 members during the previous year.[8] Moreover, during this same year (1930), only seven out of 50 state missionary organizations reported the establishment of eight new churches. After the Clarke Fund had been reorganized into the Christian Restoration Association, an even more aggressive program, reminiscent of earlier frontier days under the American Christian Missionary Society, of planting new churches was begun. Evangelists, under the encouragement and auspices of the CRA scattered throughout the land to establish local atonomous congregations after the order of the New Testament pattern, free of affiliation with the Disciples of Christ and the oversight of the state missionary societies.

Baptizing and gathering disciples into new congregations were the main thrust of CRA evangelists in the early years of the organization. In 1925, when the Clarke Fund became the Christian Restoration Association, 1,212 people were baptized and 14 new churches were established.[9] Four evangelists were supported by the CRA: J. S. Rauns, T. H. Adams, C. C. Root, and Edward Clutter. The following year,

---

7. *Restoration Herald*, Feb. 1932, p. 5.

8. James DeForest Murch, "A Mission For Home Missions," *Restoration Herald*, Feb. 1932, pp. 5-6.

9. *Restoration Herald*, March 1926, p. 20.

1926, 1,023 were baptized and 13 new churches were planted.[10] A fifth evangelist, P. O. Gates, was added by the CRA and was personally responsible for the establishment of five of the thirteen new congregations in 1926. In 1927, 785 people were baptized resulting in 12 new churches being started.[11] Tents were now being extensively used by CRA evangelists. The number of CRA evangelists doubled in 1927 from five to ten full-time evangelists. In 1928, 551 people were baptized and seven new churches established.[12] In 1929, Murch, editor of the *Restoration Herald*, called for an even greater effort in new church planting.

> In the beginning of the program, churches and individuals pledged themselves to plant more than 100 new churches by Pentecost, 1930. Through the liberality of a Missouri brother, F. W. Strong was added to our staff. Plans were inaugurated by which an evangelist for every state will eventually be added to the staff. The aim of this department is to "Cover North America with the Plea."[13]

In 1932, Murch claimed that the goal of 100 new churches had been reached,[14] for in the ten year period between 1921 and 1931 (during which time the Clarke Fund became the Christian Restoration Association) Murch reported that 122 new churches had been planted, of which 111 were still functioning. There had also been 6,553 people baptized during this period (for an average of over 650 a year).

Home evangelism as well as foreign missions caught the imagination of conservative churches and individual Christians among the Disciples of Christ. In 1932 James DeForest

---

10. *Restoration Herald*, March 1927, p. 15.
11. *Restoration Herald*, March 1928, pp. 20-21.
12. *Restoration Herald*, March 1929, p. 21.
13. *Ibid.*
14. *Restoration Herald*, Feb. 1932, p. 5.

Murch in the pages of the *Restoration Herald* called for "A Million for Home Missions."[15] Citing the neglect of the UCMS in establishing new churches, Murch called for a $1,000,000 Fund to be raised to support preachers and evangelists in planting new churches. Funds poured in to the Christian Restoration Association designated for the support of evangelists and the planting of new churches. Wealthy individuals often underwrote the full support of individual evangelists, as in the case of A. D. Milroy, who supported the work of a CRA evangelist in Texas and upon his death in 1934, willed the CRA the equivalent of $125,000 for the support of New Testament evangelism.[16] This type of support, both spiritual and financial, attracted capable evangelists to the ranks of the CRA. One capable CRA evangelist was Frances W. Strong, originally a merchant who soon became a well-known evangelist even outside the ranks of the Christian Restoration Association.

> F. W. Strong . . . spent almost a decade in mercantile business before he finally yielded to importunities of friends to give his life to preaching. . . . When he finally yielded . . . (he) sold his business, moved to Denton (Texas) and then to Fort Worth, where he spent six years in Brite Bible College.
>
> He has been distinctively an evangelist. Each summer while at T.C.U. he had more calls for meetings than he could answer. For three of these years he led the Texas preachers in numbers of converts, and for eight years his converts were equal to half of those won by the whole staff.[17]

---

15. James DeForest Murch, "A Million For Home Missions," *Restoration Herald*, Feb. 1932, pp. 5-6.

16. *Restoration Herald*, Feb. 1932, p. 6.

17. "The Merchant Turned Evangelist," *Christian Standard*, April 1, 1939, p. 291.

F. W. Strong was responsible for the establishment of more new congregations than any other evangelist of his day.[18] In 1939 he took over a small Bible institute in northwest Arkansas that had all but closed down and began what later became Ozark Bible College. He moved the college to Joplin, Missouri in 1941 and remained closely associated with this preacher training school until his death in 1947.

In the early years of the Christian Restoration Association, no essential differentiation was made between missions and evangelism, except foreign evangelism was generally called missions and home missions evangelism. The goal of either, as far as the CRA and conservative Disciples were concerned, was the evangelization of the lost, baptizing them and gathering them into functioning congregations. Anything that contributed to the achievement of that goal was called evangelism or missions. Consequently, according to the CRA, Bible College and seminaries were classified as evangelistic agencies (i.e., home missions) of the Christian Churches, because they contributed in a direct way to the training of preachers and missionaries to evangelize the world. Moreover, such institutions were free of the United Christian Missionary Society (and the UCMS Board of Higher Education) and received financial support direct from churches and individuals as any foreign missionary did.

Even before the Christian Restoration Association came into existence the Bible College was considered a legitimate mission in the Restoration Movement. The first four Bible Colleges established in the Restoration Movement were totally evangelistic in nature. Indeed, as Marshall Leggett

---

18. This was stated by F. W. Strong in a personal communication to the author's parents (circa 1941).

states, they "manifested the intense desire to reach people with the message of Christ and the plea for the restoration of primitive Christianity felt by many late nineteenth century and early twentieth century leaders of the Movement."[19] The four colleges were Johnson Bible College (1893), Northwest Christian College (1895), Minnesota Bible College (1913), and Kentucky Christian College (1919). Two people prominent in these early years were Ashley S. Johnson, who founded Johnson Bible College, and Eugene Sanderson. Both men had the vision of using education as a means for evangelizing the lost. Of the two, Sanderson had the greater vision, but unfortunately was unable to realize all his dream.

In 1895 Sanderson moved to Eugene, Oregon, and established Eugene Bible University (later Northwest Christian College) adjacent to the University of Oregon. Under the inspiration of Sanderson, David Olson, a graduate of Eugene Bible University, returned in 1908 to his home state of Minnesota and began working with C. S. Osterhaus, a former Norwegian Lutheran minister. Together Olson and Osterhaus established the Scandinavian Christian Missionary Society (1912), which was reorganized the following year into the International Christian Missionary Association.[20] The purpose of the Association was to evangelize immigrants residing in America, and to train foreigners to return to work among their people. To facilitate this purpose, the International Christian Bible College (later Minnesota Bible College) was founded in 1913 in Minneapolis. The college,

---

19. Marshall J. Leggett, *Historical Factors in the Rise of the Bible College*, unpublished M.A. thesis, Butler University, 1961, p. 12.

20. Henry E. Webb, *A History of the Independent Mission Movement of the Disciples of Christ*, unpublished Th.D. dissertation, Southern Baptist Theological Seminary, 1954, p. 235.

however, ran into financial problems and had to be put into the hands of receivers in 1921. Two years later Sanderson organized the International Bible Mission and incorporated both the International Christian Bible College and the International Christian Missionary Association into its structure. The International Bible Mission was an ambitious program, intending to establish a network of Bible Colleges (including other agencies) all over the United States.[21] By 1928 the mission listed the following institutions.

> Eugene Bible University—including Eugene Bible College, School of Elocution and Oratory, and School of Music; Home and School for Girls, Home for the Aged, Pacific Christian Hospital and Nurses' Training School at Eugene, Oregon; Seattle Bible College at Seattle, Washington; Minneapolis Bible College at Minneapolis, Minnesota; Colorado Bible College at Fort Collins, Colorado; Kansas Bible Bible College at Manhattan, Kansas; Home and School for Boys, El Monte, California; Home and School for Boys, Turner, Oregon; Missouri Christian College at Camden Point, Missouri.[22]

The International Bible Mission collapsed in 1929, and all of its institutions either folded or managed to survive as independent enterprises. Undaunted Sanderson moved to Los Gatos, California, and founded in 1932 the Evangel University which later became San Jose Bible College.[23]

There was still another reason why Bible Colleges were considered missions in the Direct-Support missionary movement. As was noted above, many Christian Churches had

21. Marshall J. Leggett, *Historical Factors in the Rise of the Bible College*, p. 24.

22. Henry E. Webb, *A History of the Independent Mission Movement of the Disciples of Christ*, pp. 237-238.

23. Marshall J. Leggett, *Historical Factors in the Rise of the Bible College*, pp. 25-26.

closed their doors and ceased to function under the steward-
ship of the United Christian Missionary Society and the
various state societies. It was, for example, estimated that,
of all the churches which had been established in the State
of Missouri, approximately half of them had closed their
doors by the opening of World War II. In Illinois, it was reported that between 1913 and 1943, 174 Christian Churches
had died.[24] The mission, therefore, perceived by conservative Disciples was to reopen these closed churches. Since
many of these churches had been closed because of the lack
of preachers, the strategy used to reopen them was the
establishment of Bible Colleges to recruit and train preachers
who in turn would reopen closed churches. From this perspective, establishing a Bible College became a mission
enterprise in its own right, since its ultimate purpose was
not education for its own sake but the fulfillment of a broader
mission of regaining for the Restoration Movement what had
been lost by the Disciples of Christ. In response to this need,
seventeen Bible Colleges had been established by 1945.

The *Restoration Herald* was not the only journal reporting and promoting evangelism in America during the early
years of independency from the United Christian Missionary
Society and the various state societies under its control.
The *Christian Standard* likewise devoted space to the pro-
mulgation of new church evangelism in the USA. During
the darkest days of the Depression (1929-1939), when funds
for home missions were at their lowest, C. J. Sharp, through
the pages of the *Christian Standard*, promoted a volunteer
service of home evangelism called Contributed Work. This
was volunteer evangelism donated without remuneration.

24. Earl C. Hargrove, "What Faith and Vision Can Accomplish," *Christian
Standard*, March 6, 1954, p. 145.

Contributed Work (consisted) of revival efforts conducted for any church that cannot and would not otherwise have a revival, or for a closed church or unentered point, or in an outpost. The work may also consist of Sunday afternoon or week-night preaching, for any of the above it may consist of schoolhouse preaching, gospel-band and gospel-team work for needy or unentered points, or of volunteer missions, mission Bible schools, etc.[25]

For the years of 1931 to 1934, the reported results of such volunteer evangelism were tabulated and given an estimated cost equivalent.

If one will add (up) . . . the . . . "closed churches reopened," "new churches planted" and "outposts maintained," it becomes apparent that the gospel was preached in 417 places where otherwise it would not have been preached at all.

The number of days contributed is equal to fifty-six evangelists giving full time for one year each. To have hired this work done would have taken $100,000. This work was contributed, for the most part, by humble workers, many of them were on very short pay, and some with no income at all.[26]

The emphasis among Christian Churches in independent home missions in the years before World War II was on new church evangelism. However, there were also at this time "home missions" in a more traditional sense of the term, namely establishing religious and educational institutions in an economically depressed area of the United States and supporting such by mission contributions from more affluent areas. Perhaps the earliest example of this

---

25. "Contributed Work," *Christian Standard*, June 15, 1935, p. 570.
26. *Ibid.*
27. "How the Restoration Movement Entered a Mountain Country," *Christian Standard*, 1942, p. 884.

was the Grundy Mountain Mission of Grundy, Virginia.[27] Evangelists of the Restoration Movement preached at Grundy as early as 1910 and performed several baptisms in this mountain community. In 1912 a church was finally established, and in 1921 a mission school was organized under the direction of Sam R. Hurley to serve the mountainous area of western Virginia through evangelism and education. On the other side of the USA during this same time, churches in Arizona were evangelizing among the Indians.[28] In 1931, the Apache Mission in Phoenix was established under the oversight of three elders of the Central Christian Church of Phoenix. Mission work among other Indian tribes and ethnic minorities was established by Arizona Churches. An interesting footnote to mission work in Arizona was the organized way in which it was conducted, i.e. the Arizona Churches conceived themselves as a state convention of churches conducting home mission work among the Indians by means of a (state) missionary society. However, as R. E. Elmore, a minister in Arizona at the time, explained this did not imply any affiliation with the UCMS.

> A clear word concerning the Arizona work should be given. First, this is a mission field. Long drained by general promoters, for many years the churches have struggled for existence, some dying. The brethren co-operating in this convention few years ago decided to shuffle off outside yokes, and get down to the business of evangelizing and edifying the local churches in the state. This decision was the turning point, and from that day to this the cause has prospered.

---

27. "How the Restoration Movement Entered a Mountain Country," *Christian Standard*, 1942, p. 884.

28. R. E. Elmore, "Arizona Churches Thriving and Launching Churches Among the Indians," *Christian Standard*, 1931, pp. 373-375.

Second, Arizona has been a favorite field for ecclesiastical adventures, floating preachers hunting a soft snap. The churches have no stomach for any more of this sort. There is a welcome here for Christian preachers who love the church, who are willing to sacrifice, not afraid of hard work, who can stick and see the thing through.

. . . It is the spirit of the Christian pioneers with their capacity for sacrifice, that the Arizona brethren are setting up the banners of the New Testament faith in this pioneer state.[29]

In Oregon the churches conceived a new type of mission which was to set a precedent for home missions among Christian Churches in later years. In 1934 the Turner Memorial Home was established for retired ministers of the Christian Churches. The Home was formerly a school for boys enrolling as many as 34 boys at one time; however, the need for a home for aging ministers was more pressing. The Home opened its doors to retired ministers but shortly afterward elderly people other than retired ministers applied to live there. With this development Turner Memorial expanded to become a nursing home for the aged and was operated as a mission to the elderly, supported by the churches and individual Christians of Oregon. After World War II other nursing homes were established by Christian Churches as missions to the elderly of America.

1946-1976 Branching Out

After World War II home missions among Christian Churches and Churches of Christ increased dramatically, both in number of (home) missionaries and types of mission

---

29. *Ibid.*

work being performed. As mentioned above, the number of home missionaries has only recently drawn abreast to the number of foreign missionaries. This equality in number has not always been the case, especially in the years immediately following the War. In fact, it took several years after the War for the number of home missionaries to catch up with the number of foreign missionaries. In 1946, there were 90 missionaries, and approximately 60 were serving outside the USA, leaving 30 home missionaries.[30] In 1963, the first year that Mission Services through its publication *Horizons* began keeping separate statistics on the number of foreign missionaries and home missionaries in the Christian Churches, the number of foreign missionaries was 394 while the number of home missionaries was 330 (for a grand total of 724 Direct-Support missionaries). Figure 1 shows graphically the relative growth in the numbers of home and foreign missionaries published in *Horizons,* at two year intervals from 1964 to 1976. According to the graph, the rate of growth in the number of home missionaries has in general, with one exception, paralleled the growth rate for foreign missionaries. The exception was in 1970, when home missionaries briefly outnumbered foreign missionaries, then fell off sharply to resume a rate of growth comparable to foreign missionaries. A major reason for the drop in home missionaries around 1970 may have been the sudden and

---

30. The number 90 missionaries is taken from an article by W. E. McGilvrey entitled, "North American Action in Christian Mission," and published in *Horizons,* August 2, 1975, p. 4. The number 60 foreign missionaries is taken from Carr's book, *The Foreign Mission Work of the Christian Churches* (privately published, 1946). Assuming that the number 90 includes both home and foreign missionaries, the difference between McGilvrey's and Carr's counting is taken to be the number of home missionaries in 1946.

abnormal increase in the number of foreign missionaries at the same time. Only after this sudden increase had "spent itself" could home missions regain what they had lost and continue at a parallel rate.

GROWTH IN
FOREIGN AND HOME MISSIONARIES COMPARED

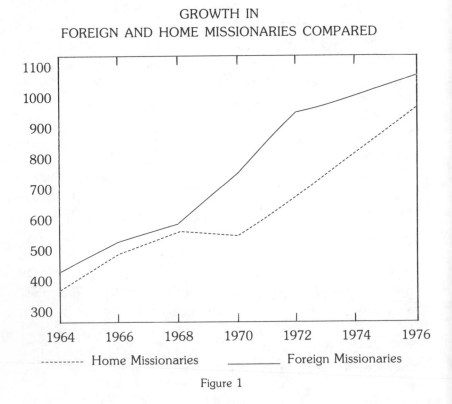

Figure 1

In addition to an increase in the number of home missionaries at the end of World War II, there has also been an increase in the types of home mission work performed by Christian Churches in the USA. It is impossible to list all the types of home missions that have been established since

1946; on the other hand, all of the home missions fall into one of four broad categories: *New Church Evangelism, Minority Evangelism, Youth Evangelism* and *Handicapped Evangelism*. It should be noted that, even though four categories are discernible, the main orientation of all home missions among Christian Churches is still evangelism, i.e. preaching, baptizing, and conserving the lost and/or unchurched population of our nation. Other traditional orientation in home missions, e.g. benevolence, are also involved, but such orientations are viewed as aids in accomplishing the main goal of all home missions — evangelism.

New Church Evangelism

One of the main emphases of the Christian Restoration Association under the leadership of James DeForst Murch was the establishment of New Testament congregations throughout America. "Cover America with the Plea" was the slogan which the CRA used in carrying out this emphasis. However, as with its other emphasis, foreign missions, the CRA moved away from concentrating on new church evangelism and into other brotherhood concerns after Murch left the organization in 1933. Yet, this did not mean the end of new church evangelism among Christian Churches. On the contrary, despite the decline of the CRA in this area, the work in new church evangelism which the CRA had already accomplished became the example for others to follow, and, after the CRA had been established and had worked in new church evangelism, other organizations dedicated to planting new congregations were formed. One of the earliest organizations of this type was the Calumet (Illinois) Evangelistic Association established by C. J. Sharp around 1905.[31]

---

31. C. J. Sharp, "The Chicago-Calumet Evangelistic Association," *The Evangel* (Organ of Chicago District Evangelistic Association), June, 1951.

Several churches in the Chicago, Illinois area were planted under Sharp's leadership. These churches were mobilized to support the Association, and with added financial support from interested individuals, Sharp was able to employ D. Emmet Snyder as a full time district evangelist. In 1925 this organization became the Chicago District Evangelistic Association (CDEA).[32] After its reorganization, Robert M. Lillie was employed as the first full-time evangelist.[33] Lillie worked with the CDEA until 1954 when he moved to Colorado to establish the Rocky Mountain Christian Mission.

Indeed, in the years following World War II, literally scores of evangelistic associations sprang up across America, each one dedicated to mobilizing existing churches of a particular area for the task of planting new churches in places of strategic importance where no Christian Churches exist. From just a few of these associations, which were in operation after the War, their number had grown to over one hundred by 1976, several of them employing full-time evangelists.[34]

In addition to evangelistic associations, there arose between the years of 1946 and 1976 other agencies devoted to establishing new churches. Elmer Kile, in 1946 established the Go Ye Chapel Mission in the greater New York areas as a new church planting mission. This in turn spurred the establishment of other missions (e.g. New England Christian Evangelizing Association) to evangelize in New England. In 1956 The Christian TV Mission (of Homestead USA fame) was organized by four brothers (Bill, Bob, B.J. and Don

---

32. Carl W. Moorhous, "A Short History of the Chicago District Evangelistic Association," *The Evangel*, May 1974.

33. "Robert M. Lillie (1912-1977)," *The Evangel*, Sept. 1977.

34. *Directory of the Ministry*, Springfield, Illinois, p. F-55 (1976).

Vernon) with the goal of covering America with the Restoration Plea via television. In the ensuing years this TV mission has been responsible for establishing fifteen churches. At the same time that the Vernon Brothers were starting, Cecil Todd was beginning in general evangelistic work which included tent campaigns with the view of establishing new congregations. As Todd's work grew, he organized Revival Fires, Inc., branching out into television, radio, literature and foreign evangelistic campaigns. By 1976, the Revival Fires organization had been responsible for establishing more than 50 new churches.

In the early 1970's Paul Benjamin of Lincoln Christian College and Seminary (Illinois), together with a few other brotherhood leaders, decided to join the Key 73 Campaign, an interdenominational campaign designed to place in every American household in America a Bible and Christian literature calling for commitment to Jesus Christ. It was hoped that many new converts would be obtained from this campaign and gathered into new congregations. Key 73, however, fizzled and nothing of substance in new church evangelism was accomplished for Christian Churches. In 1975 a new brotherhood-wide campaign, a Bicentennial Venture in Evangelism, was instituted, again under the direction of Paul Benjamin, with the goal of establishing 300 new congregations by June 30, 1977. At the end of 1976, only about 40 new congregations had been established.[35] Yet, despite the disappointing results of Key 73 and the Bicentennial Campaign, new church evangelism remains a major emphasis in home missions among Christian Churches/Churches of Christ.

---

35. *Christian Standard*, Feb. 6, 1977, p. 132.

Minority Evangelism

Since World War II Christian Churches have been active in establishing mission work among the various ethnic and other minority groups in the US. The purpose of such mission work, like all other Christian Church mission work, is the evangelization of the lost and the goal of forming functioning, i.e. self-supporting, congregations among ethnic minorities. Evangelism among the various Indian tribes began early in the Direct-Support mission work of the Christian Churches, beginning with the Indians of Arizona before World War II. After the war evangelists entered other American Indian tribes. One example was A. B. McReynolds who retired in 1940 to the Kiamichi Mountains in eastern Oklahoma to regain his health; by 1950 he was evangelizing the Choctaw Indians and other groups in that region. In 1946 the McKinley Indian Mission was established at Yakima, Washington. In 1951 Don Larson moved to evangelize the Indians in Montana. From this time other works have been established among Indians in New Mexico, and Seattle, Washington.

Jewish evangelism in Direct-Support missions dates back even earlier than mission work among the American Indians. At the outset of the Christian Restoration Association the Christian Witness to Israel under the direction of Charles Wiesenberg was listed as a free agency in the *Restoration Herald*.[36] Wiesenberg was converted in 1921 and immediately organized the Christian Witness to Israel as a personal mission to the Jews of New York City. In 1924, a young Jew, Harry Bucalstein was converted by this mission and soon became an evangelist among his people. Bucalstein

36. *Restoration Herald*, March 1926, p. 19.

continued to be associated with the Christian Witness to Israel until after World War II.

In 1967, Emiterio "Terry" Reyes, a preacher from the Philippines arrived in New York City to begin a mission work among Filipinos in that city. A similar mission work among the Koreans has been estalished in Chicago under the direction of a Korean evangelist, Soongook Choi. In addition to those home mission ventures, there is evangelistic work among Spanish speaking minorities in Florida and Texas.

Evangelism and church planting activities among the Black population of America deserves special mention. While there are several Black missions currently in operation, all are continuations of a long effort in the Restoration Movement to evangelize the Black minority of our nation. Even before the Civil War churches were established among Black freedmen of the South. With the establishment of the Christian Woman's Board of Missions after the Civil War, Disciple missionaries were sent to work among Blacks in Mississippi. As a result the Southern Christian Institute was established in 1875 at Edwards, Mississipi, and in 1890 the Negro Board of Education was established. Evangelism among the Blacks flourished until 1910 when a decline set in.[37] As a consequence, during the years of turmoil over theological liberalism and open membership, the state of evangelism among the Blacks was overlooked. After the break between liberals and conservatives in 1926, Black churches found themselves in the middle and largely neglected but usually claimed by the Disciples of Christ.

---

37. Tibbs Maxey, "Negro Evangelism in the United States," *Christian Standard*, June 21, 1947, p. 438.

In the meantime there were leaders among Black Christian Churches who attempted to keep the Restoration Movement growing.[38] One of these was George Calvin Campbell, born in 1872 at Pinetown, North Carolina. Campbell was one of the few blacks of his time able to receive a high school, college and graduate training. After several ministries he served with the National Home Finding Society (1937) which operated an orphanage at Irvington, Kentucky. Another man working to promote the Restoration Movement among Blacks was Isaiah Henri Harrison Moore. Moore was born in 1882 in extreme poverty at Green County, Tennessee. His parents died when he was still a boy and for a while he went to live in the county poor home. Later he was raised by relatives and thus began his education in the Restoration Movement. Moore managed to receive training at several institutions, including free tutoring from Ashley Johnson, founder of Johnson Bible College. It was perhaps Ashley Johnson, more than anyone else, who won Isaiah Moore's heart to the Restoration Movement, because after their first meeting together in 1902 Johnson tipped his hat to the young Black preacher as they departed.[39]

A third person was W. H. "Baltimore" Taylor, who was converted from the Episcopal Church and became minister of the Mt. Olivet Christian Church in Baltimore, Maryland in 1933.[40] Taylor disagreed with the Disciples over open membership and soon quit as minister of the church. For the next Lord's Day, however, he invited the public to hear him preach at a club house. He extended an invitation and

---

38. Tibbs Maxey, "Negro Evangelism in the United States," *Ibid.*

39. Tibbs Maxey, *One Wide River* (Louisville: College of the Scriptures, 1960).

40. *Ibid.*, p. 24.

63 people accepted. From this group the Emmanuel Christian Church was formed free from any Disciples of Christ oversight. Taylor went on to influence the National Christian Missionary Convention, a convention of Black Disciples, to remain free of control by the United Christian Missionary Society. In 1944 Taylor served as its President.

Despite the efforts of Campbell and Moore, Black Christian Churches after 1926 were dying and Black evangelism was in general lacking. Few Black leaders were being trained. This situation became known and was discussed in the *Christian Standard*.[41] However, the Depression of the 1930's and World War II, including the general social climate of the time, prevented much of anything from being done. But in 1943 Tibbs Maxey, while a student of the Cincinnati Bible Seminary, decided to dedicate his life to Black evangelism.[42] He immediately planned to open a training school for Black preachers. At first only training institutes were held, the first one being at Paris, Kentucky, and New York City in 1944. The following year the College of the Scriptures was open in Louisville, Kentucky, to three students (a fourth student was added later in the first semester). Faculty included Tibbs Maxey, George Calvin Campbell and Max Ward Randall.

The situation in Black evangelism after World War II was critical. Between 1930 and 1947 nearly sixty Black Christian Churches had closed.[43] There were an estimated 500 Black churches, but there were only 250 Black ministers. A Bible college training Black ministers to fill empty pulpits, reopen dead churches and plant new churches was urgently needed. But soon after the opening of the College of the Scriptures

---

41. T. R. Errett, "The Reader's Forum," *Christian Standard*, Nov. 2, 1929, p. 1046.
42. Tibbs Maxey, *One Wide River*, p. 114.
43. *Ibid.*, p. 115.

in 1945, brethren saw that another college was needed. Leland Tyrrell, who was unable to enter South Africa as a missionary, accepted an invitation in 1949 to reorganize a Black ministerial training school in Winston-Salem, North Carolina.[44] The school was associated with the Disciples of Christ but at the time was serving an interdenominational constituency. Upon agreement to be firmly aligned with the Christian Churches and Churches of Christ in doctrine and practice, the school was renamed Winston-Salem Bible College with Tyrrell as President.

Youth Evangelism

Perhaps the most exciting type of home missions started among Christian Churches since World War II has been to the youth. Certainly youth work from infants to grade school to college age has caught the popular imagination of churches and individual alike and has received widespread support. The beginning of youth evangelism occurred with the establishment of the Boise Christian Children Home in 1946 under the direction of Arnold Kernon. The Home took in unwanted children as well as children whom the courts found difficult to place in foster homes and provided them a Christian environment and instruction in the Scriptures. Naturally the goal of the Home was evangelistic, i.e. to rear children who otherwise would not learn of Jesus Christ in the Christian faith for future leadership in the church as well as Christian citizenship in America. Ten years later, Kernon helped organize the Cookson Hills Christian School in Oklahoma. With the organization of Cookson Hills, children homes

---

44. *Christian Standard,* Dec. 17, 1949, p. 801.

were established in many other places. The Cookson Hills mission itself, in addition to Oklahoma, has units in Arkansas, Missouri, Kansas and Texas. Altogether, Christian Churches support forty such children homes in the U.S., all with the same evangelistic goal of rearing children for future Christian leadership.

In 1968 Robert D. Stacy organized Christ In Youth, Inc., a mission dedicated to evangelizing the youth (Junior High, Senior High) of America. This mission holds campaigns in public schools (where permitted), in churches, and sponsors retreats. CIY teams, in 1976, operated in California, Georgia, Missouri, New York, North Carolina, Ohio and Texas.

Of all the youth ministries started since 1946, however, the Campus Ministries have probably enjoyed the most support from churches and individuals. The college and university campuses, because of perceived dangers in higher education to Christian faith, had all but been given up for redemption by Christian Churches. The main reason underlying this attitude stemmed from the rise of liberal theology in the Disciples of Christ, because liberalism in theology made its way in to the Restoration Movement by way of colleges and universities established by the Disciples of Christ. Since these were liberal arts colleges and universities, a relationship between the liberal arts education and liberal theology was naturally assumed by many in the Christian Churches, i.e., it was assumed that a liberal arts (i.e. secular) education presupposes and must inevitably lead to liberal theology. Consequently any young person attending such an institution was expected to lose his faith and be lost to the church. The turnabout in attitude occurred in 1958 when Richard Carpenter organized a Christian Student group at the University of

Kentucky.[45] By 1978 there were over 60 campus ministries supported by Christian Churches. The National Association of Christian Student Foundations serves as a cover organization for these campus ministries.

Handicapped Evangelism

Churches of the Restoration Movement have always been heavily committed to the *Word* whether in written form or proclamation. Indeed, a major part of the appeal of the Movement has been its insistence upon the "Thus saith the Lord in the Scriptures." Conservative Disciples during the days of controversy over the issue open membership, continually appealed to the written Word, the Bible, to substantiate their position. In new church evangelism as well as in the other types of home missions of the Christian Churches this tradition has been carried through. Then some evangelists discovered that the American population contained a large number of deaf people plus some 500,000 blind people, people who by their handicap were cut off in one way or another from the Word of God. To offset such handicaps deaf missions and blind missions have been established. Since 1971, when Duane King organized Deaf Missions, in Council Bluffs, Iowa, there have been over 30 such missions to the deaf in thirteen states. In 1970, Floyd Rhoades, a blind Christian, established the Christian Mission for the Sightless located at New Ross, Indiana.

Home missions among the Christian Churches and Churches of Christ continue to proliferate, branching out into new areas of missionary service than those mentioned

---

45. Charles Garrison, "They Minister to Students," *Christian Standard*, Aug. 24, 1963, p. 535. See Charles Garrison, *Forgotten Christians* (Joplin: College Press, 1967).

above. But regardless of the type of mission work created the main orientation is still evangelistic; new and different agencies are conceived as additional aids in discipling the lost and gathering the unchurched into functioning congregations. This emphasis on evangelism, so basic in Direct-Support Missions both in foreign and home missions during the first fifty years of history, will no doubt continue.

Part IV

A BRIEF EVALUATION

Chapter Nine

DEFINITIONS AND STATISTICS

Growth in Direct-Support missions since the end of World War II has been phenomenal. From less than 100 missionaries in 1946, the number of missionaries supported direct from churches grew to nearly 2,000 by 1976. This growth in Christian Church missions, moreover, paralleled the growth that took place in Christian missions in general over the same period of time. Ralph D. Winter cites that, in spite of the political retreat of the West in the years following World War II, missions from the Western nations were advancing in all areas of importance: organizational, personnel and income.[1] During these years over 150 new Protestant missionary agencies came into existence; the total number of Protestant missionaries jumped from a low of just over 20,000 in 1945 to nearly 50,000 by 1969; and total income for Protestant missions during these same years climbed from an estimated $165,000,000 to nearly $300,000,000. Furthermore, even though newly independent nations were being created on the ruins of crumbling colonial empires during these postwar years, these same nations did not in principle or in fact reject, hence impede (except in the case of total Communist domination), the spread of Christianity via missions from the West. On the contrary, new opportunities arose in these new nations for growth and expansion.

It is now time to take a closer look at the phenomenal growth in Direct-Support missions. Any type of growth brings problems associated with it and Direct-Support missions are no exception. One major problem is definition:

---

1. Ralph D. Winter, *The Twenty-Five Unbelievable Years 1945-1969* (South Pasadena, William Carey Library, 1970).

Who is a (Direct-Support) missionary? What is a missionary? or perhaps more to the point, Who should be considered and listed as a missionary in the Direct-Support method? Another major problem is in statistics: How many (Direct-Support) missionaries are there? Should we really count many of those whom we count just to say we have 2,000 missionaries? What are the effects, for good or bad, of listing so many missionaries?

There are various reasons why these questions should be raised in a book dealing with the Direct-Support missionary movement of the Christian Churches/Churches of Christ. This chapter will explore these reasons, describing the various factors, both past and present, which have given rise to such questions. But merely describing is not sufficient, since description, even though analytic in nature, does not guarantee solutions to problems revealed in the description. While solutions to problems of definition and statistics are not easily accomplished, this chapter will nevertheless take up the challenge of suggesting answers to these questions of Definitions and Statistics.

Definitions and the Modern Missionary Movement

Since its beginning the modern missionary movement has been plagued with shifting, confusing and even conflicting criteria for answering the question, " What is a missionary?" The problem has been compounded by the phenomenal growth that has taken place in recent years. It has been characteristic of modern missions, as growth has occurred, to diversify by performing many types of service other than evangelizing nonchristian populations of foreign nations. This diversification has been a major source of the shifting criterion in considering who should be counted as a missionary. A 1976 *MARC Newsletter* asked:

What is a missionary? Our last survey for the *Mission Handbook* emphasized again the problem of definition. The growing number of short-term missionaries (six months to two years) raised questions with some mission executives as to whether these people should be considered in the same way as "career" or long-term personnel. Does length of service determine "missionary" status? Or place of service? (Only across borders; or just across cultures?) Our questionnaire for North American mission agencies simply asked for the number of overseas personnel in which "overseas" was defined as serving anywhere outside the United States and Canada. Third World missions agencies . . . defined missionary as the "individual who is sent cross-culturally and/or cross-geographically and whose primary task is that of evangelism and church planting." The first definition is based upon geography by exclusion of (all other places) and the second includes geography, culture and task.[2]

As the quote indicates, there are three criteria used to determine who is a missionary: length of service (usually career, long-term service), place of service (usually foreign) and nature of service (i.e. cross-cultural). Conflict arises when the attempt is made to apply consistently these criteria to the present, diversified missionary scene. Consider, for example, a person serving a short-term assignment in a foreign country: he fulfills two of the three above-mentioned criteria, foreign location and cross cultural service. Compare this person to a long-term missionary serving in an Indian

---

2. *The MARC Newsletter*, published by World Vision, Monrovia, California, January, 1976.

tribe in the U.S. The latter likewise fulfills two of the above three criteria: length of service and cross-cultural service (but not, of course foreign location). Although in each case two of the three criteria for determining are fulfilled, usually the latter is considered a missionary while the other is not.

Yet inherent in the definition of missionary, at least in the romantic version of the term, is the idea of foreign service, a condition the former case fulfills but not the latter. Therefore, should the short-term person be considered and counted among the missionaries because of his foreign location and the career person be also counted as a missionary because of his length of service? Or should the short-term person not be considered a missionary because of his (short) length of service, and the career person likewise not be considered a missionary because of his State-side location? A satisfying answer to these questions is not easily found.

Two Missionary Lists

The Direct-Support missionary movement of the Christian Churches has not escaped these and other problems arising out of the shifting criteria for defining and counting missionaries. In fact, there are even special and unique problems of definition and statistics which arise out of the historical events and tensions which gave rise to the Direct-Support movement in the first place. One such problem is the existence of not one but two lists of Direct-Support missionaries. One list is given in the *Directory of the Ministry, A Yearbook of the Christian Churches and Churches of Christ,* which is published yearly.[3] The other list is published

---

3. *Directory of the Ministry, A Yearbook of Christian Churches and Churches of Christ,* 1525 Cherry Road, Springfield, Illinois 62704.

by Mission Services under the title, A Missionary Directory of Christian Churches and Churches of Christ.[4]

At first it might appear a simple matter to consult these two Directories, or perhaps investigate those who are listed in them, to arrive at an answer of who is a missionary in the Direct-Support movement. Unfortunately it is not that simple. It is true the two Directories, for the most part, contain the same names. Despite this high degree of overlap the two lists are not all that comparable, because of differing criteria for classifying and listing missionaries. For example, the 1976 Directory of the Ministry listed 695 missionaries. The main criterion used for inclusion in this list is service outside the 50 States of the U.S. and Canada. U.S. citizens ministering in Canada are not counted as missionaries. Puerto Rico, on the other hand, though a Commonwealth of the U.S., is considered a mission field and U.S. citizens from the "north 48" ministering there are considered missionaries by the Directory of the Ministry! Home missionaries, furthermore, are not listed, since the Directory of the Ministry has its own method of classifying those normally thought as home missionaries, usually in the States where they work as evangelists, Children's Home Administrators, teachers, etc. The 1976 Missionary Directory, on the other hand, listed a total of 1,976 missionaries of which 1,341 are in North America, a classification which includes U.S. citizens ministering in Canada but not in Puerto Rico, the latter being a different classification. This left 635 missionaries serving outside the continental 48 States. Wishing to emphasize foreign missions and that there are more foreign missionaries

---

4. A Missionary Directory of Christian Churches and Churches of Christ, W. E. McGilvrey, ed., Mission Services, Box 177, Kempton, Ind. 46049.

than home missionaries, the 1979 *Missionary Directory* subtracted 379 personnel living in the U.S. and counted them as foreign missionaries, because they are working cross-culturally in Spanish-speaking missions or an overseas mission nearby. "Following this latter plan the total 1,976 breaks into: 962 in the 48 states of U.S.A. and 1,014 outside the 48 states and in Spanish speaking missions."[5]

A major difference between these two listings, one which reflects an important difference in policy in determining who may properly be a Direct-Support missionary, is that the *Directory of the Ministry* lists overseas missionaries of the Christian Missionary Fellowship while the *Missionary Directory* does not. Mission Services, the publisher of the *Missionary Directory,* considers mission support received via the Christian Missionary Fellowship is not "direct" from congregations and individuals but is still "in the nature of a missionary society"; therefore, CMF missionaries are not Direct-Support missionaries. The 1976 *Directory of the Ministry,* on the other hand, listed 20 CMF missionaries serving in Ethiopia and Brazil plus another 22 candidates, or recruits, for missionary service.

In spite of these differences the two lists are useful in a very practical way, because they identify *who* in the brotherhood is a missionary and where he or she may be contacted for speaking and sending funds. Beyond these practical aspects, which are indispensable for the successful operation of Christian Church missions, problems of definition persist. Such problems may appear unimportant in the light of the practical and successful role these lists play in publishing names and addresses for interested churches and individuals,

---

5. *Ibid.*

but such success does not solve some of the more intrinsic problems of who is a missionary in the Direct-Support movement and, more crucially, whether a certain person should be supported as a missionary in the traditional sense or supported under some other classification (evangelist, teacher, etc.). This latter issue is crucial, because much of what passes as missionary work in the Direct-Support movement is not necessarily mission, a fact that may seem inconsequential except that those who support such work are thinking they are indeed supporting missions when in fact they are funding some other type of ministry. This of course takes away from the support of true mission work. For example, it is quite possible, for a congregation to have a mission budget of $50,000 or more only to earmark $10,000 for disbursement to overseas missionaries, the remaining $40,000 going to support such ministries as church camps, nursing and children's homes, local benevolence, perhaps even a building program for the local congregation. While these ministries are worthy, they nevertheless are not mission work properly speaking. In other words, these ministries should be supported for what they are and not be masqueraded as mission work.

What Is A Missionary?

A missionary in the traditional sense is a person who proclaims the Good News about Jesus Christ to nonchristians of other ethnic groups. In general the *Directory of the Ministry* follows this definition by listing only those who serve outside of North America as missionaries, since, except in rare instances, service outside of the North American continent ipso facto involves service among other ethnic groups. However, the list of missionaries published by Mission Services

289

does not adhere to the above definition of a missionary. Upon investigation we discover that people engaged in ministries not even remotely related to the common definition of a missionary as stated above are listed in the *Missionary Directory.*

What are the various ministries which people perform and which, right or wrong, merit inclusion by Mission Services in the *Missionary Directory?* Naturally those engaged in cross-culturally proclamation, either in the U.S. or foreign nations, of the Good News of Jesus Christ are listed. But beyond this obvious and uncontested class of personnel, the following are also listed (as Direct-Support missionaries):

Evangelists employed by evangelistic associations (e.g., the Chicago District Evangelistic Association) and serving American citizens within an American cultural framework;

Teachers and Secretaries employed by mission schools (e.g. the Grundy, Virginia Mountain Mission School);

Administrators and Houseparents serving in children's homes (e.g. East Tennessee Christian Home);

Administrators and Promotional Directors e.g. of nursing homes;

Professors of Missions who have served on the mission field but now teaching in Bible Colleges;

Returned and Retired Missionaries who are, for the most part, residing in the U.S.;[6]

Campus Ministers who are serving for the most part, white, middle-class students on the university campus;

---

6. It is the policy of the *Directory* (and Mission Services) to list returned missionaries for one year after overseas service. After this one year period, if they have not continued in some other type of missionary activity, they are dropped from the list. (See Preface of *A Directory of Missionaries, 1976-1977* published by Mission Services.)

Counterculture Evangelists as in the various "His Place" ministries;

Mission Iterns, usually Bible College students who are serving for a short time in foreign mission fields;

Missionary Recruits who have not arrived to serve on any mission field but who have made definite commitments to serve or have begun raising their support;

Children of Missionaries who are studying in universities or colleges in the U.S.;

Self-supporting Personnel, i.e. people who are supporting themselves at some secular occupation but still performing some minstry.

It is obvious from the above that the *Directory of Missionaries* published by Mission Services is not discriminating enough in listing who is a missionary. People are included in the list who are not performing services considered, in the traditional sense, missionary in nature. This judgment is not meant to deny the worth of such people, nor to deny the worth of their ministries. Even though their ministries are evangelistic in many cases, they do not constitute missionary work properly speaking. Inherent in, and necessary to, any definition of missionary as noted earlier, is the work of cross-cultural evangelism. Foreign location is normally associated with cross-cultural evangelism, but it need not be as in the case of Spanish-speaking, Indian or Korean evangelism in the U.S. Therefore, if the term missionary is to be properly and adequately defined, the factor of cross-cultural evangelism must be a determining factor. Otherwise, a person performing any type of Christian ministry can be classified as a missionary, which makes the term missionary largely meaningless.

The indiscriminate listing of the *Missionary Directory* leads to a related problem. If it were to become more discriminating, then it would be obvious that there are not as many Direct-Support missionaries as the *Directory* lists. Perhaps here is the reason why the *Directory's* listing is indiscriminate, namely there is a desire to have a large number of missionaries to advertise to ourselves and to the world. This leads to uncritically listing all types of personnel as missionaries. I am not against large numbers of missionaries, or quantitative growth in missionaries, Christians or churches; in fact, I am a strong advocate of quantitative growth in these areas. Yet, I am not an advocate of growth along these lines if it means using ill-defined criteria for classifying and subsequently listing those who shall be missionaries in the Direct-Support movement. Clearly the criteria for determining who is a Direct-Support missionary need to be tightened up, but before we tackle this problem we should consider further the problem of how many missionaries there really are in the Direct-Support movement.

How Many Missionaries Are There?

The indiscriminate listing of personnel and types of Christian service in the *Missionary Directory* published by Mission Services casts doubt on the number of missionaries that the *Directory* advertises. If there are personnel performing services not related to what is commonly understood as missionary work, then it becomes very difficult to justify their inclusion in a listing of missionaries. This problem of justification has long been known in the Direct-Support missionary method. Writing in 1972, Mark Maxey, veteran Direct-Support missionary to Japan, discussed the problem in an article entitled "How Many Foreign Missionaries?"[7] The article focused on the number of *foreign* missionaries supported directly by Christian Churches/Churches of Christ; however, the issues Maxey raised in the counting of foreign missionaries are still valid for the Direct-Support missionary movement as a whole. Furthermore, the fact that the article was written at a time when the number of missionaries was fewer than now does not invalidate many of the conclusions he made about the enumeration of missionaries in the Direct-Support method.

Maxey began his discussion by quoting Harrold McFarland.

> We list all kinds of missionaries where the intent is to evangelize and to serve God's people: the youth challenge groups, evangelistic associations, Bible Colleges, new church planting activities, child saving ministries, senior citizens' homes, and convalescent hospitals. The list may be endless.[8]

Maxey's conclusion from this open-ended method of counting missionaries was simple and straightforward: "A list that may be endless may also turn out to be meaningless. That may become the fate of the word 'missionary.' "[9] Of the foreign missionaries listed in 1972, Maxey voiced doubts as to whether many of them, nearly 20% of the total, really should have been counted as missionaries. These included recruits not yet gone to the field, (former) missionaries who had returned permanently to the U.S. and retired missionaries. In addition to these, Maxey also noted somewhat sarcastically the listing of personnel living at permanent U.S.

---

7. Mark Maxey, "How Many Foreign Missionaries Are There?," *Christian Standard*, Oct. 8, 1972, pp. 893-894.

8. Harrold McFarland, "Growth In Missions," *Christian Standard*, Mar. 19, 1972, p. 247.

9. Mark Maxey, "How Many Foreign Missionaries Are There?"

addresses under the headings of various foreign countries. To quote Maxey: "These may represent a new phenomenon, the 'absentee' missionary directing his foreign work from a U.S. base with occasional visits to the field."[10]

But Maxey voiced the strongest doubt about whether foreign nationals should be listed and counted, as is still the case in the 1976-1977 *Directory*, as missionaries in the (American) Direct-Support missionary movement:

> Foreign nationals are serving in their own homelands, in their own cultures, using their own languages. Adding their names makes our missionary statistics more impressive but in actual fact when we include them we reduce the percentage of U.S. Christians who have made a missionary commitment. Listing foreign nationals gives U.S. churches the feeling that they are sending out more of their own people than they really are.[11]

The obvious conclusion to be drawn, which Maxey implied, is that foreign nationals should not be counted. They do not, after all, fulfill the definition of missionary, i.e. cross-cultural evangelism, because they are working in their own culture among their own people. Yet, the matter is not this simple and clearcut, because there were at the time Maxey wrote, and still are, missionaries of Third World nations working cross-culturally in nations other than their own homeland. The main reason why they are listed and counted in the (American) *Directory* is that U.S. churches provide the bulk, if not all, of their financial support. Apart from such instances, however, the issue of including as missionaries foreign nationals who return to their own people is a

---

10. *Ibid.*
11. *Ibid.*

legitimate question. The fact that they are supported by U.S. churches does not ipso facto qualify them to be so listed. There are, furthermore, other issues that, even if U.S. funding were a qualifying factor, could override and cancel out this factor as a justification for considering foreign nationals as missionaries in the Direct-Support missionary movement of American Christian Churches. These issues are whether mission work should be subsidized with U.S. funds or whether mission work should be fully indigenous and self-supporting from the beginning. But this is not the place to discuss these issues.

One of the more enduring problems in counting missionaries, whether in Direct-Support missions or in Protestant missions in general, is whether wives of missionaries should also be counted. This is a difficult and highly emotional issue. On one side, many missionary wives are fulltime housewives and mothers. Just how many of course is not known, but the *Mission Handbook* (11th edition) cites a survey taken in Brazil which stated that 40% of wives of missionaries were engaged practically fulltime in homemaking.[12] Whether this percentage holds true for Direct-Support missions as a whole is unknown. If it does, or even if some other percentage holds true, then there is a legitimate question whether wives who are not engaged in evangelistic outreach or a task directly related to evangelism should be counted as missionaries. But there is another more emotional side to this issue. Mark Maxey himself, even though raising doubts about the proper inclusion of some other types of personnel in the number of Direct-Support missionaries,

---

12. *Mission Handbook* (11th edition), (Monrovia, California: Missions Advanced Research and Communications Center, 1976), pp. 26-27.

does not wish to exclude wives from the list. "I do not want to question in any way the listing of wives as missionaries. My own wife is a full and complete partner in our missionary work. I could not labor without her."[13] In other words, even if a missionary wife is not engaged in a missionary activity, her supportive role in the total missionary program is so vital that, if she were not performing this role, no missionary outreach on the part of her husband would be possible. Therefore, to exclude her from any listing of missionaries would be absurd.

But this issue is not so easily settled for Direct-Support missions as a whole. If wives of *foreign* missionaries are allowed to be listed as missionaries, then we are forced to reconsider as well wives of *home* missionaries — evangelists serving evangelistic associations, campus ministers, professors of missions in Bible colleges, and so on. Wives of these personnel should also be listed and counted as missionaries. The problem becomes more complicated when the supportive role of these wives, many of whom are homemakers or must work at secular jobs to subsidize their husband's evangelistic or teaching work, is also considered: their support, whether in homemaking or financial, is just as important to them as the wife of the foreign missionary. This being the case, it becomes a difficult problem to exclude wives of home missionaries from the lists of Direct-Support missionaries. Consequently, the *Missionary Directory* lists wives as well as husband in the ranks of Direct-Support missions.

Unfortunately the issue refuses to die at this point, since the inclusion of wives, especially those not engaged in activity directly relating to missionary outreach, in a listing of missionaries distorts the picture of how many there really are

---

13. Mark Maxey, "How Many Foreign Missionaries Are There?," *Christian Standard*, Oct. 8, 1972.

in missionary work. By advertizing several hundred missionaries while at the same time a significant number are not engaged in missionary activity, in the commonly understood meaning of the term, gives a false impression of the status of the missionary outreach of the Christian Churches. For example, the 1976-1977 *Missionary Directory* listed 1,976 missionaries. An analysis, however, reveals these classifications and numbers of *couples* (husband and wife) listed:

Over 350 couples serving outside of the U.S.;

Approximately 150 couples serving in evangelistic functions in the U.S.;

Over 150 couples serving in children's homes and mission schools (many of these are houseparents);

Some 15 couples were listed under the category of Professors in Bible colleges;

Over 100 couples were listed in a wide ranging category which included campus ministries, intercity ministries, counseling, etc.[14]

This totals 615 couples or 1,200, for half of whom there is legitimate questioning concerning their direct contribution to the evangelistic outreach of the Direct-Support movement. This is not intended to denigrate the role and function of wives of missionaries and evangelists as "team members" in missionary outreach, nor to overlook those wives who do play significant and direct roles—often in addition to household duties—in evangelism. The purpose of such an analysis is to arrive at a more realistic picture of the missionary outreach supported by Christian Churches.

---

14. This count is by no means exhaustive. These figures are given for illustration purpose only.

At this point the reader may wonder why so much space has been taken in discussing whether wives of missionary husbands should or should not be listed as missionaries. After all, we are talking only about numbers, and, regardless of how we add up the total, wives will still be included one way or another. Whether to count wives or not may seem to be an insignificant issue. But it is a significant issue for at least three reasons:

First, to count wives as missionaries gives misleading impression of our total strength in missionary outreach to the nonchristian world. Specifically if over 600 couples or 1,200 individuals are advertized as missionaries but a sizeable portion or one half of these individuals are engaged in direct missionary outreach, we have considerable fewer individuals in evangelism than we have been led to believe.

Second, if we are led to believe that we have many more in missionary outreach than actually is the case, we lull ourselves into thinking that we are indeed doing a commendable job of sending out a great number of missionaries. But if we can devise a system whereby only those engaged in evangelistic outreach—whether husbands or wives—are counted, then we could obtain a more realistic assessment of the status of the evangelistic outreach of our total missionary force and can take steps to increase the number of personnel truly engaged in evangelism.

Third, it is a matter of integrity to count those who are in fact missionaries however the term is consistently defined. Unfortunately, there has been and still is a great amount of inconsistency in defining the term missionary. Therefore, it is a point of integrity for the Direct-Support missionary movement to become more consistent in defining, listing and counting those who are engaged in worldwide missionary outreach for the Christian Churches.

How many missionaries are there in the Direct-Support movement? Perhaps not as many as we suppose. It all depends, of course, on the definition of the term missionary. As has been noted several times already through the course of this chapter, the definition of what is a missionary has not been consistent. It is time to attempt a serious and consistent definition of missionary.

Needed: Better Classifications

Who should be counted a missionary in the Direct-Support movement? A definitive answer is difficult if not impossible to achieve. One aspect of this movement which makes it difficult to arrive at a definition has been an underlying assumption which has guided the listing and counting of missionaries. This assumption has not been definitional in nature but rather methodological. That is, the criterion used in determining whether a person is to be listed as a missionary is whether that person receives financial support directly from congregations and individuals for work done in another area. The nature of his or her work — cross-cultural, children's homes, prison evangelism, etc. — was and still is inconsequential. The main issue has been the method employed in receiving financial support. This position naturally stems from our historical association with the Disciples of Christ and the United Christian Missionary Society. Because of this association the insistence at one time upon Direct-Support made sense, because funds sent through the UCMS went to support not true Biblical evangelism.

William McGilvrey of Mission Services (in a written personal communication) has offered a definition of missionary.

A missionary is one-sent. The sent-one should be of the same faith and quality of character as those sending. The sent-one should propogate the same Bible message as those sending. The sent-one is an extension partner working with the endorsement, support and undergirding prayers of those sending. The missionary is like a minister abroad for those sending . . . Church-sent Christian missionaries give the basic idea involved in this definition. . . . In another sense, all Christians being supported with funds outside the field served are sent by others.

While this communication contains a minimum definition of a missionary (one who is sent), its main import is still largely methodological, for the emphasis is upon how the missionary is to be sent and supported: ". . . the missionary is . . . an extension of the local ministry . . . is like a minister abroad . . . is church sent . . . and must receive support from outside his or her area of service." These methodological remarks continue to be the hallmark criteria for determining who is a Direct-Support missionary since the movement began.

Perhaps a definition of the term and work of a missionary is not what is needed. We have seen already how difficult it is to define the term and how even more difficult it is to consistently adhere to a definition once it is agreed upon. This has certainly been the case not only in the Direct-Support missionary movement but in Protestant missions generally. Since definition of the term missionary involves classification of different types of missionaries (e.g. evangelistic, printing, etc.), what is needed in place of a better definition is a better scheme for classifying personnel and the work they perform. Classification in missions puts the emphasis where it belongs, not on the total number of missionaries but on how many are doing what in the total missionary outreach of the church. Having access to such knowledge instead of just knowing the total number of missionaries, is an important factor in assessing effective missionary outreach into the nonchristian world. For example, Mark Maxey, writing in 1972, estimated that one-fourth of the total Direct-Support missionary force were engaged primarily in the operation of schools, hospitals, printing presses and other mission-related ministries.[15] While such work is mission related, it is not directly evangelism, proclaiming the Good News of Jesus Christ to nonchristian populations. There is no way of knowing whether, of the 1,976 missionaries listed in the 1976-1977 *Missionary Directory,* more or less of one-fourth are engaged in similar missions-related activities. No doubt a great number of these missionaries are engaged in missions-related work. Taking Maxey's figure of one-fourth as our "working" estimation, we conclude that nearly 500 of our missionaries are not primarily working in evangelism.[16]

The fact that a missionary is not primarily engaged in evangelistic outreach is not wrong in itself. The main point is that our ignorance of this leads us to believe that far more people are actively evangelizing than is in fact the case. If there were in existence a scheme to classify those engaged in mission-related or supportive activity (of whatever type) and those engaged primarily in evangelism and count the number in each accordingly, then we would have a better picture of the effectiveness and needs of our missionary

---

15. *Ibid.*

16. In a 1978 article printed in *Horizons,* Mark Maxey hazards a guess that there are no more than 250 men living and serving as Direct-Support missionaries overseas. ("Who Is A Missionary," *Horizons,* May 15, 1978, p. 15). The significance of this guess is that, for overseas, our evangelistic impact is far less than what we have been led to believe from the listing of 1,976 missionaries.

force. While supportive roles are needed in the modern missionary program, there is a greater need for evangelism. By knowing the relative strengths of support personnel versus evangelists, we can achieve a better balance between the two by recruiting according to the needs and not numbers. Unfortunately we are unable to do this because of the absence of accurate classifications in Direct-Support missions.

A classification scheme for mission work similar to what I have been discussing has been worked by Ralph D. Winter. The scheme was presented in the form of a paper to the International Congress on World Evangelism, which was held in 1974 at Lausanne, Switzerland, under the title *The Highest Priority: Cross-Cultural Evangelism*.[17] Winter's scheme takes as its basic theme that cross-cultural evangelism — evangelizing nonchristian people of ethnic groups different than that of the evangelist — must take precedent over the evangelization of other groups. However, the way the modern missionary movement has indiscriminately lumped together under one classification all who are engaged in "mission" (home, foreign, children's homes, etc.), the precedence that should belong to cross-culture evangelism is obscured and in effect buried away from sight. To overcome this effect, Winter recommended giving labels to various kinds of evangelism, so that the church can know who are performing which type of evangelism. He proposed three kinds of evangelism:

1. The first kind is *E-1 Evangelism* in which an evangelist wins a neighbor of his culture and language to Jesus Christ.

---

17. Ralph D. Winter, "The Highest Priority: Cross-Cultural Evangelism," in *Let The Earth Hear His Voice* (Minneapolis: World Wide Publication, 1974), pp. 213-225.

2. The second kind is *E-2 Evangelism* in which an evangelist wins a person from a different but closely related culture and/or language to Christ, a task that involves different skills and techniques than the first type.

3. The third kind is *E-3 Evangelism* in which an evangelist wins someone from a completely different culture and language to Christ, a task that is greatly more difficult than E-1 and E-2 evangelism.

If adopted, its advantage for Direct-Support missions would be that we would have a clearer idea of what many of the nearly 2,000 missionaries are doing. For example, it is a point of pride to advertize that there are 2,000 Direct-Support missionaries which Christian Churches are supporting, but it is another matter to realize, according to Winter's scheme applied to the *Missionary Directory,* that 962 of these are engaged in E-1 Evangelism, 379 in E-2 Evangelism and only 636 in E-3 Evangelism.[18] In other words, the fact that 1,976 *missionaries* were advertized led us into believing that we had 1,976 E-3 evangelists proclaiming the Gospel in other cultures and languages whereas we now see that at the time we had one-third more E-1 evangelists than we had E-3 evangelists, with E-2 evangelism lagging far behind. Again, this is not intended to denigrate the nearly 1,000 E-1 evangelists, who are considered Direct-Support missionaries — we need every one of them. Rather, the purpose of dividing up our total missionary force into E-1, E-2 and E-3 evangelism is to focus

---

18. No doubt if a detailed analysis were made of the *Directory* some of those classified under E-1 Evangelism would be found to be doing E-2 Evangelism, and some under E-2 Evangelism could qualify to be engaged in E-3 Evangelism. However, it is just as doubtful if the total number of any of the three classifications would be altered significantly.

on our strengths and weaknesses with the view of strengthen-ing the weak areas of the Direct-Support movement. Ob-viously this movement is weak in two areas; E-2 evangelism (which we may roughly compare to minority evangelism in the U.S.) and E-3 evangelism. However, with this scheme, we are able to focus on these two areas by specifically recruit-ing personnel for E-2 and E-3 evangelism and channeling more of our financial support into these kinds of evangelism. By focusing on these two areas we can expect to have in a short time a greater percentage of people working in these two types of evangelism than we would normally expect by a more general approach to recruitment for service in the Direct-Support movement.

Chapter Ten

FROM MOVEMENT TO SYSTEM

A new generation has arisen in the Direct-Support missionary movement, a generation which includes both missionaries and their supporters. It is a generation that is unaware of the controversies and developments which brought forth the movement, a development itself which in turn called forth this book. Yet, the coming of this generation is significant in a way that perhaps has escaped our notice, since it shows that the movement is now operating on its own. The mission dynamics introduced in the years immediately preceding and following the turn of the 20th Century are now self-generating. In short, after fifty years of struggle and success, the Direct-Support missionary movement has become a system of missions for the Christian Churches and Churches of Christ. No longer do we depend upon the controversies which revolved around the Disciples of Christ, and the United Christian Missionary Society, for the generation of new "independent" missionaries. Direct-Support Missions, as a missionary system, are now capable of sustaining themselves for the fulfillment of the Great Commission as we enter the final decades of the 20th century.

Moving from a missionary movement to a system of missions, however, poses a number of questions. The first question that immediately comes to mind is this: Given our starting point which we characterized in the Introduction as the Campbellian Dilemma, how well have Direct-Support missions resolved the tension resulting from the dilemma? How does our resolution compare with what has transpired elsewhere in the Restoration Movement? But more important than the resolution of historical tensions is the question of how well the resolution, which has since become a system

305

in its own right, is working now. Is it holding up well and accomplishing the tasks for which it was designed? Of even more importance is the future. As we close out the 20th Century and enter the 21st Century (should our Lord tarry), how well will this system work as a strategy by which Christian Churches and Churches of Christ can fulfill the Great Commission in a world becoming more populated and complex with each passing year? Are there tendencies and developments occurring now which must be checked or encouraged in order to more effectively disseminate the Gospel to an ever increasing world population?

These questions will be discussed in this final chapter. The orientation of the discussion will be systematic in nature, that is, focus on how well the brotherhood — now comprising both congregations and missionary — is implementing Christ's command to make disciples of all nations.

Freedom — With a Limitation

This book on the history of Direct-Support missions began by pointing out a dilemma that emerged soon after Thomas Campbell formulated his concept of restoration in his *Declaration and Address*. The dilemma that emerged was this: In restoring primacy to the local congregation, it was discovered that the mission of the congregation — to make disciples from all nations — could be fulfilled only inadequately unless para-church organizations were specifically created for the task. This in itself was a strange turn of events for a movement whose goal was restoring the New Testament Church, since it meant also creating an extra-Biblical form to carry out a task which the New Testament had given the church to fulfill. More seriously, though, it meant creating a form whose very existence contained within itself the capabilities to overshadow the local congregation. As expected, this dilemma gave rise to tensions within the Restoration Movement, tensions which in turn gave rise to dynamics for their resolution. In a very real sense, resolving these tensions is "what the Restoration Movement has been all about," because, in over 150 years of existence, since the publication of the Declaration and Address in 1809, there have been three main resolutions to the Campbellian Dilemma. The Direct-Support missionary system is one of the three. The Disciples of Christ and Churches of Christ (non-instrumental) are the other two.

How well have we solved the tensions which have arisen from the dilemma that the church is primary but that para-church agencies (i.e. extra-Biblical forms) appear needed to fulfill the Great Commission throughout the world? We have resolved these tensions, and the fact that our resolution, Direct-Support missions, is now operating as a self-generating system, indicates that the resolution is successful. That being the case, what is the nature of this resolution? There are two essential components to the Direct-Support resolution to Campbell's dilemma. The first is freedom, but the second is freedom with a limitation.

In Direct-Support missions, we recognize the freedom to create forms and organizations in addition to the local congregations by which to carry out the Great Commission. An individual, or a group of individuals, has the right to legally incorporate and operate an organization outside the congregation to accomplish specific tasks. An individual also has the right to mobilize brethren from several congregations by forming them into a single organization, apart from the congregation(s) involved to perform certain ministries.

307

This freedom, furthermore, is not viewed as causing tensions, either theologically or pragmatically, between the congregation(s) and organization; no conflict of interest is seen in this arrangement. Both the congregations and para-congregation organizations of the brotherhood see no Scriptural principle being violated by this combination. In fact, the brotherhood generally looks upon this juxaposition as having the best of both worlds: the local congregations can retain their primacy and autonomy, as is biblically correct, while simultaneously employing the para-church organization, because of its proven efficiency in recruitment and service.

While we have accepted the idea that the church has the freedom to create and use organizational structures other than itself to perform various ministries, it is nevertheless a freedom to be exercised with care. This limitation to freedom was a lesson concluded from the traumatic experience with the United Christian Missionary Society in the 1920's. At that time we saw that, while there was freedom to have a multiplicity of agencies and societies for mission work, benevolence, etc., this freedom did not allow us to unite all such organizations into one larger organization, for at this point, it was observed that the para-church organization did indeed overshadow the local congregation in power and importance. In other words, a denominational structure is created and the local congregation becomes buried out of sight by a vast and complex ecclesiastical overlay. When this happens, we have come full circle back to the situation which compelled Thomas and Alexander Campbell to call forth the Restoration Movement in the first place. When it does happen, as it did with the formation of the United Christian Missionary Society, it is time to call for a renewal of the principles of restoration and return to the original plea of the Restoration Movement. For even though we have freedom, it must not be allowed to destroy the primacy which the local congregation enjoys in God's scheme for the redemption of mankind.

In other words, the freedom we enjoy ends at the creation of a plurality of para-church agencies to perform specific tasks of the churches. James DeForest Murch first enunciated this limitation to congregational freedom when he began editing the *Restoration Herald*. He spelled out seven principles governing the existence of para-church agencies.[1] Murch's seventh principle is of particular interest in this regard. In this principle, in which he labeled "Agencies are Merely Expediencies," Murch proclaimed the right of a congregation to make use of several agencies to perform various tasks, or several congregations may use several agencies to perform a single task. To deny or violate this right, Murch went on to claim, would tend toward a centralized ecclesiasticism and the ultimate overthrow of the Restoration plea. In order to keep agencies as servants of the churches, they must be kept separate, organically, one from another. Otherwise, their combination would create a power structure that would overshadow the autonomy of the local congregation, the restoration of which is the hallmark of the Restoration Movement.

How does the above resolution compare with the way which other segments of the Restoration have handled the Campbellian dilemma? The Disciples of Christ and the Church of Christ (non-instrumental) have likewise had to live with this dilemma and find their own respective resolutions. Actually the Disciples of Christ would probably not

---

1. See above, Chapter Six.

agree with us that such a dilemma as we have stated really exists. In fact, to formulate the problem we see as a dilemma is, from their viewpoint, to ask all the wrong questions. From the perspective of the Disciples of Christ, the real questions which arise from Thomas and Alexander Campbell are those which revolve around the unity of the church. Taking this as the basic issue, we see in effect a different dilemma emerging, namely if local congregations have the right to utilize para-church organizations, then the existence of so many organizations, standing in opposition to the congregation, flies in the face of the Plea of the Restoration Movement for church unity. The tension which arises from this formulation is this: If the para-church organization is performing the work of the church, but is not an integral part of the church, then it cannot be claimed that the brotherhood is unified. But, as was stated in the Introduction, a tension creates dynamics for its own resolution. For the Disciples of Christ, this tension set in motion certain dynamics to resolve their formulation of the dilemma, i.e. unifying first of all the para-church agencies into one organization, and then as occurred during their Decade of Decision (the 1960's), complete the process by "restructuring" both congregation and para-church organization into a single unified structure.[2] Yet, at this point, the process is still not complete either, for there is a greater unification to be achieved with other

---

2. The Disciples of Christ have not been alone in this development. Ralph D. Winter writes that by 1950 nearly all the mainline denominations had moved to the concept of the unified budget as a further step toward centralization. (Ralph D. Winter, "Protestant Mission Societies: The American Experience," Missiology, Vol. VII, No. 2, April, 1979, pp. 139-178). The Disciples of Christ, as has happened at other times in their history, picked up the theme of centralization, added their own theological justifications and proceded with a restructuring program.

denominational bodies. Consequently the Disciples of Christ are still in the process of resolving the Campbellian Dilemma, as they have perceived it for themselves, in the modern denominational world.

It is obvious that, in interpreting the Restoration Movement, the main difference between the Christian Churches/ Churches of Christ and the Disciples of Christ corresponds to the difference between unity and relationship. To the Disciples of Christ, the existence of so many autonomous churches and agencies, regardless of the relationship among them, is antithetical to the concept of unity. To the Christian Churches/Churches of Christ, who advocate the primacy of the local congregation and the freedom to create para-church organizations, unity is achieved only when the proper relationship between the two is maintained. For the Disciples of Christ, unity is accomplished when integration of the two has occurred, no matter what the resulting relationships turn out to be. For the Christian Churches/Churches of Christ, unity is accomplished when the two are kept separate with the latter (the organization) serving the former (the congrega-tion). This difference, unfortunately, has created a divergence between the two groups far greater than what appears on the surface. Such a divergence, moreover, given current theological and pragmatic perspectives on the issues in-volved, appears irreversible.

If the respective solution of the Disciples of Christ and the Christian Churches/Churches of Christ to the Campbellian Dilemma are not in the end comparable, a comparison be-tween the Direct-Support method of the Christian Churches/ Churches of Christ and the third segment of the Restor-ation Movement, the (non-instrumental) Churches of Christ, holds much better promise of being productive. In fact, it was this segment which first clarified the Dilemma for the Restoration Movement. Long before the official division of 1906, this segment was pointing to the tensions that arose when para-church agencies were created and employed to carry out the work that was given to the congregation in the first place. To these brethren, such organizations were human innovations, which the Biblical doctrine of freedom was not meant to cover. In short, freedom ended with the local congregation. Since freedom did not include para-church missionary organizations, the resolution to the Campbellian Dilemma which the Churches of Christ have formulated is this: The local congregation must be educated to the point where it will initiate and sponsor directly missionary outreach around the world. In general, this has been accomplished by the Churches of Christ.[3]

This brief sketch of the Churches of Christ's approach to the Campbellian Dilemma reveals both similarities and dissimilarities with the Direct-Support missionary method. The two are similar in that both uphold the primacy of the local congregation and that there must be a direct relationship between the congregation and missionary. However, the similarity ends here. For the Christian Churches, there is freedom to utilize para-church agencies, as long as the agencies maintain a proper relationship to the brotherhood. For the Churches of Christ, congregational freedom does not extend that far, hence, theoretically, para-church organizations are not legitimate. On the other hand, when we move from the theoretical to the practical we see a great deal more similarity to Direct-Support missions in this regard than meets the eye. For example, interpretations differ in the Churches of

---

3. Phillip Wayne Elkins, *Church-Sponsored Missions* (Austin, Texas: Firm Foundation, 1974).

Christ over what congregational freedom means and how far it may in reality be extended in order to fulfill the Great Commission in today's world. Essentially there are three interpretations: 1) no cooperation among congregations is legitimate, so each congregation must be able to completely sponsor a mission project or it must not be done at all; 2) cooperation among congregations is permissible as long as no para-church organization is thereby created and the autonomy of the local congregation is not destroyed; 3) organizing and legally incorporating a group to accomplish a specific task of the church is permissible. The first two interpretations are not similar to Direct-Support missions, although the second may be more so than the first. The third appears to be no different than what has taken place in Direct-Support missions. According to Phillip Wayne Elkins, this last interpretation is becoming more of a tendency among Churches of Christ.[4] If this tendency continues and spreads, there will ultimately be little if any difference in the resolution at the Campbellian Dilemma which has developed in Direct-Support missions. In fact, Elkins claims that in recent years the Churches of Christ have used para-church organizations more often than not to implement the Great Commission in the world.

> The organization role played by periodicals, educational institutions, foundations and leading individuals partially explains why the local congregation was not really the sole missionary agency within the Church of Christ. Most congregations would have to be categorized more as "responders" than "initiators." They responded positively or negatively to someone's appeal for . . . (a) project.[5]

---

4. *Ibid.*, p. 33.
5. *Ibid.*, p. 43.

While this "centralization," as Elkins characterizes it, is definitely gaining ground among the Churches of Christ, it has not proceeded as far as the same process has in Direct-Support missions.

Given the similarities between the Direct-Support mission and what is developing among the Churches of Christ (non-instrumental), we may confidently say that such a mission system is working well for the two groups involved with respect to the Cambellian Dilemma. The system allows the local congregation to maintain its autonomy while providing an efficient strategy for fulfilling the Great Commission. There is one potential flaw in the system, however, and I would be remiss not to mention it. I have already referred to this flaw in the closing pages of Chapter Seven. There it was mentioned in the context of Christian Churches only, but since the Churches of Christ also share a similar system of missions, we should reconsider the flaw in the context of both groups. That flaw is this: as more and more para-church agencies are used, more and more responsibility for world evangelization is being transferred by congregations to the agency. Such transference, if not checked, is wrong, for the Great Commission was given to congregations to fulfill. A para-church agency is meant only to be a servant of the churches, i.e. to serve each church in a manner so that the church itself may more readily and efficiently implement the Great Commission. When the agency is not leading the congregation in this way — or congregations refused to be reminded of their responsibility in world evangelism, then the relationship between agency and congregation is wrong.

Paradoxically, the ideal of congregational autonomy, which both Christian Churches and Churches of Christ uphold, may serve to reinforce this tendency of transferring

314

congregational responsibility in world missions to agencies. That is to say, congregational autonomy is often taken to mean autonomy from not only other congregations but also from the world as well. Evangelizing the nations of the world is not viewed as an obligation, or a debt, as the Apostle Paul viewed it (Rom. 1:14). Such obligation belongs to the agency not the congregation. The congregation, after all, is "autonomous." Unfortunately, there is evidence a considerable number of Christian Churches and Churches of Christ (non-instrumental) have drawn such a conclusion from the doctrine of congregational autonomy. If this is indeed the case, then the doctrine has been wrongly formulated and the formulation must be changed. Congregational autonomy must not be used, intentionally or unintentionally, to cancel out the Great Commission. Congregational autonomy in this regard is meant to ensure congregational freedom to puruse the most direct way possible in performing its task in world missions, not as a convenient means of transferring responsibility and thereby escaping the task of world missions.

It is impossible to say how much transference to para-church agencies has taken place among Christian Churches and Churches of Christ (non-instrumental). Whatever the facts really are in this regard, this tendency should be closely watched, checked and reversed whenever there is evidence it is becoming too strong. The great strength in world missions of both groups is an openness to directly mobilize congregations and individuals in congregations for the task of making disciples of all nations. This openness should be zealously guarded and enhanced, because in the final analysis, the task of world evangelism is given to every one in the Kingdom and not to just a few.

Some Strengths and Weaknesses

How well is the Direct-Support system of missions operating now in being a strategy whereby Christian Churches can fulfill the Great Commission in today's world? The limited scope of the chapter, indeed of the whole book, prevents a full-scale review of the strengths and weaknesses of the Direct-Support method; nevertheless, to the extent that is possible here a brief evaluation of the method is given. We must remember at this point that the Direct-Support method is being viewed as a system in which the processes of recruitment, training, supporting and reporting are interrelated to make a whole. In looking at some of the strengths and weaknesses of this system we are investigating how well it is functioning as a strategy of missions for the brotherhood. As we shall see, there are several strong points to Direct-Support missions as well as a number of corresponding weak points. By noting the weak points, we should not be unduly alarmed; but rather, as I will show toward the end of this section, we should let these weaknesses suggest ways to improve the system.[6]

The first strength in Direct-Support missions, and one which is most apparent when considering the graphs in Chapter Eight, is the growing number of missionaries, both home and foreign, who are responding to this method of performing mission work. In fifty years, a whole host of people have responded to God's call through this method. In Direct-Support missions the challenge to a person to do

---

6. This section is a condensation of a three-part article which I wrote for the Christian Standard in 1974. (See "A Critical Look at Independent Missions," by David Filbeck, *Christian Standard*, Aug. 18 (pp. 745-746); Aug. 25 (pp. 771-772); Sept. 1 (pp. 793-795), 1974.

something for God is limited only to his own personal, God-given abilities. This method challenges a Christian *positively* to leave what he has—whether it is a job, pulpit, houses, or land—and go to perform a work. Such a challenge does not go unheeded, as witnessed by the increasing number of people responding. A corollary to this strong point is that Direct-Support missions allows a person to exercise his faith to the maximum. Great things for God are accomplished only by men of great faith in God. The genius of the Direct-Support system of mission among Christian Churches has been the removal of organizational shackles on the exercise of great faith setting men free to go throughout the world to preach the gospel.

Yet, there are corresponding weaknesses to the above strengths in inspiring an ever increasing number of people to serve as missionaries. Perhaps the greatest weakness of Direct-Support missions has been, and still is, is increasing fragmentation of the work force into small units, each unit doing its own thing. Thus the strength we saw above be-comes, in a sense, self-defeating, because there is no central authority in an essentially independent method to concentrate a great force to accomplish a major project. In both theoretical and practical terms we must face up to this problem of fragmentation.

In any fission process there is an initial explosion and a great many particles are thrust outward. But they are only a mass of energy, and as the individual particles recede in time and space from the initial explosion, entropy sets in and the amount of energy contained in the mass actually decreases, eventually ceasing to be a force, unless, the entropy is reversed and the energy mass harnessed in some way. Direct-Support missions today can be compared to a great mass of energy which is largely unharnessed for an efficient and sustained drive in the cause of Christ around the world. And herein, I believe, is where our weakness becomes most conspicuous: we have allowed an "independent" movement, with its strength of thrusting out even more new missionaries, to become an uncoordinated and often ineffective force. Because of this our system of missions stands in danger of suffering a decrease in per-unit effectiveness, partially because we have sent out a mass of 2,000 missionaries.[7]

A corollary to the above weakness is the retention of the word "independent" in our mission vocabulary. The term, during the last fifty years, has undergone a subtle change in meaning. Originally it meant freedom from the United Christian Missionary Society in order to preach New Testament Christianity. Independence has been won, and it is no longer an issue whether our missionaries shall or shall not be under the control of a mission board. Yet every missionary recruit, including those born less than twenty-five years ago, still goes out as an "independent" missionary. So what has the term "independent" come to mean to the missionary in our movement today? Unfortunately, it is taken to mean only what it can mean some fifty years after the fact, viz. a missionary working on a mission field independently of all other missionaries on the same field, who in turn are working independently of everyone else.

---

7. In other words, we may by now have simply outgrown our own system, and will continue to suffer a decrease in missionary impact *per person* as more new missionaries enter the system. A "law of missiology" can be stated here: Growth in individual units does not ensure a corresponding growth in impact. True, our system can thrust missionaries out into the field, but it has no effective means of harnessing their power for a collective assault upon the kingdom of Satan in this world. Solving this problem will be one of the major tasks in Direct-Support missions in the years to come.

I do not believe that the pioneers of the "independent" missionary movement had in mind the concept of working independently of one another when they set out to work independently of the United Christian Missionary Society. Rather, they envisioned a group of missionaries, supported directly rather than by any society, working together as the apostles worked together in planting New Testament churches.

However, in many of our mission fields men independently supported are also working independently of each other. As a consequence the fruits of such a field have often not been proportionate to the number of missionaries working there; nor have they been comparable to those of other missions, whether denominational or interdenominational, which have coordinated their work force to accomplish their own ends. Even among ourselves we can see that those direct-support missions which make a greater impact are those which have been able to amass and coordinate a large staff. The lone Christian church missionary, justifying his independence because he is an "independent" missionary, can seldom match the accomplishments of his better coordinated colleague.

Another strong point in Direct-Support missions is the type of person who is usually attracted to this system. Direct-Support missions attract a certain personality type—usually the strong-willed person, a person not easily defeated by obstacles and unwilling to take "no" for an answer. It is the strong type that cuts through red tape and gets things done. When such a person sees a need—a hospital must be built, a printing ministry must be established for a national language, or a nation must be opened up to New Testament Christianity—he turns his back on security, begins with nothing except a handful of personal recommendations, raises funds, arranges visas, and then performs his task to

319

the maximum of his abilities. He does not submit a proposal to a mission board, wait for an appointment, wait even longer for funds to be appropriated, and then humbly accept it when headquarters reduces funds after the project is started.

Direct-Support missions do not attract very many weak-hearted people, an asset of the system for which we should be thankful. Think of the condition New Testament Christianity might be in today in New York City had Elmer Kile not had a strong personality. As a fledgling missionary recruit in Bible college I once asked Mr. Kile about helping him in New York for a summer. Instead of giving the expected pat on the back he bluntly informed me of what I as a Midwesterner would have to do to get to New York and to survive as a preacher in the big city. I left my interview with Mr. Kile a somewhat shaken but wiser recruit. I knew more about what it took to be a missionary!

Yet, this is not to say that the Direct-Support missionary is a perfect person. The strong personality type, in spite of his ability to get things done, also brings along his share of trouble. For strong personalities often clash in getting things done! And I see no more glaring problem in Direct-Support missions than the personality clashes that erupt between strong-willed "independent" missionaries upon the field. Such eruptions never fail to affect the work of the missionaries involved nor — even worse — do they escape the notice of the national Christians on the field. Individualism is a trait highly valued in American society, and our system of Direct-Support mission is well suited for the full exercise of this trait especially on the foreign mission field. However, while this may be a strong point for the system in an American context, it can be a severe handicap in another culture. Consider, for example, the missionary going into a society where individualism is not valued but is regarded rather as a personality trait to be suppressed. Mission work suffers when a rugged individualist confronts a culture in which his personality is not appreciated but is perhaps even considered unchristian according to the cultural understanding of the Christian faith on the part of the nationals.

Still another strong point in the Direct-Support system of missions is the flexibility given to missionaries in formulating their own theories of mission work. As applied to missions, theory refers to how things ought to be done in order to do the best job of evangelizing and establishing the church in a different country. In this respect a mission theory may be good, bad or rigid, and rigid mission theory is always bad. But in Direct-Support missions, no one procedural theory gains precedence over others. Direct-Support missions are eclectic, allowing a missionary to take an empirical approach to solving the problems of his field. There is freedom to change from an unprofitable method, to experiment and innovate right on the spot. Several different missionaries may try different approaches to a particular problem if they so wish. Many missionaries under the control of mission boards have expressed their envy of the freedom of the Direct-Support missionary to change and innovate *now* in order to take full advantage of an opportunity.

The strength of Direct-Support missions is the freedom to innovate; but a weakness is that there is no authority to make a missionary innovate. In short, freedom of theory is sometimes understood as freedom from theory. Missionaries may use their freedom to select and try one or any number of theories, or may choose to do nothing. The outstanding performance of many Direct-Support missionaries, in other words, may speak well not of the sytem but of the individual involved.

321

The problem of setting goals, working out methods to achieve them, and then of evaluating one's work is a continual one in Direct-Support missions. It is often a temptation to an "independent" missionary to do one of two things: to fall into a self-contented, self-perpetuating rut, or simply to set no goals for accomplishment during his tenure on the field. The latter course is often justified by saying, "I am out here just to do however the Lord leads." Of course, if the Lord does not lead, then the Direct-Support missionary is released from all responsibility for using his mind and abilities (which the Lord created in him) to set goals and accomplish them for the Lord.

Another weakness in "independent" missions is apparent when there is a dispute among missionaries over theory — that is, the correct way of doing missionary work. There is no authority above the individual missionary to settle disputes and, as often happens, individuals split with each working independently of the other. This only weakens the impact that Direct-Support missions can have in a mission field.

Having reviewed several strong and weak points of the Direct-Support system of missions, let us discuss ways of improving the system to enhance the strengths while minimizing the weaknesses. In doing this, though, we must be careful not to destroy the strong points of our system of missions in trying to correct its differences. Most of all, we do not want to destroy the capability of the system to challenge and send into the field an ever increasing number of new missionaries. That would be a tragedy out of proportion to the cure. Without new and more workers the Christian Churches/Churches of Christ would be ill-equipped indeed to carry New Testament Christianity into other lands. Since

1960, when I first became a missionary, the total missionary force of our movement has more than doubled. If a similar proportionate increase continues, there will be more than 3,000 missionaries of our churches by 1990. A method that can do this is not to be tampered with in any radical way.

Neither do we want to destroy the flexibility and freedom inherent in Direct-Support missions. The modern world is too complex for a mission system to be restricted to any single theory. Moreover, modern society changes too fast and radically, even within the lifetime of a missionary on the field, to adhere rigidly to one way of doing mission work. The modern missionary must be flexible to meet the changing demands of our age. There is perhaps nothing more pathetic to see than the veteran missionary clinging to outmoded mission theories in face of a changing society and justifying his lack of results by the correctness of his theories. Such ossifying does occur in our missionary force, but the freedom of the Direct-Support system hopefully prevents it from becoming a habit.

What improvements can we make within our system of Direct-Support missions to enhance their strong points while diminishing their weaknesses? It would be presumptuous for me to tell two thousand missionaries and their supporting churches what to do to improve their performance. This is not a subject that may be settled once and for all; it is one that requires continual study and reevaluation from all concerned. An improvement in one decade may become a weakness in the next. Here are, though, a few guidelines that might help us improve our total effectiveness as a missionary force.

First, we should drop the word "independent" from our missionary vocabulary. This word has lost its original meaning

—of being independent from the United Christian Missionary Society—and its continual use tends only to foster an isolationist attitude among us, which is robbing our movement of the strength that comes from coordinated, cooperative action. The term "independent" has most certainly outlived its usefulness in our movement, and its elimination should help remind our missionaries that we are not independent of one another but are "servant one to another" in the great service of evangelizing the nations. Henceforth our method should be known exclusively as Direct-Support missions.

Second, we should be training recruits to be problem-oriented missionaries as well as pioneering evangelists. The missions fields are different from what they were one hundred or even fifty years ago. The Gospel has been preached in many areas of the world, and few places remain where a new missionary can strike out on his own and begin from scratch. A problem-oriented missionary is one who is able to enter an already-established mission work; take a critical look, analyzing the strengths and weaknesses of the fields; and select a weak area and work in coordination with other missionaries and national leaders to bring growth and improvement to that area. The missionary for this closing part of the twentieth century should not be oriented to reduplicating what others have already done but should orient himself to doing what they have been unable to accomplish, to "reap where others have sown."

Third, we should have a better educational program to teach supporting churches what it means to be a Direct-Support missionary. Churches should become aware of the strengths and weaknesses in our system. At the present, when a crisis or problem comes up in a mission, the churches directly involved may be unable to handle it because they do not understand it. They have not learned to analyze the causes of the problem and to see how they often compound to affect the situation.

The Next Fifty Years

In the first two sections of this chapter, we have considered the question of how well the Direct-Support system of missions measures up in solving a major dilemma posed by the Restoration Movement. The criteria for that measurement have been more theological than ecclesiastical, because in the Restoration Movement we consider ecclesiology—the doctrine of the church—as one of the most important items theology must define. The result we have come up with for the Direct-Support system is an optimistic one. According to the problem as we have perceived it, the system is functioning well in solving the problem. Admittedly, however, this is an internal and to some degree subjective evaluation of the system. We must look into the future as much as we can and try to estimate how well the Direct-Support system will measure up as a strategy for fulfilling the Great Commission in the world. In this arena of comparison, the criteria of measurement are not theological but sociological. Jesus Christ commanded us to preach repentance to all the nations (Luke 24:47) and to make disciples from these nations (Matthew 28:19). Therefore, what are the conditions among "the nations" in which we must seek to win disciples? This is a sociological question and not a theological one.

We must remember that the term "nation" in the Great Commission is translated from the Greek word *ethne,* a word which is also the source for our word "ethnic." The Greek word would probably be better translated as "ethnic group" instead of "nation"; this latter word is much too limited in meaning now due to the emergence of the nation-state whose main characteristic is not ethnicity but territorial boundaries. Within each modern nation-state of today, one is likely to discover a citizenry composed of several ethnic groups. Since a main characteristic of an ethnic group is the language it speaks, and since there are over 5,600 languages in the world,[8] there are over 5,600 ethnic groups in the world. It is from all these ethnic groups, therefore, regardless of the territory of political domain they inhabit, that the Great Commission commands us to make disciples.[9]

What are the sociological conditions among all the ethnic groups of the world where we must implement the Great Commission? The answer to this question is obviously much too broad for the purpose of this section. However, as we look into the future to see if and how well the Direct-Support system of missions might function, one overwhelming sociological fact dominates our concern. That one factor is population, more precisely the growth of the world's population over the next fifty years. How well might the Direct-Support system of missions, in the second fifty years of its existence (1976 to 2025), function in evangelizing an increasing world's population? To rephrase the question more bluntly: Given the certainty of a greatly expanding population, are we prepared through the Direct-Support

---

8. *Ethnologue* (Huntington Beach, Summer Institute of Linguistics, 1974), p. XII.

9. This linguistic criterion for defining *where* we are to evangelize is not an unscriptural concept. In Rev. 7:9, there is the promise that "people—from every race, tribe, nation and language (standing) in front of the throne and of the Lamb, dressed in white robes and holding palm branches in their hands." (TEV). For this promise to be fulfilled, we must make disciples from every language group of the world.

mission strategy to meet the challenge of world population over the next fifty years?

The world's population is now increasing at alarming proportions. It was not always this way, however. Demographers estimate that between 4000 B.C. and the time of Christ, world population grew from less than 100 million to perhaps 200 million; it took four centuries for the world's population to double itself. From the time of Christ to 1650 A.D. the world's population grew to 550 million. From this date the increase in population began to accelerate rapidly. By 1850, the world's population had doubled to over one billion people, and by 1950 that population figure had again doubled to over two billion people. Now demographers estimate the world's population is doubling every 35 years! The challenge that the church faces from an expanding world population is this. Will the church be able to keep up in evangelizing and gathering into its fold the many billions more who will be born and live over the next half century?

In 1975, the world's population reached four billion people. It is now over four billion. The earth's population, moreover, keeps increasing at more than 1% per year. At this rate, by the year 2000 there will be upwards to seven billion people on the earth; and by 2025 — a year well within the lifetime of many of our readers — the world's population will hover around eleven billion people. Naturally, these numbers are only estimates. Some estimates of future population project fewer people on earth than the figures given here; others project more! In any event, the population of the world will be greatly more than what it is at the present time.

Of the four billion people who inhabited the world in 1975, approximately 1.3 billion belonged to some form of the Christian religion. Christianity throughout the world, furthermore, has been increasing at a rate slightly greater than 2% per year, a rate which is slightly greater than the growth rate of the world's population. While this greater growth rate in Christianity is commendable, we should not let it lull us into thinking that all is well, or will be well, in the task of evangelizing the world. For, while the greater growth rate of Christianity will eventually overtake the lower growth rate of the world, resulting eventually in the predominance of Christians over nonchristians, the differential in the meantime between the number of Christians and the number of nonchristians in the world, especially during our lifetime, underscores how far we will have to go in evangelizing the world. For example, in the year 2025, when the world's population is expected to be eleven billion, we may expect the Christian population to number four billion people. In other words, while in the next fifty years the number of Christians will more than triple in number, there will still be in 2025 some seven billion nonchristians, *twice as many nonchristians as in 1975.*

What these statistics and projections of future population, both Christian and nonchristian, mean is that Christianity over the next fifty years must greatly increase its efforts in evangelizing the world just to maintain the 1975 differential of 2.7 billion between the number of Christians and nonchristians. Just maintaining the present growth rate in the expansion of Chrisianity, even though greater than the growth rate in population, is still to fall far short of what is really needed in world evangelism. To assure that there be only 2.7 billion nonchristians in the year 2025 means that Christianity must grow to 8.3 billion people. But to achieve this number by 2025, Christianity must increase 638% over the intervening years or more than double its current projected growth under the present growth rate.

The preceding projection deals with a comparison between Christian (however broadly defined) and nonchristian populations. But what about the Restoration Movement and world population? A projection for the Restoration Movement from now until 2025 reveals that a similar if not greater effort must be expended in order to meet the challenge of world population. The Churches of Christ (non-instrumental), Disciples of Christ and the Christian Churches/Churches of Christ, throughout the world numbered approximately 6,000,000 adherents in 1976. This amounted to only .15% (more than 1/10th of one percent) of the four billion people who inhabited the earth at this time. To maintain this percentage of the world's population in 2025, the Restoration Movement must in the intervening years grow to a worldwide membership of 16,500,000 adherents. The Restoration Movement must grow by 275% to maintain the status quo.

In coming closer to home, however, we see that the statistical projection for the Christian Churches/Churches of Christ looks just as challenging. At the end of 1976, it was estimated that the combined membership of Christina Churches/Churches of Christ in the U.S. and Canada stood at 1,040,000 people.[10] Overseas membership at the time did not exceed 250,000 Christians. Together the worldwide membership of Christian Churches/Churches of Christ in 1976 was approximately 1,300,000 people, or .0325% (slightly more than 3/100th of one percent) of the world's population of the time. To maintain even this small percentage in the year 2025, when the world's population will be eleven billion, the worldwide membership of our churches must be 3,575,000

---

10. Ralph McLean, editor, *Directory of the Ministry, A Yearbook of Christian Churches and Churches of Christ* (Springfield, IL: p. F-54, 1977).

adherents. We must triple our numbers between 1976 and 2025 just to keep pace with the growing world's population.

Biological growth among our membership (i.e. Christian families raising children who will remain faithful to the church) and normal outreach into the nonchristian population should assure the above amount of growth in the Christian Church by the year 2025—except for one disturbing statistic that was noticed at the end of 1976. There was reported a loss of 3,319 members, or .3% (3/10th of one percent) in membership for the year.[11] This loss may seem small, but, if it foreshadowed a tendency that might continue over the full fifty year period, the total loss would be significant indeed. At this writing it is too early to determine whether this loss is a general tendency or was only a temporary dip in a more general growth pattern of Christian churches.[12] This is an observation that only future students can validate. Whatever the case may be, a decline in church membership for any reason—especially at the beginning of this new fifty year period!—does not bode well for achieving the continuous future growth necessary just to stay even with the projected world's population of 2025 as members of our brotherhood.

The challenge is clear to the Christian Churches/Churches of Christ and the Direct-Support missionary movement. How well prepared are we to meet the challenge of a greatly expanding world population? Actually the question of preparedness in this respect is quickly reduced to the question

11. *Ibid.*, p. F-54.

12. Ralph McLean, editor of the 1977 Directory, attributed the loss to a different method of reporting church membership. The loss, he speculated, was due not to a decline in real numbers, but to the tendency of counting only active members. If this is true, then such a tendency must be figured in as a factor in determining growth patterns of the Christian Churches.

of distribution: How strategically are Christian workers distributed throughout the world's population to achieve the necessary growth by the year 2025? Unfortunately, the distribution of Christian workers—preachers, song leaders, church secretaries, missionaries, etc.—supported by our brotherhood suggests that we are ill-prepared to meet the challenge. For example, for 1976, a total of 10,251 personnel supported by Christian Churches/Churches of Christ was reported.[13] This is an impressive number, except when we consider where they were located at the time relative to the population of the world. Of all the personnel listed, only 696 were working outside the U.S.A. and Canada as foreign missionaries. That left 9,602 personnel working in North America. Now the total population of both the U.S.A. and Canada was approximately 240,000,000 people, or nearly 6% of the world's population in 1976. What these statistics mean is that 93.2% of our ministerial force at that time was working among only 6% of the earth's population, while only 6.8% of our work force was ministering among 94% of the earth's population.

At this writing the above distribution of Christian workers in the Christian Churches, relative to the world's population, has not changed in any significant way. Nevertheless it must change if we hope to achieve the growth mentioned above. I am sure that our current church leaders and membership are thinking about growth, but, according to the distribution of our full time workers in the world, I seriously doubt if they are thinking in the magnitude of 3,575,000 members worldwide by the year 2025. Fortunately, we are only a few years into the second fifty year period of the Direct-Support missionary movement, so there is still time to make

---

13. McLean, *Directory of the Ministry*, p. F-56, 1977.

the adjustments in our thinking and planning for the magnitude of worldwide growth we must achieve by the early years of the next century. What must we do to become prepared to meet the challenge that the world's population will present us from now until 2025? For the conclusion of this book, I offer five suggestions.

Become oriented to evangelism. This suggestion may seem strange to a brotherhood historically evangelistically oriented. But, recent statistics indicate that our orientation may now be otherwise. The 1976 Directory of the Ministry reported a total of 9,171 personnel working in U.S.A. churches and church related agencies. The 1977 Directory reported 9,421 personnel, an increase of 250, or nearly 3%, in the number of Christian workers in one year. But the same Directory also reported a slight drop in overall membership for the brotherhood during the same period. Obviously the new personnel gained during the year were other than ministers and evangelists who are engaged in converting and incorporating the lost into the Church of Jesus Christ. This observation, moreover, proves to be true when we investigate who these 250 new personnel were. There was an increase of only 27 ministers, from 5,028 in 1976 to 5,055 in 1977, for a miniscule .5% increase. The number of evangelists, on the other hand, dropped sharply, from 291 in 1976 to 188 in 1977, an astonishing 35% decrease. Some nonevangelistic categories which showed sharp increases were Benevolent Personnel 28%, Day School Personnel 22%, Campus Ministers 15%, and Church Secretaries 5%. But the category that showed the greatest increase in number of new personnel was the miscellaneous—camp and bookstore personnel, chaplains, editors, printers, etc.—which grew from 313 in 1976 to 418 in 1977, a whopping 34% increase. In other words, we gained as many "miscellaneous" personnel as we lost in evangelists. No wonder Christian Churches/Churches of Christ declined in membership in the year between 1976 and 1977!

Become oriented to World Evangelism. This, too, may seem odd to a brotherhood whose very emergence was due to issues revolving around missions and world evangelism, but to show how far we have moved from this orientation we need to look no further than to the statistics over how many missionaries we have versus how many of these are actually overseas. Mission Services of Kempton, Indiana reports that our brotherhood supports over 2,000 missionaries; however, as mentioned above, in 1976, only 696, or one-third of our missionary force, were serving in foreign locations. The fact that 66% of our missionary force is located in the U.S.A. and Canada is strong indication that our orientation is not worldwide. Yet, we must become so oriented, for the bulk of the world's population is outside of North America; and it is outside of this continent where the future growth of the Church must occur in the massive proportions needed to keep pace with the world's expanding population. It is estimated that by the year 2000, the majority of Christians in the world will be Asians, Africans and Latin Americans. We must go there now to reap the harvest of souls who will be receptive to the Gospel over the next five decades.

Promote world evangelism in the Church. Obviously, if we hope to achieve a minimum worldwide growth to 3,575,000 members by 2025, we must begin now to do a better job in mobilizing the brotherhood to become more effective in evangelizing the world. Promotion in the local congregation is the modus operandi in mobilizing the Church today. It is the link between the church and the missionary outreach of the church into the world at large: without promotion a church has no way of knowing needs and opportunities to preach the gospel in various parts of the world, nor is a missionary able to raise the financial support needed to "redeem the time" by taking advantage of opportunities in evangelizing other areas of the world.

Encourage more of our young people to become world evangelists. Many Christian parents, unfortunately, do not wish their children to become full time Christian workers in the U.S.A., much less encouraging them to become missionaries. The hymn, *O Zion Haste* expresses well what we need to do in this regard.

> Give of thy sons to bear the message glorious;
> Give of thy wealth to speed them on their way;
> Pour out thy souls for them in prayers victorious
> And all thou spendeth Jesus will repay.

The Mormons have 20,000 young missionaries throughout the world who are supported by parents and families. The Mormons already have 4,000,000 adherents worldwide, and with 20,000 young evangelists this cult will no doubt double, perhaps even triple, in membership by 2025. If we hope to achieve the same growth over the same period of time, the Christian Churches/Churches of Christ must adopt a similar program of encouraging young people to become world evangelists.

Break out of the bottleneck that is inherent in our Minister-Pastor system. Ministers of Christian Churches/Churches of Christ are becoming more like the "pastors" of denominational churches. This means that nearly, if not all, of the requests for an opportunity to promote a missionary cause in a congregation must be channeled through the minister. Several reactions have resulted from this development. First, since a minister can accept only so many requests, the majority are thrown in the wastebasket; after a time it becomes easier to throw all such requests away instead of choosing which ones to honor. Another reaction, one that arises more directly from the emerging "pastor" system in our churches, is that the minister perceives such requests from missionaries as threats to his popularity in and control over the congregation. Consequently, few missionaries are allowed to speak before the congregation, or, at the very most, allowed to speak under very controlled conditions. If we are to achieve the growth needed to keep up with the increase in world population, we must find ways which will allow missionaries to approach directly church members in order to enlist them in giving and supporting from their wealth the evangelization of the world.

Up to now I have been talking about a minimum standard of growth which Christian Churches/Churches of Christ must achieve by the early years of the next century. The reason for emphasizing this minimum is that from present indications as revealed by the above statistics, we will probably not achieve it. However, instead of minimum growth, we should be discussing the *maximum* growth which we should be able to achieve over the same period of time.

What is maximum growth? I believe it is certainly more than the growth to 3,575,000 members by 2025. Yet, it is difficult to set some upper number for the maximum growth which we would be capable of achieving if we truly dedicated ourselves to achieving it; since however much we would increase in membership, it would still be far short of evangelizing the masses of people that shall inhabit the earth. Whatever the case, we should not be satisfied with achieving only minimum growth.

105518

The reason that we should not be satisfied is that God would not be satisfied if we just keep pace with the increase in world population. God wants His Church not only to grow but to *multiply* and *extend* into every part of the world. Christian Churches/Churches of Christ, therefore, dare not be slothful in fulfilling the Great Commission as the world enters the 21st Century. We must become prepared now to meet the challenge of evangelizing and gathering into congregations the many billions who will be born and live over the next half century!

336